THE PUERTO RICO RECONSTRUCTION ADMINISTRATION

The
Puerto Rico
Reconstruction Administration

New Deal Public Works, Modernization,
and Colonial Reform

Geoff G. Burrows

UNIVERSITY OF FLORIDA PRESS

Gainesville

Copyright 2024 by Geoff G. Burrows
All rights reserved
Published in the United States of America

29 28 27 26 25 24   6 5 4 3 2 1

Library of Congress Cataloging-in-Publication Data
Names: Burrows, Geoff G., author.
Title: The Puerto Rico Reconstruction Administration : New Deal public works, modernization, and colonial reform / Geoff G. Burrows.
Other titles: New Deal public works, modernization, and colonial reform
Description: 1. | Gainesville : University of Florida Press, [2024] | Includes bibliographical references and index. | Summary: "This book explores the history and impact of an important New Deal program that improved living conditions across Puerto Rico in the wake of destructive hurricanes and the Great Depression, while at the same time resulting in a strengthened colonial relationship between the island and the United States"—Provided by publisher.
Identifiers: LCCN 2023054128 | ISBN 9781683404132 (hardback) | ISBN 9781683404385 (pdf) | ISBN 9781683404507 (ebook) | ISBN 9781683404309 (pbk.)
Subjects: LCSH: Economic development—Puerto Rico. | Puerto Rico—Economic policy. | Puerto Rico—Economic conditions. | BISAC: HISTORY / United States / 20th Century | BUSINESS & ECONOMICS / Economic History
Classification: LCC HC154.5 .B86 2024 | DDC 338.97295009/043—dc23/eng/20231201
LC record available at https://lccn.loc.gov/2023054128

University of Florida Press
2046 NE Waldo Road
Suite 2100
Gainesville, FL 32609
http://upress.ufl.edu

This book is dedicated to Vanessa, Charlotte, and Ysela

CONTENTS

List of Figures   ix

Acknowledgments   xi

List of Abbreviations   xv

Introduction   1

1. San Felipe, San Ciprián, and the Election of 1932   19

2. From Relief to Reconstruction   37

3. *Para Permanencia*   63

4. The Road to Modernization   90

5. Rural Electrification   114

Conclusion: From the New Deal to Today   138

Notes   155

Bibliography   213

Index   225

FIGURES

Figures follow page 82.

1. Cataño cement plant under construction, Guaynabo
2. Model house and subsistence garden for rural workers and homesteaders, Arroyo
3. Puerto Rico Reconstruction Administration employee baseball team
4. Directors of El Falansterio Cooperative
5. Members of Puerto Rico Rug Cooperative
6. Inauguration of the Lafayette Cooperative, Arroyo
7. Puerto Rico Reconstruction Administration officials inspecting the construction of brick houses in Castañer
8. Central plaza with American flag and concrete houses at the Caserío La Granja, Caguas
9. Distribution of fertilizer to resettled farmers from workers in the Rural Rehabilitation Section of the Engineering Division
10. Delivery of keys to resettled farmworkers in the coffee zone
11. Recently completed construction of the main library and teachers college of the University of Puerto Rico, Río Piedras
12. Vegetable planting at a Puerto Rico Reconstruction Administration farm near Cayey

ACKNOWLEDGMENTS

The arguments in this book are based on primary sources located in both Puerto Rico and the continental United States. The bulk of the research was conducted in New York City at the National Archives regional branch at Bowling Green and its former location on Varick Street. Additional research was conducted at the Library of Congress, the Franklin D. Roosevelt Presidential Library, the Archivo General de Puerto Rico, the Fundación Luis Muñoz Marín, and the Museo de la Historia de Ponce. These sources were enhanced by archival newspaper collections held by the library system of the University of Puerto Rico, Río Piedras, that were digitized as part of the U.S. Caribbean and Florida Digital Newspaper Project and photographs held by the Biblioteca Digital Puertorriqueña and the Archivo de Arquitectura y Construcción, both of the University of Puerto Rico, Río Piedras. Many thanks to all of the archivists, curators, and librarians who assisted me with patience and expertise and to the many other specialists who work in these institutions daily. Their service in collecting, preserving, and making available the foundations of Puerto Rican history—in the face of extraordinary obstacles—is truly appreciated. Humanities research would not be possible without them. Special thanks to Elena M. García Orozco, Nathalie González Torres, Julio Yamil Mercado Avila, Javier Almeyda-Loucil, Julio Quiros-Alcala, Dax Collazo, and Hilda Teresa Ayala.

My interest in the PRRA originated with a suggestion from Laird W. Bergad during a seminar on modern Latin America and, under his guidance, developed into the research that became the foundation of this book. For their mentorship and support, I would like to thank Laird, David Nasaw, Gerald Markowitz, Teresita Levy, and Herman Bennett. Special thanks to Albert G. Way of *Agricultural History* and to Karen E. Eccles and Debbie McCollin of the University of the West Indies, St. Augustine, for publishing parts of this research and granting permission to republish some of that material in this book. Initial work on this project was funded by the CUNY Graduate Center and the Franklin and Eleanor Roosevelt Institute.

Thanks also go to numerous friends and colleagues who read parts of this work in its earlier phases and shared their knowledge, sources, suggestions, critiques, and ideas with me over email exchanges and phone calls, at conferences and workshops, and during lunches and dinners. While some are old friends, I met others as a direct result of this work. The list of readers includes (but is not limited to) Aldo Lauria Santiago, Manuel Rodríguez, César Ayala, Mark Healey, Anne Macpherson, Raymond Laureano, Julio Ortiz Luquis, Ismael García-Colón, Harry Franqui-Rívera, Ann Zulawski, Leandro Benmergui, Carlos E. Chardón, and Juan Guisti. More recently, several friends read drafts of the manuscript and offered valuable comments and suggestions. Many thanks to Judy Adkins, Jorell Mélendez-Badillo, Mike Murphy, Dan Sack, and Vanessa Burrows for your time. I owe each and every one of you a drink. At the National Endowment for the Humanities, I am grateful to work in the company of such smart and generous colleagues—particularly my friends in the Division of Research, who have listened to me talk about this project for years. Thank you all. Extra thanks to Russ Wyland, Chris Thornton, Tony Mitchell, Derika Ferdinand Walker, and Marlo Blue for their assistance and support.

Special thanks also go to Stephanye Hunter of the University of Florida Press. Her steadfast support, valuable suggestions, and clear communication are exactly the things you hope for in an editor. The book has benefited from the entire editorial team at the press who helped bring it over the finish line. Many thanks also to the anonymous readers who provided insightful feedback; their ability to discern the manuscript's flaws and strengths were of tremendous value as I revised it for publication.

I'd like to offer special thanks to my family for their love and support over the years, without which this book would not have been possible. Much love to George Burrows, Deby Romero-Clopton and Jim Clopton, Holly and Bruce Dahm, Russell Burrows, Barbara and Al Weller, Sam Weller, Kathryn Weller, and Gwen Demming. Above all, this book is dedicated to Vanessa, Charlotte, and Ysela Burrows for their love, kindness, humor, creativity, knowledge, inspiration, wisdom, and dedication to making every moment count. In the early stages of my research, Vanessa and I made numerous excursions through the Cordillera Central and coastal regions of the island to observe and photograph extant New Deal public works. A boat ride across Dos Bocas was particularly memorable. It is with great joy that so many years later we have been fortunate enough to take Charlotte and Ysela to Puerto Rico as I prepared the book for publication.

Disclaimer: The arguments expressed in this book are my own and do not reflect those of the NEH or federal government.

ABBREVIATIONS

AAA	Agricultural Adjustment Act
AES	Agricultural Experiment Station
ASA	Aqueduct and Sewer Authority
CCC	Civilian Conservation Corps
CGT	Confederación General de Trabajadores (General Confederation of Workers)
CWA	Civil Works Administration
DIVEDCO	División de Educación de la Comunidad (Division of Community Education)
ELA	Estado Libre Asociado (Free Associated State) or Commonwealth of Puerto Rico
FERA	Federal Emergency Relief Administration
FLT	Federación Libre de Trabajadores (Free Federation of Workers)
FSA	Farm Security Administration
FWA	Federal Works Agency
NIRA	National Industrial Recovery Act
PPD	Partido Popular Democrático (Popular Democratic Party)
PRCC	Puerto Rico Cement Corporation
PREPA	Puerto Rico Electric Power Authority
PRERA	Puerto Rico Emergency Relief Administration
PRHA	Puerto Rico Housing Authority
PROMESA	Puerto Rico Oversight, Management, and Economic Stability Act
PRRA	Puerto Rico Reconstruction Administration

PWA	Public Works Administration
RA	Resettlement Administration
RFC	Reconstruction Finance Corporation
SSA	Social Security Administration
TVA	Tennessee Valley Authority
UFF	Utilización de las Fuentes Fluviales (Water Resources Utility)
UPR	University of Puerto Rico
WPA	Works Progress Administration
WRA	Autoridad de las Fuentes Fluviales (Water Resources Authority)

Introduction

This book considers the history and legacy of the Puerto Rico Reconstruction Administration (PRRA), the most important New Deal agency to operate in Puerto Rico and the largest established for any of the U.S. territories. Created by Franklin D. Roosevelt in 1935, the PRRA (pronounced as one word, the "Pra") replaced the Puerto Rico Emergency Relief Administration, which had been formed in 1933. Funded with over $1.7 billion in U.S. tax dollars, the PRRA functioned as an immediate relief and long-term modernization program. While providing disaster and work relief from two devastating hurricanes and the effects of the Great Depression, the PRRA implemented a program of economic development and colonial reform that precipitated the island's transition from an agrarian to an industrial society. At its peak in 1937, the PRRA employed over 58,000 people, the vast majority of which were Puerto Rican, including 90 percent of all administrators and 99 percent of all other workers. While the number of employees declined after 1938, Puerto Ricans from all backgrounds played a central role in how the agency operated and gained valuable training and experience in federal public service from New Deal employment.[1]

The PRRA's attempt to move beyond providing immediate relief from the Great Depression toward constructing more permanent solutions to entrenched social, environmental, and economic problems was characteristic of other Second New Deal programs. As a locally run federal agency operating in a tropical colony of the United States, however, the PRRA was quite distinct from any other New Deal agency. Using previously untapped archival sources and a wide range of published primary and secondary texts, this book situates the PRRA's public works and colonial legacy in both their Puerto Rican and New Deal contexts. In providing the first institutional history of the agency, it also engages with the question of how its programs reconstructed U.S. colonial control in the unincorporated territory of Puerto Rico.

The Puerto Rico Reconstruction Administration argues that disaster recovery programs following San Felipe and San Ciprián became catalysts for modernization and sparked a program of colonial reform. Akin to the Dust Bowl in the midwestern United States, the twin hurricanes were central to how the Great Depression was experienced in Puerto Rico. The scale of their environmental and economic effects went beyond the routine occurrence of smaller storms and was crucial to how reconstruction plans were developed and implemented on the island. Although this book does not engage with environmental determinism, it analyzes how the catastrophic magnitude of the storms created opportunities for Puerto Rican engineers, experts, planners, and other technocrats to initiate programs of social reform and economic modernization. Their programs represented a significant shift from previous colonial policy in Puerto Rico. Changes in the U.S. political system, beginning with the election of Franklin Roosevelt in 1932, had a profound impact on socioeconomic and political conditions in Puerto Rico. The PRRA, which was the clear manifestation of the Second New Deal on the island, created jobs for thousands of new federal public servants whose collective labor began the process of transforming Puerto Rico from an agricultural-based society to a modern industrial economy. Puerto Rican administrators and workers took such an active and leading role in designing, theorizing, and building its public works programs that the PRRA operated, in many ways, like a bilingual and bicultural federal agency. While this might be accurate, it should be stressed that the PRRA was in fact a federal entity that operated out of the executive branch and that its charter could be altered, revoked, or judged unconstitutional at any time. With social work, legal contracts, and health care administered in Spanish to Puerto Ricans by Puerto Ricans, however, the PRRA can rightly be seen as a Puerto Rican–run colonial agency. By the end of the 1930s, the New Deal in Puerto Rico was more accurately the Puerto Rican New Deal.[2]

In addition to its archival source base, the arguments put forth in this book draw upon several distinct historiographical traditions: that of natural disasters and economic development in Latin America and the Caribbean; the history of Puerto Rico; and the history of the New Deal. In doing so, this book simultaneously considers Puerto Rico as a Latin American country and a jurisdictional possession of the United States. While historical scholarship on Puerto Rico has long acknowledged the New Deal, there has yet been little critical examination of the PRRA by historians of Puerto Rico or by scholars of the United States. In fact, most works on the New Deal do not mention the island at all, thereby missing an opportunity to investigate how federal domestic policy impacts daily life in the unincorporated territories and extends the global reach of the U.S. empire. Contemporary Puerto Ricans, however, like other pragmatic observers of the American political system, recognized the enormous changes that marked the transition from Herbert Hoover's New Era to Roosevelt's New Deal.[3]

Despite the fact that thousands of public works constructed by the PRRA continue to have a physical presence in Puerto Rican daily life, the agency has never been the subject of sustained historical inquiry. Among scholars of the United States, for example, there has been little to no academic analysis of the PRRA nor any other aspect of the New Deal in Puerto Rico, even by specialists, despite the voluminous list of works on Franklin Roosevelt and the New Deal. While historians, political scientists, and anthropologists of Puerto Rico are familiar with the New Deal and have used some aspects of the PRRA in their work, the addition of an archivally grounded history of the agency will be useful to a broad range of scholars. This book does not intend to simply fill the gap in the literature, however. Rather, it seeks to make three significant contributions.

One, this book shows how U.S. colonialism in Puerto Rico changed over time. While the PRRA did not solve the crisis of the Great Depression, it, like relief and recovery programs in the continental United States, acted as a kind of holding operation for Puerto Rican society until more decisive changes occurred after World War II. Just as critics in the American Left criticized the Roosevelt administration for propping up and strengthening corporate capitalism and lamented that the New Deal did not go far enough to extinguish the combined forces of racism and poverty (while conservative critics argued that the New Deal was the beginning of a socialist state), we can see today that the PRRA did not work to dismantle U.S. imperial power on the island. Through its direct intervention into the daily lives of all Puerto Ricans and robust commitment to constructing a new public health infrastructure, however, the PRRA tangibly and symbolically demonstrated that the federal government would be a permanent part of Puerto Rican social and economic life for years to come. Employment in the PRRA, whether in temporary work relief or permanent professional training, created many lasting ties to the federal government, informed a negotiated colonial relationship, and was used by many Puerto Ricans as a form of social mobility.[4]

Two, this book provides the first institutional history of the PRRA. In doing so, it introduces readers to a range of Puerto Rican– and American-born New Dealers. Some of the figures were elected officials, partisan appointees, and political leaders. Others were ordinary citizens who were inspired by the election of Roosevelt to enter public service. All of them made pragmatic choices to align with the PRRA.

Three, this history of the PRRA heightens our understanding of the global reaches of the New Deal. What does it mean to view the New Deal through a colonial lens? In Washington, where the PRRA was valued for its diplomatic possibilities as a showcase for the Good Neighbor Policy in Latin America, the New Deal in Puerto Rico meant one thing. On the island, where Puerto Rican New Dealers viewed the PRRA as a vehicle for long-range social and economic reform, it meant something entirely different. After the attack on Pearl Harbor, the PRRA was imbued with a new global significance: the agency's public works became essential to the defense of the Caribbean from deadly U-boat attacks and instrumental to the Allied victory in the Battle of the Atlantic, a necessary precursor to the defeat of Nazi Germany in Europe. The Second World War, as West Indian scholars have argued, could have been lost in the Caribbean at least two years before D-Day.[5] While hurricane recovery predated and overlapped with the PRRA's efforts in economic development and hemispheric defense, its modernization programs became preconditions for the island's rapid postwar transformation and a leading case for U.S. economic intervention in Latin America during the Cold War.

All aspects of the Great Depression in Puerto Rico were exacerbated by two powerful hurricanes, San Felipe and San Ciprián. The first of these, San Felipe, struck the island on September 13, 1928, during the last months of the Calvin Coolidge administration. Its 150 mph winds and torrential rains were even greater than those of San Ciriaco, which had hit Puerto Rico in 1899 at the dawn of U.S. military control. Not only did San Felipe arrive one year before the collapse of the New York Stock Exchange and beginning of the Great Depression, the so-called once-in-a-lifetime storm struck just four years before the equally devastating San Ciprián made landfall in September 1932. Together, the two hurricanes leveled trees and crops, ravaged the infrastructure, and worsened a range of public health crises on the island. Along with the resultant soil erosion and loss of external markets for major crops such as sugar, coffee, and tobacco, environmental damages from the storms hindered agricultural production, put strains on subsistence farming, and plagued rural and urban regions of the island for the rest of the decade. By imperiling nearly all aspects of daily life in the agrarian sectors, the hurricanes compounded the local social and economic effects of the global economic crash. By laying bare the precariousness of the built environment in agricultural and urban regions, the storms invited recovery plans that required scientific, technical, and engineering-based solutions.

Puerto Rico was not the only island in the Caribbean struck by the monstrous force of major hurricanes between 1925 and 1935, as Cuba, the Bahamas, the Dominican Republic, and nearly all other polities of the region witnessed large and frequent storms during this ten-year period. As Stuart Schwartz has shown, the intense hurricane activity of the late 1920s and early 1930s conditioned a wide array of sociopolitical responses to the Depression, including labor unrest and organization, nationalist uprisings, and the formation of populist political coalitions that oversaw state-led welfare and development programs. While disaster recovery programs in the region varied, they shaped local politics in meaningful ways. In Puerto Rico, the 1928 and 1932 hurricanes exposed weaknesses in the colonial relationship that constrained the available strategies of response to the crisis. They also, as we will see, presented engineers, planners, doctors, architects, and other professionals with a chance to design and implement plans for a transformative and lasting recovery. As it did in the continental United States, the New Deal in Puerto Rico responded to environmental crises as much as economic ones.[6]

But there were vast differences between Puerto Rico and the continental United States. Unlike other areas of New Deal intervention, Puerto Rico was an unincorporated territory of the United States and the centerpiece of its strategic interests in the Caribbean, and this colonial history informed how New Deal programs played out on the island. After four hundred years of Spanish colonial rule, Puerto Rico became an internationally recognized possession of the United States on December 10, 1898, when the Treaty of Paris officially ended the Cuban-Spanish-American War. The small archipelago, whose main island measures about 3,500 square miles, had been invaded and occupied by U.S. troops as a strategic consequence of the Cuban war for independence against Spain when the USS *Gloucester* harbored in the southern bay of Guánica in July 1898. A few months later, U.S. soldiers planted the American flag on Puerto Rican soil for the first time. Control of the island was not simply a spoil of the war, however, and should not be reduced to a mere symbol of a new American empire but was rather a central component of the United States' global commercial and military power that had expanded westward during the nineteenth century and spread overseas at the turn of the twentieth. The island's geostrategic value for the remainder of the twentieth century loomed large as a gateway to the Caribbean and thus protector of the Panama Canal and Gulf of Mexico, as the heart of joint naval defenses in the Atlantic theater of World War II, and, later, as both a buffer from and symbolic counterpoint to Fidel Castro's Cuba during the Cold War.[7]

After two years of military rule, Puerto Rico was transferred to civilian colonial control by the Foraker Act, which was signed by William McKinley on April 12, 1900. Under the new law, the Puerto Rican government was undemocratically controlled by Washington as the president had the power to appoint nearly all local leadership without popular consent, including the governor, cabinet, executive council, justices of the Supreme Court of Puerto Rico and U.S. district court, and the resident commissioner (a nonvoting representative to the U.S. Congress). The only exceptions were thirty-five members of the insular legislature who were directly elected. The Foraker Act also established the dominance of federal law over the island and gave Congress the right to veto insular legislation without recourse or appeal.

The Foraker Act was challenged but ultimately sanctioned by the Supreme Court, which ruled that Puerto Ricans did not have protections under the citizenship clause of the Fourteenth Amendment and could thus be governed differently than persons living in the continental United States. Through a series of rulings known as the Insular Cases (ca. 1901–1922), the court changed U.S. territorial policy by defining islands such as Puerto Rico to be ancillary possessions that were not actually parts of the United States. Key to this ruling was the court's finding that Puerto Rico was an unincorporated territory—which is important because unlike incorporated ones, unincorporated territories are legally defined as areas in which only selected parts of the Constitution apply. Defining Puerto Rico as an unincorporated territory consequently justified the imperial nature of U.S. rule without offering the promise of statehood or independence, turning Puerto Ricans into subjects of a growing empire. The Insular Cases were largely decided by the same justices who ruled in favor of racial segregation in the *Plessy v. Ferguson* decision of 1896, and the new legal doctrine of unincorporated colonial rule was undergirded by the justices' racist views of Puerto Ricans, who they wrote were an "uncivilized race" of "fierce, savage and restless people" that were "absolutely unfit" for inclusion into the United States.[8]

Although the island's unincorporated status remained unchanged, Puerto Ricans became birthright citizens of the United States by the passage of the Jones-Shafroth Act, signed by Woodrow Wilson on March 2,

1917. The Jones-Shafroth Act (or Jones Act) replaced the Foraker Act as the guiding colonial framework. In addition to extending U.S. citizenship to Puerto Ricans born on the island, the Jones Act offered greater local autonomy by restructuring the insular government. Despite allowing for the direct election of senators and the resident commissioner, however, the president retained exclusive power to appoint the island's governor, cabinet, and all federal judges. The Jones Act also exempted the sale of Puerto Rican bonds from federal, state, and local taxes. Under the new law, Puerto Ricans occupied an even more ambiguous place in the U.S. legal system, transforming into both citizens and subjects at the same time with no clear path to resolve this contradictory legal position. Further, since the birthright citizenship of Puerto Ricans remains statutory rather than constitutional, its status in U.S. law is more precarious than other forms of citizenship.[9]

Between the passage of the Jones Act and the time of the New Deal, insular politics were dominated by a series of partisan alliances formed around positions on local sovereignty. As a direct result of the ambiguous position of Puerto Rico in the U.S. colonial system, the status question loomed over all other partisan matters and concerns. The question can be boiled down to whether Puerto Rico should be admitted as a state or become an independent nation. The election of 1932 is illustrative of the degree to which Puerto Rican politics had calcified around these two positions. The election, which took place just a few months after San Ciprián, featured four political parties: the conservative, pro-business, and pro-statehood Republican Party, which was often associated with the island's sugar producers; the pro-labor and pro-statehood Socialist Party, which had close ties to the island's largest labor union, the Federación Libre de Trabajadores (Free Federation of Laborers or FLT); the mildly pro-independence Liberal Party; and the more radically pro-independence Nationalist Party. While the Liberal Party received the most total votes of any single party in the election, it failed to gain control of the legislature due to the formation of the Coalition, a strange and at times tenuous alliance between Republicans and Socialists who were united by their support for statehood.

The PRRA was in part shaped by these partisan political divisions. The Coalition emerged as the leading opponent of the New Deal on the island, teaming up with appointed governors to thwart, delay, and criticize the implementation of several initiatives. The PRRA, notably, was conceptualized and run by intellectuals and technocrats in the Liberal Party who viewed economic reform as a necessary precursor to political independence. During the 1930s, Liberals saw cooperation with the Roosevelt administration as the best path toward economic modernization, colonial reform, and eventual independence. At first glance, the Coalition's opposition to the PRRA may seem counterintuitive. Why would a pro-statehood party look to frustrate the federal government? Wouldn't it naturally seek common cause with Congress and the executive branch? But while the Coalition no doubt supported some of the New Deal's policies and programs, its conservative wing was adamantly opposed to business regulations and labor reforms—particularly those that impacted the sugar and other agribusiness sectors, from which came an influential portion of the Republican Party's leadership. Additionally, Coalition leaders charged the Liberal Party with exploiting its relationship with the Roosevelt administration to disproportionately control relief dollars, contracts, and patronage on the island.

Ironically, however, none of the four major political parties survived the Great Depression intact as each fractured under the weight of political tumult, violence, state repression, the lingering effects of natural disasters, and the worsening socioeconomic conditions of the Great Depression. There was also a significant generational shift within party leadership underscored by the imprisonment of Nationalist Pedro Albizu Campos in 1937 and the deaths of three major political figures: Liberal Antonio Barceló in 1938, Socialist Santiago Iglesias in 1939, and Republican Rafael Martínez Nadal in 1941.

The question of how and why the New Deal operated in Puerto Rico animates much of this book. Keeping the political struggles of the 1930s in mind will help, in part, explain why a sizable contingent of Puerto Ricans aligned themselves with the PRRA. More broadly, the election of 1932 was also one of the most important turning points in U.S. political and economic life during the twentieth century. Roosevelt's victory that year ushered in a New Deal for American workers that sharply contrasted with the laissez-faire political economy of his three Republican predecessors, Warren G. Harding, Calvin Coolidge, and Herbert Hoover. By insisting that the federal government had the responsibility to ensure the economic security of all citizens, Roosevelt enhanced the power of the government to more directly intervene in the daily lives of citizens. Doing so, his administration believed, would minimize the factors that exacerbated the economic inequality that had deepened the impact of the Great Depression. Ranging from enhanced financial regulations, protections for organized labor, and a federally secured social safety net to the construction of capital-intensive public works and new interventions in public health, the New

Deal shifted more power to American workers, spurred new understandings of the American public, and created new political coalitions around those understandings. As Marlene Park and Gerald Markowitz have argued, although its "goals were inadequately pursued and implemented, the New Deal . . . broadened the concept of democracy and based it in the economic sphere."[10] Indeed, as Morton Keller has written, the New Deal's "flood of new laws, government action, and social planning after 1932" produced long-range effects, as "never before—save in wartime—had the activities of the [federal] government had such profound and far-reaching consequences for the [American] way of life."[11] The extension of the New Deal to Puerto Rico was an unexpected development that provided Puerto Ricans on the island, who had been U.S. citizens since 1917, access to the long-term changes that Keller describes.

On the island, the New Deal was closely watched by political observers on all sides of the status question. Federal intervention arrived in two phases that map onto the contours of the broader New Deal. There was a First New Deal between 1933 and 1935 that aimed at agricultural reform and hurricane relief and a Second New Deal that looked toward social and economic planning, infrastructural modernization, and colonial reform. While some continental New Deal laws and programs were extended to Puerto Rico, others were designed to exclusively operate on the island. Among the most important elements of the First New Deal that were extended to Puerto Rico were the Agricultural Adjustment Act (AAA), which was intended to stabilize and boost agricultural prices through the reduction of crops, livestock, and other farm products; the Civilian Conservation Corps (CCC), an environmental improvement and work relief program; the National Industrial Recovery Act (NIRA), which implemented wage and price codes across many industries; and the National Labor Relations Act (or Wagner Act), which encouraged collective bargaining. Created in 1933, the Puerto Rico Emergency Relief Administration (PRERA) was specifically designed for the island to provide stopgap disaster and work relief to alleviate the most intense suffering of the Depression's darkest years. While programs like the AAA roiled Puerto Rican politics and were opposed by the island's sugar producers, the PRERA was a subsidiary of the Federal Emergency Relief Administration (FERA), which was itself designed as a short-term work relief program. Whereas the NIRA and AAA were struck down by the Supreme Court in 1935 and 1936, FERA was dissolved in 1935 with most of its work being taken over by the newly created Works Progress Administration (WPA) and Social Security Administration (SSA).[12]

The Second New Deal in Puerto Rico also included many elements of larger programs extended to the island. Among these were the Fair Labor Standards Act of 1938, which applied minimum wage and other labor laws to Puerto Rico (though minimum wages in Puerto Rico and the U.S. Virgin Islands were drastically cut in 1940 after extensive protest from employers in the island's sugar, needlework, and tobacco industries), and the SSA, some aspects of which—such as child welfare services—were applied to the island after 1940. Other well-known programs, such as the WPA, the Public Works Administration (PWA), and the Federal Works Agency (FWA), also operated in Puerto Rico on a limited basis.

One of the most important aspects of the Second New Deal on the island was the Puerto Rico Reconstruction Administration, which was created in 1935 and officially operated until 1955. While the PRRA's goals, methods, and outcomes overlapped with those of the PRERA, its more direct style of intervention into urban and rural daily life created longer-lasting effects than any First New Deal program. The PRRA benefited from direct congressional appropriations and a change in the island's jurisdiction from military to civilian control when it was moved out of the War Department's Bureau of Insular Affairs to the Department of the Interior's newly established Division of Territories and Island Possessions.

The PRRA's tenure can be divided into three distinct phases. The first was between 1935 and 1937 when its initial administrator, Ernest Gruening, sought to use the agency as a showcase for the changing U.S. role in Latin America and the Caribbean under the Good Neighbor Policy. Gruening's diplomatic focus conflicted with the ideas of assistant administrator Carlos Chardón and other Puerto Rican New Dealers. It was also at odds with influential members of Roosevelt's cabinet, particularly Harold Ickes, the secretary of the interior, to whom Gruening directly reported.[13] The second phase lasted between 1937 and 1942 when, led by Puerto Rican engineers, planners, and technocrats, the PRRA made its most lasting reforms to the country's infrastructure and environment. During this period, which is the primary focus of this book, the PRRA headquarters were moved from Washington to San Juan under the leadership team of Miles Fairbank and Guillermo Esteves.[14] The third phase was the long, winding path from World War II to the agency's dissolution in 1955. Overseen by Esteves, this period was almost entirely focused on liaising with the insular government and managing the broad range of public works created during the middle phase.[15]

Historians of the United States have formed a general consensus that the New Deal's emphasis on progressive reform waned after the 1938 midterm elections and had completely ended by the onset of the Second World War. This consensus rests in part on the idea that the shift from domestic spending on public works to wartime expenditures on defense signaled the end of the reform era. In Puerto Rico, however, the influx of New Deal dollars and creation of jobs in the island's economy between 1937 and 1942 manifested a new federal presence on the island as Puerto Rican New Dealers helped transform hurricane and job relief into a broader program of economic reconstruction. The reform emphasis in Puerto Rico, in other words, was only beginning to hit its full stride in 1938. Though few in Washington understood or cared about local developments in Puerto Rico at the time, the New Deal proved to be a pivotal turning point from decades of previous colonial policy.[16]

The shift from relief to reconstruction was not simply a discursive turn but rather a material one that spurred a series of significant social and economic changes in Puerto Rico. By constructing the Caribbean's first modern cement plant, for example, and undertaking widespread rural electrification through the building of seven major hydroelectric dams in the interior mountains of the island, the PRRA created a new public health infrastructure that enhanced physical and social mobility for decades to come. Beyond its considerable socioeconomic impact, the PRRA also had a lasting influence on local politics. By providing a concrete example of how the colonial system changed over time, this book shows that the cost of redoubled federal intervention was in fact a reformed colonial relationship with the United States. While the Puerto Rican New Deal can be seen as a break from previous colonial policy, it should be stressed that it operated at all times within the existing political structure; its inability to confront or challenge the nature of the island's relationship with the United States resulted in a reconstructed but strengthened form of colonialism.

The PRRA was divided into seven basic divisions that overlapped with its principal concerns of public works, public health, job creation, and economic modernization: (1) Administration, Planning, and Personnel; (2) Cooperatives; (3) Engineering; (4) Legal and Finance; (5) Forestry; (6) Rural Electrification; and (7) Rural Rehabilitation. These divisions, which integrated rural and urban reform, were supplemented by various subdivisions such as those dedicated to the cement plant, "slum clearance," housing management, the University of Puerto Rico, public health, social work, sanitation, work relief, research and publicity, and the special mid-decade census of the population that was conducted by the PRRA in 1935. Workers in these divisions and subdivisions performed the kind of labor undertaken by a multitude of the New Deal's so-called alphabet soup agencies in the continental United States. For starters, PRRA programs included the kind of work performed by the WPA, PWA, CCC, Resettlement Administration (RA), Farm Security Administration (FSA), and Tennessee Valley Authority (TVA). In fact, while some of these agencies also operated on the island, their work was almost always managed by PRRA administrators and staffed by PRRA employees.

The PRRA was as essential to the improvement of social, economic, and political conditions on the island as any domestic-facing agency that operated in the continental United States, and it made lasting contributions to the physical well-being of thousands of Puerto Rican families through the construction of hurricane-proof houses, schools, hospitals, roads, bridges, storm drains, and modern water supply and waste disposal systems. This new public health infrastructure contributed to one of the largest increases in life expectancy and opportunity in the island's history. At the same time, improved transportation and communication networks built by PRRA engineers enabled Puerto Ricans in both rural and urban areas to communicate and move in newfound ways. Combined with land reform and increased industrialization, movement and mobility were key elements of the island's mid-century modernization project and became part of a trend toward urbanization and suburbanization, fostering internal migration from rural areas to growing cities such as San Juan, Mayagüez, and Ponce, and outward migration toward metropolises like New York, Chicago, and Philadelphia.[17]

This book largely focuses on the Engineering Division, which emerged as the most significant component of the PRRA during its most active period. Led by Puerto Rican engineers like Guillermo Esteves and Antonio Lucchetti, the PRRA spent large outlays of federal capital and other resources that had never before been available on the island or elsewhere in the Caribbean. Through the construction of capital-intensive public works and creation of the island's first public authorities to administer them, the Engineering Division built a hurricane-proof infrastructure capable of addressing three interrelated goals: increasing life expectancy through concrete interventions in public health; providing more egalitarian access to the built environment; and limiting the monopolistic power of private corporations to control the island's natural resources. The realization of these goals was contingent on an alliance between Puerto Rican workers and the Roosevelt administration, as many on the island saw the New Deal as the only viable option during the troubled times of the decade.[18]

Intellectual, agrarian, and working-class alliances with the Roosevelt administration were not unique to Puerto Rico but rather hallmarks of the broader New Deal. While critiqued by conservatives as a monolithic governmental program imposed from the top down, the New Deal was in fact oftentimes shaped by the local control of federal resources. Demonstrating its creative, flexible, and experimental nature, Roosevelt often shifted resources from one agency to another to negotiate the New Deal's many political ups and downs. Often, policy changes were the result of contentious challenges from Roosevelt's left and right, ranging from erstwhile governor and then senator Huey Long, the so-called populist dictator of Louisiana, who stood poised to challenge Roosevelt in the 1936 Democratic primary with his Share Our Wealth campaign, to conservative southern Democrats such as senators Carter Glass (D-VA), Thomas P. Gore (D-OK), and Millard Tydings (D-MD). As any historian of Puerto Rico can tell you, Tydings also emerged as one of the island's foremost antagonists in the 1930s. Placing the punitive Tydings Bill for Puerto Rican independence in the context of his growing opposition to the progressive wing of the New Deal, this study sketches a fuller picture of Tydings than previous historical scholarship on Puerto Rico.

When San Felipe struck in 1928, there was no publicly funded social safety net on the island. The population, as in many areas of the continental United States, was almost completely vulnerable to natural disasters and almost wholly dependent on external charity to provide relief. Underfunded, the insular government's public works agencies were unable to develop or implement long-range reconstruction plans. Within a decade, however, Puerto Ricans working for the PRRA had contributed to the development of internal markets, built structures that provided greater protection from hurricanes, and established publicly owned corporations and authorities that assured technocratic control of the island's natural resources. The two most important public authorities created by the PRRA were the Puerto Rico Cement Corporation (PRCC) in 1939 and the Puerto Rico Water Resources Authority (WRA) in 1941, both of which were modeled on New Deal–era public corporations in the continental United States and served as models for the island's postwar expansion of the public sector vis-à-vis the creation of insular public authorities and corporations during the Operation Bootstrap era. Historians of the New Deal will not be surprised to learn that the PRRA put its public works construction into high gear after Harold Ickes replaced Gruening as administrator in 1937.

New Deal public works helped legitimize the expanded role of the federal government in Puerto Rico. Legitimization was necessary since the PRRA was a reformed colonial agency that operated through negotiation and alliance. Increased spending on public works underwrote acceptance of the New Deal by creating both jobs and lasting physical infrastructure. By the end of the 1930s, the newly formed Partido Popular Democrático (Popular Democratic Party) stepped into the political vacuum created by the breakdown of the existing party structure by—in part—linking itself with popular PRRA programs. Led by former Liberal Party senator Luis Muñoz Marín, the Popular Democratic Party successfully presented itself as the only political faction able to secure continued federal support for public works and rural rehabilitation. Indeed, even though he had little direct influence on the PRRA after 1937, Muñoz Marín positioned himself as the leader of a populist political coalition that was formed around a combined program of public works and land reform. After winning control of the Puerto Rican Senate in 1940 and later becoming the first elected governor in the island's history in 1948, Muñoz Marín maintained local power in Puerto Rico until the late 1960s.

Indeed, much of the governance structure of the Estado Libre Asociado (Free Associated State or ELA), or Commonwealth of Puerto Rico, after 1952 was put in place during the previous decade and modeled on the PRERA and PRRA. Between 1941 and 1945, Muñoz Marín and Rexford G. Tugwell—the first New Dealer and last American-born appointed governor—wrote and signed laws that enhanced the role of New Deal liberalism on the island.[19] Together, Muñoz and Tugwell created at least nineteen new public agencies modeled on the PRCC and WRA, including the Puerto Rico Transportation Authority, Development Company of Puerto Rico, Puerto Rico Agricultural Development Company, Puerto Rico Aqueduct and Sewerage Service, Puerto Rico Land Authority, Development Bank for Puerto Rico, and the Puerto Rico Communications Authority. The creation of these public agencies highlighted the ways in which the rise of political populism in Puerto Rico corresponded to both mass-based support for New Deal liberalism in the continental United States and contemporary political developments throughout other regions of Latin America and the Caribbean.[20]

This book is divided into five chapters. Chapter 1, "San Felipe, San Ciprián, and the Election of 1932," examines two major hurricanes that struck the island at the onset of the Great Depression and the politics of natural disaster relief as it existed during the Spanish and U.S. colonial eras before the New Deal. While the hurricanes contributed to the political tensions of the decade, emerging plans for relief invited a more federal approach to local recovery efforts. This chapter analyzes the environmental history of San Felipe and San Ciprián while noting how they ravaged the infrastructure of the island, severely depressed the agricultural economy, and increased some of the island's most dangerous threats to public health. Chapter 1 also provides a brief analysis of insular politics during the early 1930s, particularly the election of 1932 and the great wave of labor unrest that rocked the island in 1933 and 1934.

Chapter 2, "From Relief to Reconstruction," observes the formal shift from providing emergency relief during the PRERA to the beginning of long-term reconstruction under the PRRA. This chapter focuses attention on how New Deal programs were developed and deployed and how they reshaped the landscape of recovery. It covers some of the familiar faces of 1930s while introducing the reader to characters such as Miles Fairbank and Guillermo Esteves, who ran the day-to-day operations of the PRRA during its most active period. The coincidental pairing of Fairbank, a mid-level farm bank administrator from Baltimore, and Esteves, one of the island's most important civil engineers, was as fruitful as it was unlikely. This chapter also explores how some of the most explosive events of the decade—including the assassination of police commissioner Francis Riggs, the Tydings Bill for independence, and the Río Piedras and Ponce massacres—affected the administrative structure of the PRRA.

Chapter 3, "*Para Permanencia*," argues that the construction of the island's first cement plant was one of the most significant events of the New Deal years. Built by PRRA engineers between 1936 and 1938, ownership of the Cataño cement plant was transferred to the PRCC, an independent public authority created by the insular government to operate the plant. This chapter also examines how locally produced cement was central to the agency's "swamp drainage" and "slum clearance" programs, through which PRRA engineers sought to remove residents from improvised houses constructed in the island's *arrabales* and *barriadas* (peripheral working-class neighborhoods) and resettle them into newly constructed houses and apartments. Especially important to this chapter are the door-to-door surveys of barriada residents, as the data collected by PRRA social workers offered health officials, urban planners, and engineers insight into daily life among the island's most vulnerable citizens.

Chapter 4, "The Road to Modernization," analyzes some of the PRRA's most critical infrastructure projects such as the construction of hurricane-proof houses, schools, roads, hospitals, health clinics, sanitation and water delivery systems, recreation facilities, agricultural and craft industry cooperatives, and rural rehabilitation centers. By examining how cement from Cataño was used to build a new public health infrastructure, this chapter shows how Puerto Rican engineers, experts, and planners sought to make long-range interventions into social life for residents in both urban and agrarian areas of the island.

Chapter 5, "Rural Electrification," examines the capital- and labor-intensive project to bring hydroelectricity, indoor plumbing, and clean drinking water to the small landowners and landless workers who lived in the Cordillera Central, or interior mountains of the island. This chapter also considers the political fight for rural hydropower and the protracted struggle to break up utility power monopolies on the island. As with the cement plant, all property, constructions, and lands of the rural electrification program were transferred to the local government, which established the WRA to administer the water and electric resources of the island. While the local control of natural resources represented a break from previous colonial policy, it should not be viewed as a lessening of U.S. imperial control of Puerto Rico, which was in many ways strengthened during this era.

The conclusion, "From the New Deal to Today," is dedicated to examining the effects and legacies of the PRRA public works program. This section considers the decline of public authorities and corporations on the island and examines how New Deal programs inadvertently contributed to current and ongoing environmental and financial crises in Puerto Rico caused by the expiration of Section 936 of the U.S. tax code and the recent hurricanes María, Irma, and Fiona. It also examines the PRRA's contributions to the war effort and postwar industrialization program and its impact on the emergence of a Puerto Rican brand of populism under Muñoz Marín.

The story of the PRRA is one in which local factors, decisions, and choices take center stage. Like all people affected by the Great Depression, Puerto Ricans struggled to find appropriate responses to the social, environmental, and political crises of the decade. As elsewhere, their decisions were conditioned by external factors such as the collapse of the stock market, the precipitous decline of international trade, and the rise of totalitarianism in Europe and Japan. Their choices were also shaped by internal dynamics such as insular political upheavals and local environmental conditions. Although these factors presented challenges and limitations to their response to the Depression, the ideas and labor of Puerto Ricans from all backgrounds were central to formulating visions of a lasting recovery, and a cross-section of civil engineers, teachers, academics, doctors, farmers, and other workers found common ground on pragmatic solutions made possible by new alliances, choices, and compromises. To be sure, Puerto Rican choices were constrained by the widespread repression of nationalist and radical voices undertaken by federal and insular police agencies during the 1930s. This story, however, is neither one of simple resistance to colonialism nor a lament for the limits of personal and collective agency in the face of great or arbitrary power. Rather, it is the story of how professional and working-class Puerto Ricans negotiated with the imperial structure of U.S. control during the New Deal era, gained prominent positions within relief and recovery programs, and made enduring improvements to living conditions in all areas of the island.[21]

To tell this story from an archival perspective, however, two considerations were necessary. First, the book takes the work of Puerto Rican engineers and other experts seriously. While the chapters that follow do not adopt their technocratic point of view wholesale, they refrain from dismissing such actors as colonial agents whose elite status and American educations permanently stained their efforts to build a new Puerto Rican society and economy. Instead, this book examines how Puerto Rican technocrats attained influence over the shape and pace of colonial reform. The PRRA, for the Puerto Rican experts discussed in this book, was an infrastructural development program that considered ideas about science, progress, and modernity central to finding solutions to the island's entrenched socioeconomic problems, its vulnerability to natural disasters, and its colonial dilemma. Well versed in U.S. political and economic discourse, Puerto Rican technocrats found common ground with American-born counterparts by skillfully articulating their visions to align with the goals of the Roosevelt administration. As the PRRA could not have functioned without close cooperation between these two groups, it is important to keep in mind that many of these Puerto Rican experts and planners shared the class-, gender-, and race-based biases of their American allies regarding the impoverished and largely uneducated mass of rural farmers, sharecroppers, and wage workers, often referred to as jíbaros or peasants.

At the same time, working within the colonial system revealed conflicting and contradictory impulses in the work of the highly educated technocratic classes discussed in this book. Working within the system provided a means of enacting lasting hurricane recovery, constructing a new public health infrastructure, and electrifying the countryside. Aligning with the federal government not only secured an influx of New Deal dollars but also created an opportunity for Liberals to operate independently from the Coalition-controlled legislature and oppositional governor's office. Yet working within the colonial system perpetuated and strengthened that system as well. Because the technocratic sector of the population has been little studied in the historical literature, this book uses all available source data to analyze the plans for modernization developed by a variety of Puerto Rican professionals ranging from medical doctors and nurses, agronomists, and educators to architects, urban planners, and social workers. It considers not only the executive level of the professional class but also the many junior white-collar men and women who used work experience in the PRRA as a means of social mobility for themselves and their families— many of whom continued to work in professional public service positions in insular, state, and federal governments during the postwar period. Since few bureaucrats, engineers, or public servants leave behind memoirs and written records, it has been necessary to study their public works and actions instead.[22]

Second, this book has had to confront the limits of the federal archive that at times includes only marginal insight into the identities and ideas of many Puerto Ricans who worked for the PRRA and participated in its programs. Wherever possible, this book has pulled their voices and stories from a variety of sources including legal contracts, demographic surveys, payroll documents, disciplinary records, newspaper articles, letters of support, photographs, and letters of complaint. For example, while the research for this book uncovered limited archival data regarding race, archival photographs reveal the actuality of Black Puerto Rican doctors working for the PRRA.[23] With no extant list of all PRRA employees found, this book could not put names behind all of the data regarding the employees mentioned in its pages. Often, when a name was present in planning documents, personnel records, or letters, this book has included it in the text or notes. While further ancestral and ethnographic research could tell us more about the longer trajectory of their lives, such a project is beyond the scope of the current book.

1

San Felipe, San Ciprián, and the Election of 1932

On Thursday morning, September 13, 1928, those living on the southern coast of Puerto Rico awoke to a suspicious wind coming onshore. For some residents in the sugarcane regions of the island, the swirling wind did not alter their daily routine; for others, such as Don Taso Zayas, the informant of Sidney Mintz's *Worker in the Cane*, the gathering wind meant that work would be cancelled that day. After closing the irrigation conduits to the cane fields, Don Taso sent home the seven or eight workers he supervised. Walking by the beach before lunch, he noted that the waves were strong and the tide was already passing underneath the sea grape trees that grew along the shore. An hour later, the hurricane known in Puerto Rico as San Felipe II struck the thatched palm– and zinc-roofed houses and improvised wooden structures of Barrio Jauca, Santa Isabel. While officials in San Juan received radio reports that a well-formed tropical storm had been reported about a thousand miles southeast of Guayama by the SS *Commack*, a cargo ship sailing from Bahia, Brazil, to Philadelphia, others relied only on experience, intuition, and door-to-door messages. Although residents of the sugar-growing south coast had experienced hurricanes before, few could have realized how dramatically San Felipe would affect nearly all aspects of social, economic, and political life during the coming decade of the 1930s.[1]

San Felipe, which was called Okeechobee in the continental United States, was the most powerful hurricane to ever strike Puerto Rico. Measured by the Saffir-Simpson Hurricane Wind Scale in use by the National Hurricane Center since the 1970s, San Felipe was a Category 4 major hurricane. Having ravaged the island of Guadalupe the day before, the storm continued northward across the Bahamas on Friday and Saturday and struck the south coast of Florida somewhere between Jupiter and Boca Raton on Sunday, September 15. In Florida, nearly two thousand people died when the waters of Lake Okeechobee flooded, disproportionately killing African Americans and West Indian immigrants who worked in the southern Florida sugarcane fields. By September 20, a week after it struck the southern coast of Puerto Rico, San Felipe had crawled up the Eastern Seaboard and crossed New York State before dissipating over the cool waters of Lake Ontario and southern Canada.[2]

The exact death toll in Puerto Rico from San Felipe is unknown; the official report was 312 killed, though recent studies estimate that more than 1,500 people may have actually died as a direct result of the storm. Over one-third of the island's population was rendered homeless by San Felipe, with somewhere between 500,000 and 700,000 people needing immediate relief shelter before the construction of permanent housing could even be contemplated. Among these, approximately 250,000 to 300,000 residents of the island's three major agrarian zones would need at least 50,000 new houses. San Felipe's sustained winds and intense rain caused catastrophic infrastructural damage, with about 10 to 12 inches falling on coastal areas and between 20 and 48 inches in the Cordillera Central. Official reports and newspaper coverage painted a grim portrait of the destruction: the storm flooded Ponce and the southern coast of the island; demolished wooden-framed houses; disorganized telephone and telegraph systems within the island and to the outside world; interrupted railroad service used for exports; destroyed over seven hundred rural schoolhouses and caused significant damage to many others; tore away the roof of the tuberculosis clinic and destroyed the leper colony quarters; and caused the destruction of essential water, sewerage, and irrigation systems. Damages to many of the insular government's unfinished public works set completion back years or decades. The hurricane destroyed at least 70 percent of the houses and 30 percent of the commercial buildings in greater San Juan and caused between $40 million and $85 million in island-wide property damage (between $845 million and $1.8 billion today).[3]

In addition to infrastructural damage, San Felipe disrupted the agrarian economy of the island. All major agricultural industries were impacted, with crops and trees in the sugar, coffee, tobacco, and citrus-growing regions uprooted or otherwise destroyed. A recent study by Teresita Levy illustrated the devastation suffered by tobacco farmers, with over six thousand tobacco ranches destroyed and more than 25 percent of all tobacco seedbeds washed away in the uncompromising wind and rain.[4] For tobacco, coffee, coconut, and citrus farmers, the hurricane amplified existing financial strains caused by debt and created even higher barriers to sustainable recovery. In tobacco, for example, San Felipe compounded the disastrous 1927 crop, when the price paid to tobacco farmers had decreased by 48 percent due to the effects of San Liborio, a small hurricane that had struck the year before. As Levy has explained, the sharp price decrease was also due to years of overplanting that the market could not absorb, as consumer tastes shifted away from cigars toward cigarettes in the late 1920s. In the coffee regions, planters suffered nearly $9.5 million (about $201 million today) in losses from the amount of matured coffee beans that were washed away and scattered in the mud. The millions of dollars in losses were exacerbated by the destruction of shade trees and the fact that newly planted coffee bushes take several years to yield fruit. For coconut farmers, who lost over 227,000 trees in the hurricane and approximately $500,000 ($10.6 million today) in mature coconuts, the wait for new trees to mature would be six to eight years once they were able to be planted. Clearing the fallen trees involved huge expenses, arduous labor, and time. Citrus farmers, who had exported over a million crates of fruit in 1927, lost about 150,000 fruit-bearing trees to San Felipe as 35,000 trees were uprooted and at least 125,000 more were damaged by the furious winds, flooding, erosion, and mudslides. While countless oranges and grapefruits were blown from their limbs and ruined in the mud, fallen trees were placed back in their original holes wherever possible in hopes they would take root once again. Losses in citrus totaled $2.5 million (about $53 million today) for commercial farmers and an estimated $500,000 ($10.6 million today) for subsistence farmers in the area. For commercial and subsistence banana and plantain growers, the devastation was nearly complete as the island lost an estimated 40 million bunches of fruit in the wind and rain, which dealt a serious blow to supplemental food supplies across the island.[5]

Recovery from San Felipe was incomplete when San Ciprián struck Puerto Rico four years later, making landfall overnight between September 26 and 27, 1932, and moving horizontally across the northern length of the island where it directly impacted about two-thirds of Puerto Rico's seventy-six municipalities. Around 6:00 a.m. on Monday morning, September 26, the U.S. Weather Bureau in San Juan received reports from Antigua about a possible hurricane. Three hours later, when the report was confirmed by communications with Saint Kitts and Saint Martin, the bureau issued official warnings to all parts of the island. San Ciprián's 120 mph winds, which would be considered a Category 3 hurricane today, devastated the islands of Culebra and Vieques before hitting the east coast of mainland Puerto Rico between Ceiba and Fajardo around 9:00 p.m. That night, as San Ciprián skirted the north side of the Cordillera Central, it struck San Juan just after midnight and caused the most intensive damage between 12:30 and 1:30 a.m. It hovered over Dorado and Arecibo and trudged along the northwestern coast past Aguadilla before exiting the west coast of the island just before dawn on the morning of September 27 and eventually abating near the coast of the Mexican Yucatán.[6]

San Ciprián killed hundreds, left over 400,000 people homeless, and, like San Felipe, caused extensive damage to the infrastructure and agriculture of the island. The hurricane destroyed over 90,000 houses and inflicted almost $600,000 (about $12.7 million today) in rural and urban school property damage. In agrarian areas, San Ciprián left 1.6 million farm buildings in ruins, killed nearly 500,000 livestock animals, and exacted a staggering $30 million (about $636 million today) in financial losses to all major agricultural industries: $11.5 million ($244 million today) in sugar, $3.7 million ($78.5 million) in coffee, $1.9 million ($40 million) in citrus, $11.5 million ($244 million) in coconuts and palm trees, and $750,000 (about $16 million) in tobacco. In San Juan, the School of Tropical Medicine and its hospital were flooded with water and caked with heavy layers of sand and mud but otherwise withstood the storm intact. While San Ciprián caused minimal infrastructural ruin to the school itself, countless hours of research time and analysis were lost due to so-called minor damages. For example, while many experimental animals were saved, a number of chickens and guinea pigs were killed, making the research data collected from them valueless. Similarly, power outages rendered many hours of research in the Department of Bacteriology worthless as the lab's refrigerators stopped working and spoiled the school's unique collection of cultures. The Department of Bacteriology was also struck by a large sheet of flying zinc that broke through the windows, allowing the rain and wind to wreak havoc among the various bottles of chemicals and other glassware in the lab. Taken together, San Felipe and San Ciprián touched nearly every community on the island and affected nearly all aspects of daily life for the rest of the Great Depression. The combined damage of the two storms was over $175 million (more than $3.7 billion today).[7]

Although these numbers are striking, it is impossible to measure the economic damage caused by the storms by lost income or dollars alone. As César Ayala and Laird Bergad have demonstrated, there were vast social and economic differences between the three primary crop zones of coffee, tobacco, and sugar. In the coffee highlands, for example, *agregados* (resident farm workers or service tenants who received housing and, in some cases, wages) often grew their own food thanks to the social and legal practice of granting usufruct rights to workers for the production of subsistence agriculture. Usufruct rights, which allow land occupants to use and benefit from a property they do not own, are an important factor in Puerto Rican social history. In rural areas ravaged by San Felipe and San Ciprián, therefore, it was not simply property damage, loss of crop revenue, or the decline of wages that were factors; the devastation of the terrain itself meant that workers could not grow their own food as they customarily did. The three major agrarian zones were not all the same, however, and the sugar and tobacco areas contrasted with the customary use of usufruct rights in the coffee region. In the coastal plains where sugar dominated, wage labor prevailed and workers did not usually have access to subsistence gardens. In tobacco zones dominated by family farming, small landowners relied on subsistence crops to such an extent that they often devoted as much or more land to planting food crops for personal use than they did for tobacco, their cash crop.[8]

The four years separating San Felipe and San Ciprián were especially challenging, as two major Puerto Rican banks failed and a large number of private businesses went into bankruptcy between 1929 and 1932. The early years of the Depression were also marked by San Nicolás, a smaller hurricane that made landfall in 1931, and an influenza epidemic that began in the summer of 1932 and resulted in over fifty thousand cases across the island before finally subsiding that October.[9] While hurricanes and other natural disasters and environmental phenomena are worthy of historical study, they are more broadly significant for the ways in which they became catalysts for large-scale social, economic, and political transformations in Puerto Rico. By mid-decade, as we will see, many Puerto Rican engineers, planners, workers, and farmers aligned with the New Deal to help foster a shift from emergency relief to long-range reconstruction.

To understand the coming of the New Deal to Puerto Rico we must recognize what contemporary Puerto Rican technocrats knew well: that existing models of relief were in fact contributing to the island's intertwined economic and public heath emergencies. Indeed, previous systems of relief not only failed to relieve the immediate suffering but made the crisis worse in two clear ways. First, by relying on a decentralized model of charitable fundraising developed under earlier periods of Spanish and U.S. colonial rule, disaster relief after San Felipe and San Ciprián deepened fundamental inequalities in Puerto Rican society by enhancing the power of large landowners. Second, the wide range of temporary relief houses built after the 1928 and 1932 storms actually *increased* some of the most lethal public health crises confronting the island during the 1930s, such as malaria, hookworm, and pervasive malnutrition.[10]

A decentralized approach to hurricane relief was developed under the Spanish colonial system, which had extensive experience with Atlantic hurricanes dating back to the end of the fifteenth century. By the time San Narciso came ashore near Fajardo on October 29, 1867, about eleven months before the Grito de Lares rebellion against Spanish rule, the Crown had been confronted with numerous hurricanes of various sizes in all of its major Caribbean possessions, including Santo Domingo, Cuba, Puerto Rico, Florida, and along the circum-Caribbean coasts of New Spain and New Granada. In Puerto Rico, for example, at least twenty-five major hurricanes were recorded between the sixteenth and nineteenth centuries. Despite this experience, however, the Spanish spent only an estimated 3 percent of its colonial budget on building basic infrastructure that could buffer the destructive fury of tropical storms. Relief was distributed to farmers, workers, and their families through petitions and appeals to local landowners and officials in the colonial government. By distributing royal relief funds through private estates, the Spanish system turned large landowners into de facto government contractors who were empowered to make all essential decisions regarding the distribution of necessary funds, food, and supplies.[11]

After the occupation of Puerto Rico in 1898, the United States merged the Spanish relief system it inherited with leading ideas of the Progressive era regarding philanthropic, religious, and private charity. Like the Spanish system, the U.S. system before the New Deal provided adequate relief when necessary but failed to make structural interventions in public health or the physical security of residents. Military officials, who were in charge of Puerto Rico between 1898 and the passage of the Foraker Act in 1900, were immediately tested by the arrival of San Ciriaco on August 8, 1899. Viewing the powerful hurricane as an opportunity to demonstrate the efficiency and efficacy of their rule, the U.S. Army developed a more centralized approach than the Spanish Crown—though its foray into providing relief once again strengthened the hand of local landowners. In fact, in the three decades since San Narciso, large landowners in some parts of the island had increased the proportion of their holdings by considerable amounts. In the coffee zones, for example, land concentration, rural landlessness, and the emergence of an agrarian working class developed during the second half of the nineteenth century. While William McKinley and officials in his cabinet sought to praise the military response and politicize its relief efforts, the new insular political parties that had formed since 1898 likewise used relief as a means to garner political influence.[12]

Damages caused by San Ciriaco were severe. The storm, which struck the southern third of the island, killed over 2,700 people and left approximately 250,000 homeless in a horizontal line from Humacao to Mayagüez. Wind gusts of 140 mph were accompanied by a foot of rain in some areas while tidal waves on the southern coast submerged residential areas with saltwater. In the central mountains, flooding, soil erosion, and mudslides resulted in an estimated $20 million ($425 million today) in property damage—about half of which occurred in the coffee sector, which was hit particularly hard. As a result, coffee exports in 1899 were only 10 percent of their average in the preceding five years between 1894 and 1898.[13]

Relief efforts were overseen by Brigadier General George W. Davis, who had served in the Cuban-Spanish-American War and was the last military governor of Puerto Rico. Fashioned on the Spanish system, military relief relied on local officials and landowners. Davis, who was later appointed chair of the Central Committee of the American Red Cross and governor of the Panama Canal Zone by Theodore Roosevelt, pressed for food and other relief supplies from Secretary of State Elihu Root, who organized a campaign to promote charitable relief directed at the general public coordinated through mayors of large U.S. cities. Meanwhile, on the ground in Puerto Rico, Davis and Major John Van Rensselaer Hoff, a surgeon in the U.S. Army, established the Board of Charities to facilitate relief aid donations imported from the continental United States. Like relief efforts in the Spanish colonial era, U.S. military responses to San Ciriaco strengthened the position of elite landowners through their participation on the Board of Charities and the Planters' Relief Initiative. Landowners, in turn, submitted applications for relief on behalf of their resident tenants and farmworkers. Davis, Hoff, and other military officials distrusted the local population, considering jíbaros and other rural workers untrustworthy. In private, Davis characterized agrarian workers as "primitive peons" and assured Puerto Rican elites that only the "best citizens" would serve on the auxiliary relief committees that controlled the distribution of food and other necessities. "The greatest difficulty," he wrote, is "discriminating between those who are really needy and those who pretend to be so."[14]

In terms of actually managing and coordinating relief and distribution efforts, however, the military improved upon the Spanish model by swiftly moving food and supplies along centralized supply lines from the port of San Juan outward. Since the island was still in a state of occupation, Davis used military post commanders as relief inspectors that supervised depots and subdepots at major supply points in each municipality. While the army relied on roads and ships to move supplies swiftly, transportation on the mountainous dirt roads—many of which were washed out by the hurricane—was ineffectively provided by wooden carts, mules, and horses as it had been during the preceding centuries.

As Nicole Ferraiolo has argued, the military's experience with San Ciriaco and focus on philanthropic aid influenced all disaster relief policy in the continental United States for the next thirty years. Prior to the Great Depression, the idea of relief was dominated by a combination of Progressive-era charity and laissez-faire individualism, the prevailing economic philosophy of business leaders during the 1920s. Throughout this time, the social safety net was composed of a variety of private community and corporate organizations. Stitched together by churches, charities, unions, settlement houses, community organizations, immigrant societies, fraternal orders, agricultural associations, and welfare capitalist employers, the private safety net worked in tandem with local, county, and state governments to provide temporary assistance in times of natural disaster, environmental crisis, or economic recession. Before the New Deal, it was to these local and private institutions—not the federal government—that public welfare was entrusted.[15]

After the Great Mississippi Flood of 1927, for example, Calvin Coolidge relied on the American Red Cross to coordinate disaster response despite growing calls for more direct intervention from the federal government. That spring, when the Mississippi River overflowed its banks and levees, an area 500 miles long and 50 miles wide experienced massive flooding that killed hundreds and forced millions of people to evacuate their homes in parts of Illinois, Missouri, Oklahoma, Arkansas, Kentucky, Texas, Tennessee, Mississippi, and Louisiana. As people across the continental United States listened to radio reports in their homes and watched newsreel footage in movie theaters, Coolidge initially refused to intervene in relief and rescue efforts. A week later, he relented to the pleas of state governors and asked Secretary of Commerce Herbert Hoover to coordinate a federal relief plan with the Red Cross, selected cabinet departments, and the military.[16]

Hoover's plan for flood relief combined short- and long-term strategies. Largely based on charity and credit, it also attempted to turn evacuation camps into rural rehabilitation sites that featured education in agriculture, personal health, hygiene, and home economics. Hoover sought to rebuild the flooded region through federally supported credit and loaned money to cotton planters and sugar growers on more generous terms than private banks. To raise money for the relief loan program, Hoover leaned on the largest U.S. corporations for support and received approximately $13 million (about $275 million today) from General Electric, Standard Oil, Ford, General Motors, Dodge, Sears Roebuck, Marshall Field, Proctor & Gamble, Allied Chemical, U.S. Steel, the New Orleans Cotton Exchange, and the Pennsylvania Central and Illinois Central railroads. This loan money supplemented the $17 million (about $360 million today) donated directly to the Red Cross by private citizens. Inching closer to a centralized system of federal intervention, Hoover supported the passage of the Mississippi Flood Control Act of 1928 that authorized the Army Corps of Engineers to design and build flood control systems for the region and beyond—a major innovation in U.S. disaster preparation and relief policy.[17]

Changes to the U.S. model of relief during the Great Mississippi Flood are significant for two reasons. On one hand, Hoover was able to raise his national profile by positioning himself once again as the progressive engineer and humanitarian who had led famine relief efforts in Belgium and Russia after the First World War. By doing so, he enhanced his chances in the 1928 presidential election, which he won in a landslide. On the other hand, relief policy after the Mississippi flood was more centralized than ever before and turned the Red Cross—to many observers—into a quasi-official extension of the federal government itself.[18]

The following year, this public-private partnership between the federal government and the Red Cross was tested in Puerto Rico when the Red Cross took charge of relief efforts after San Felipe in coordination with the Puerto Rico National Guard. On September 14, the day after San Felipe made landfall, the Red Cross assembled an experienced group from the Mississippi flood who traveled by train to Charleston, South Carolina, where they boarded the USS *Gilmer* and sailed for San Juan. Meanwhile, the Red Cross sent fundraising appeals to its chapters across the country for donations. On September 16, the first supplies of beans, rice, and salted cod were shipped to the island by the U.S. Bureau of Insular Affairs and the Red Cross. While credit slips allowed Puerto Ricans to purchase extant food and supplies from local merchants, charitable contributions exceeded $5.9 million (about $125 million today) including $50,000 (about $865,000 today) from the Red Cross Reserve Fund. "Without the aid of the American Red Cross," wrote Governor Horace Towner, "it would have been impossible for Porto Rico to have met the demand occasioned by the hurricane."[19]

On the island, the Red Cross worked with the governor's office and insular legislature to distribute relief supplies. Many figures who would later be associated with the New Deal were directly involved in the relief efforts, including Carlos Chardón and Guillermo Esteves, who would each run the PRRA in future years. Chardón and Esteves served on a variety of relief committees and boards with American- and Puerto Rican–born members, such as Colonel Clarence S. Ridley of the Army Corps of Engineers and local business leaders Félix R. Hilera, Adolfo Valdés, Eduardo Soler, and Xavier Mariani. Together with the insular government, these committees enlisted over 800 police officers, 1,500 members of the National Guard, and nearly all of the island's 4,000 schoolteachers to survey the damage caused by San Felipe. (The teachers were temporarily out of work due to the closing of schools that had been damaged or destroyed in the hurricane.) Dividing the island into a hierarchical system of districts to facilitate communication, the movement of personnel, and the speedy distribution of supplies, the relief committees oversaw the clearing of roads, repair of telegraph lines, and restoration of schools and public buildings into usable shape.[20]

By the end of 1928, an Executive Committee of Supervision and Relief was formed; members included Emilio del Toro (chief justice of the Puerto Rican Supreme Court), Pablo Baerga (a district court judge), Colonel George W. Helms (regimental commander of the Sixty-Fifth Infantry), Jorge Bird Arias (chair of the Puerto Rican chapter of the American Red Cross), and Cecilio Moran (the president of B. Fernández and Hnos, a major distributor and vendor of packaged foods and household goods). Advised by Guillermo Esteves, the Executive Committee favored the hierarchical system of relief that was already established. Esteves, who was born in Aguadilla and educated at Tufts University, was a staunch believer in Progressive-era ideas about progress, efficiency, and the maintenance of hierarchical racial and social strata. The centralized system favored the *colono* class of small family farmers that Esteves believed to possess the highest moral character of all Puerto Ricans. Under his variation of the system, small family farmers—rather than elite landowners—were entrusted with the distribution of relief loans and supplies while the island's sharecroppers, agregados and other tenant farmers, wage workers, urban poor, and prison inmates were contracted by the local government to labor on construction projects. Their meager wages were paid with a 10/90 structure: a small amount in cash and the rest in food rations.[21]

In December 1928, Congress created the Porto Rico Hurricane Relief Commission to make loans to small farmers as part of an agrarian rehabilitation program. Sponsored by Senator Hiram Bingham (R-CT) and

Representative Edgar R. Kiess (R-PA), the Hurricane Relief Commission was managed by the collector of customs at San Juan, the insular Department of Agriculture, and the Army Corps of Engineers. In 1930, as the global economy sank further into the Depression, Hoover requested an additional $3 million (about $63.6 million today) for the Hurricane Relief Commission, noting that Puerto Ricans were still suffering from the effects of San Felipe and needed increased access to loans.[22]

Like other federal farm loan programs that had been extended to Puerto Rico during the previous decade, the Hurricane Relief Commission was formed in part as a reaction to the pressure put on Congress by Puerto Rican farmers who closely followed all federal relief activities and found spaces in the colonial system to strategically lobby, protest, and negotiate in their own interests. Farmers in nearly all agrarian sectors participated in agricultural leagues and associations. The Asociación de Agricultores Puertorriqueños (Puerto Rican Farmers Association), for example, was an island-wide group founded in 1924 that lobbied for its members' interests through its newspaper *El agricultor puertorriqueño* and by sending contingents to San Juan and Washington. As Teresita Levy has written, "Governors, presidents, senators, and other administrators were visited by the representatives of Puerto Rican tobacco growers, publicly challenged, and criticized." By actively promoting their own rights and interests, Puerto Rican farmers became active political participants within the colonial system and won much-needed relief as "insular and federal officials responded to such pressure by altering legislation, providing economic relief, and including Puerto Ricans in their decision-making" processes.[23]

When San Ciprián struck in 1932, Hoover had already created the Reconstruction Finance Corporation (RFC), a federal agency designed to provide aid and loans to both public institutions like state, county, and municipal governments and private corporations such as banks, railroads, insurance companies, and home lending agencies. The RFC, which can be seen as a stepping stone between the laissez-faire capitalism of the 1920s and the direct federal intervention of the New Deal, was a tacit acknowledgment that the social safety net based on private charity was inadequate. Following San Ciprián, however, the RFC was largely ineffective at making loans to Puerto Rico because the insular government had depleted its legal borrowing capacity—demonstrating the futility of Hoover's approach to relief and recovery based on loans rather than direct intervention. As before, hurricane relief efforts were coordinated by the Red Cross, the governor's office, locally elected representatives, cabinet officials, and a variety of private citizens. With lack of widespread radio ownership, the insular government used a semaphore system of signal flags flown from the churches and public buildings of each town in an effort to warn the population of the approaching hurricane about six hours before it hit.[24]

Teachers were again enlisted to undertake local surveys of the population; in some cases, they were ready to begin this work the morning after the storm. Because the hurricane struck large cities and urban areas on the northern coast, some of the 225 official deaths were caused by the collapse of buildings, being struck by flying debris, and drowning in flash floods in the barriadas and other working-class neighborhoods on the periphery of San Juan. Aerial surveys conducted after the storm revealed that the northern two-thirds of the island had severe damages while the southern third was virtually spared, looking practically untouched to observers.[25]

The Red Cross established a Committee of Medical Aid, which was chaired by Rafael Bernabe, a doctor and the president of the Medical Association of Puerto Rico. The Committee of Medical Aid assisted the insular Department of Health in providing medical relief for the population, with at least thirty-six doctors and sixty-two nurses tending to patients along the northern coast. In addition to emergency medical care, over three-quarters of all patients were treated with tetanus shots and 66,651 residents received typhoid inoculations. In the mountain towns of Gurabo and San Lorenzo, located to the east of Caguas and southwest of El Yunque National Forest, the aftermath of San Ciprián brought an epidemic of dysentery that was attended by overworked doctors, nurses, and volunteers from the Department of Health and the Red Cross. The Sixty-Fifth Infantry and the Puerto Rican National Guard, which also delivered medical care across the island, oversaw the construction of temporary relief houses built by an assemblage of soldiers, members of the American Legion, students from manual training and vocational schools, community volunteers, and prisoners from the insular penitentiary who were conscripted for the work. This diverse team, which consisted of 162 brigades of relief workers in eight municipalities, constructed 1,339 relief shelters and distributed nails, wood, and other building supplies to homeowners whose properties had been damaged—but not destroyed—by the hurricane.[26]

While the Red Cross, Committee of Medical Aid, and other relief committees undertook this work, the larger process of recovery from San Ciprián occurred amid one of the most pivotal election cycles in Puerto Rican history. A four-way race, the election of 1932 featured candidates from the Republican, Socialist, Liberal, and Nationalist Parties. While each party campaigned to lead relief efforts from the storms and the broader effects of the Great Depression, the most important issue was the island's colonial status. Although the Republican and Socialist Parties were ideologically far apart on most issues, they were steadfastly united in their support of statehood and formed a political partnership for this election known as the Coalition. By gaining a legislative majority in both the House and Senate, the Coalition was the big winner that November, and for the rest of the decade, Republican Rafael Martínez Nadal and Socialist Santiago Iglesias Pantín dominated insular politics as the elected president of the Senate and resident commissioner, respectively. Analysis of the polling data demonstrates the effectiveness of the Coalition's alliance, as Iglesias was elected resident commissioner only through the combined votes of Republicans and Socialists. Whereas Liberal Party candidate Benigno Fernández García received 170,168 votes (44.3 percent of the electorate), Iglesias was elected by the combined tally of 208,232 votes: 110,794 from Republicans (28.9 percent) and 97,438 (25.4 percent) from Socialists.[27]

The election of 1932 was also noteworthy for one entry and one withdrawal from electoral politics, both of which influenced the larger course of political life in Puerto Rico for decades to come. First, the election marked the political debut of Luis Muñoz Marín, who was elected to serve as a senator for the Liberal Party. Muñoz Marín was the son of Luis Muñoz Rivera, a towering figure in Puerto Rican politics and letters who had helped lead the movement for political autonomy within the Spanish empire. Muñoz Rivera was a leader of the Autonomist Party in the nineteenth century and, after the U.S. invasion, cofounded the Union Party in the early twentieth century. The first editor of *La Democracia*, Muñoz Rivera served as resident commissioner between 1911 and his death in 1916. His son, Luis Muñoz Marín, was born in 1898 and lived in both Puerto Rico and the continental United States during his formative years. A bilingual and bicultural advocate of political independence, he began editing *La Democracia* in 1926 before running for the Senate in 1932.

Second, the election represented the beginning and end of the Nationalist Party's participation in electoral politics during the 1930s when Julio Medina González, their candidate for resident commissioner, received just 5,257 votes (1.4 percent). The Nationalist Party had been founded by José Coll y Cuchí in 1922 and was, a decade later, led by Medina González and Pedro Albizu Campos. Following their defeat, many members of the party gravitated away from the leadership of the elderly and venerable Medina González (who was first elected to public office in 1905) toward the call for direct action articulated by the younger Albizu Campos, who had lost his own senatorial bid in 1932. As Albizu Campos moved away from electoral politics, he became the leader of an anti-colonial independence movement that employed violence in its struggle with the federal and insular governments, particularly after 1936. It should be noted that the emergence of Albizu Campos as the leader of the Nationalist Party was in many ways a reaction to the success of the Coalition—as his supporters believed that the electoral victory of the Republican and Socialist Parties would result in a renewed push for statehood.[28]

The Coalition's rise to power in 1932 is also significant for understanding the timing and shape of the New Deal in Puerto Rico. Despite the internal contradictions of an alliance between pro-business Republicans and pro-labor Socialists, the two statehood parties expected to capitalize on their legislative power. Somewhat ironically, however, the Coalition did not align themselves with the New Deal and worked against their own interests by not cultivating a close relationship with the Roosevelt administration. Today, their opposition can be seen as a political miscalculation that privileged local electoral victory over furthering the statehood movement vis-à-vis control of federal relief and recovery programs. But at the time, many Republican leaders had direct interests in thwarting reform and rehabilitation plans, particularly the New Deal's efforts to redistribute land, build worker-run agricultural cooperatives in sugar and other agribusinesses, and break up power and water monopolies. The most influential anti–New Deal voices in the Republican Party included Senator Pedro Juan Serrallés of Ponce, owner of several *centrales* (sugar mills); senator and "utility king" Alfonso Valdés Cobián, vice president of the Mayagüez Light, Ice, and Power Company and cofounder of the Compañía Cervecera de Puerto Rico in 1937; and Speaker Miguel Angel García Méndez, a lawyer for the South Porto Rico Sugar Company.[29]

The Socialist Party joined the Coalition because it viewed statehood as the optimum vehicle for social reform via organized labor. Their decision to align with the Republican Party was particularly fraught as, in hindsight, the coming of the New Deal could have been an opportunity for the party to push for progressive labor reforms and position itself as the embodiment of the Roosevelt administration on the island. But that was not to be. Despite decades of labor agitation as the political arm of the

Free Federation of Laborers (FLT), the oldest and largest labor union in Puerto Rico, the Socialist Party could not escape the colonial nature of Puerto Rican politics. Favoring a push for statehood, the party's alliance with Republicans was formed amid rising calls for independence from both the Nationalist and Liberal Parties. Independence, in their view, was a threat to working-class social and economic reform. As the Liberal Party became identified with the Roosevelt administration, however, Socialist leaders like Iglesias increasingly found themselves at odds with Puerto Rican workers who admired Roosevelt's rhetoric and hungered for the kinds of reforms that were being encouraged and financed by many parts of the New Deal on the island.[30]

The incongruity of the Socialist Party's position became increasingly acute between 1933 and 1934 when the island was gripped by the largest and most diverse wave of strikes in its history. The strike wave was mostly composed of independent and uncoordinated strikes, walkouts, and boycotts in several industries. As Rafael Bernabe has explained, it did not begin where you might expect it—in the island's urban centers or sugarcane fields. Rather, the wave began in the interior tobacco and coffee zones and was led by poorly paid semiskilled workers, most notably women in the tobacco stripping and needlework industries. By the summer of 1933, the wave expanded to urban areas and included strikes by cigar factory workers in Caguas, Juncos, and San Lorenzo; women needleworkers in Lares and Mayagüez; bakers in Santurce, San Juan, and Ponce; and large groups of unemployed workers in San Juan. By the fall of 1933, a large strike by the Asociación de Choferes (drivers' association) limited *publico* (taxi) service and crippled mobility and commerce in Mayagüez, San Germán, Ponce, San Juan, Cayey, Vega Baja, Bayamón, Trujillo Alto, Río Piedras, Humacao, Gurabo, and Aguadilla. By December, the Partido Comunista Puertorriqueño (Puerto Rican Communist Party) led strikes of dockworkers in Arecibo and San Juan as taxi drivers staged gasoline boycotts in Mayagüez.[31] The mobilization of women workers in the strikes and boycotts was significant. Indeed, women were active members of at least nine unions in needlework by 1934 and later formed the Congreso Obrero de Mujeres (Women's Labor Congress) in support of the New Deal's Fair Labor Standards Act in 1938, which temporarily increased the minimum wage for needlework and other nonagricultural workers on the island.[32]

Major strikes by organized workers in the cane-growing regions also occurred during these years. Unlike many urban strikes, boycotts, and demonstrations that had begun in nonunionized industries, organized sugar workers soon began looking for leadership outside of the FLT and Socialist Party. In January 1934, seventy thousand sugar workers paralyzed the eastern and southern parts of the island when they rejected a new labor contract signed by the FLT. Just as dockworkers had turned to the Communist Party, sugar workers in Guayama asked Pedro Albizu Campos to help organize and lead their strike. When insular police and the National Guard were mobilized to the area, Albizu blamed the entire insular government for low pay, poor living conditions, and inadequate seasonal unemployment in the region. The sugar workers' appeal to Albizu and the Nationalist Party indicated that the leadership of the FLT and Socialist Party no longer spoke for many rank-and-file Puerto Rican workers. The Socialist Party had in some ways traded its trust with workers to maintain the short-term electoral advantage offered by the Coalition.[33]

By spring 1934, the strike wave took another interesting turn as the gasoline demonstrations turned into broader boycotts against several electricity monopolies that controlled water and power in Mayagüez, Río Piedras, Ponce, and San Juan. Power companies, which operated as unregulated local monopolies, were influential supporters of the Republican Party. In Mayagüez, a series of boycotts and demonstrations against the Mayagüez Light, Power, and Ice Company were led by the Liga de Defensa de Mayagüez (Defense League). In Río Piedras and San Juan, boycotts against the Ponce Electric Company and Porto Rico Railway, Light, and Power Company were led by Comites de Defensa Social (Social Defense Committees). The wave of strikes lost steam in the summer of 1934 as the workers and interests involved were too far flung and diverse to sustain their momentum for a second year. Before dying out, however, labor unrest had spread to include garbage collectors, telephone workers, and—believe it or not—patients from the leper asylum who escaped from their facilities and marched to San Juan, where they held a rally in a public plaza before being apprehended. The leper colony, which had been partially destroyed by San Felipe, was later rebuilt by the PRRA.[34]

The strikes of 1933 and 1934 revealed widespread dissatisfaction with the existing colonial situation and the inability of insular political parties to foment a lasting recovery from San Felipe, San Ciprián, and the Great Depression. The Coalition's opposition to the New Deal was partly driven by its desire to drive a wedge between progressive technocrats in the Liberal Party and their counterparts in the Roosevelt administration. From their own perspectives, Republicans and Socialists both feared that the growing alliance between like-minded intellectuals, agronomists, scientists, engineers, and civil servants could upend local politics. These fears were not unfounded; as we will see in the following chapter, a group of notable Puerto Rican intellectuals associated with the Liberal Party began articulating ideas and strategies for lasting reform and recovery. With a shared belief that science, technology, and economic modernization could solve the most pressing problems of the 1930s while pointing the island forward, a group including Carlos Chardón (the chancellor of the University of Puerto Rico with a background in mycology), Rafael Menéndez Ramos (an agronomist associated with the Agricultural Experiment Station), and Rafael Fernández García (the commissioner of agriculture and younger brother of the Liberal Party's Benigno Fernández García) focused on improving the sugar industry through land reform, repairing the agricultural damage of the hurricanes, and finding a way to resurrect the moribund coffee, tobacco, and citrus industries.

Chardón, Menéndez Ramos, and Fernández García focused much of their attention on the 500-Acre Law, which had been designed to limit corporate and absentee landholding in excess of five hundred acres but had never been enforced. Outside of the status question, no issue divided Republicans and Liberals more than land reform; whereas Liberals sought to enforce and strengthen the 500-Acre Law, the Coalition desired to overturn it completely.[35] The major takeaway of the Chardón Plan, as the group's report was called in the press, was its intention to break up large corporate-owned sugar plantations and distribute parcels to landless cane workers. The plan also advocated for several significant economic programs outside of the sugar sector, including in coffee, citrus, and tobacco and a variety of other agricultural, financial, and light industrial initiatives.[36]

In just a few short years, the Chardón Plan became the blueprint for the Puerto Rico Reconstruction Administration—marking one of the rare instances in U.S. history that an entire federal agency was designed based on the ideas of colonized subjects. For the remainder of the 1930s, the Coalition stepped up its attacks against the New Deal and repeatedly charged that the PRRA favored the Liberal Party and denied jobs to Republicans and Socialists. Ironically, even though Liberals were against statehood (mostly supporting gradual independence and, later, increased political autonomy within the colonial system), a cross-section of the party's leading figures forged pragmatic and lasting alliances with progressive elements in the Roosevelt administration. By combining forces with the reform impulse of the New Deal, these leaders wrested control of relief and recovery away from the Coalition legislature and into the hands of two new federal agencies, the Puerto Rico Emergency Relief Administration in 1933 and the PRRA in 1935.[37]

2

From Relief to Reconstruction

One of the most important developments in Puerto Rico during the 1930s was the introduction of the New Deal. In the wake of the hurricanes and worsening Great Depression, amid labor strikes and nationalist uprisings, and in spite of sustained opposition from conservative factions in the Coalition, the New Deal inaugurated a series of reforms that had profound impacts on social, economic, and political life on the island. Through the establishment of the Puerto Rico Emergency Relief Administration (PRERA) and the Puerto Rico Reconstruction Administration (PRRA), the Roosevelt administration intervened in the organization of relief, recovery, and reconstruction from overlapping environmental and economic crises. Much as similar programs had done in areas of the continental United States, New Deal interventions began a process of modernization that transformed the island from an agrarian to an industrial society between the 1930s and 1950s. These Puerto Rican New Deal agencies differed from their continental counterparts, however, by establishing a reformed colonialism on the island that made its status as an unincorporated territory of the United States more palatable, while not actually altering that status.

The creation of the PRERA and the PRRA were made possible by the election of Franklin D. Roosevelt in 1932 and buoyed by his three subsequent reelections. While there was considerable overlay between the two agencies in terms of their goals and methods, they should not be confused or thought to be synonymous with one another. Rather, when analyzing their operations and outcomes, it is clear that the ways in which the two agencies differed were profound. Most important was the kind of funding with which each agency operated. Whereas the PRERA primarily relied on subfunding provided by other New Deal agencies, the PRRA was funded by direct appropriations from Congress that allowed for greater flexibility and somewhat more autonomy from larger, continentally focused New Deal entities. Additionally, while the PRERA was co-administered through the insular legislature and the appointed governor's office, the PRRA bypassed insular politics and reported to the Department of the Interior, a cabinet-level department run by one of the Roosevelt administration's staunchest supporters of public works. Taken together, however, the PRERA and PRRA brought new and unprecedented changes to the island, and the evolution of their focus from relief to reconstruction mirrored the paradigm shift between the broader First and Second New Deal. While the PRERA and the PRRA were not the only New Deal agencies to operate in Puerto Rico, they are worthy of examination since they were the only two specifically created for the island and the largest established for any of the U.S. colonial possessions.[1]

The PRERA and the PRRA each depended on close collaboration between Puerto Rican– and American-born public servants and on the popular support of the island's urban and agrarian workers. The Puerto Rican farmers, workers, and professionals who actively designed, labored on, contested, and benefited from New Deal programs sought to find permanent solutions to the island's most pressing problems. Like the New Deal in the continental United States, however, the New Deal in Puerto Rico had many shortcomings. It was underfunded. It went through several administrative changes. It drew considerable opposition. It was susceptible to corruption. It was used as political fodder. It overreached. It did not accomplish all of its goals. It was designed to be temporary. Political opponents in both the Republican and Nationalist Parties derisively referred to the PRRA, in particular, as a colonial supergovernment that functioned without democratic consent. From our perspective today, we can add that it was too often skewed by class-based contemporary assumptions about race, gender, and ethnicity. Most of all, to supporters of statehood and independence alike, the New Deal did not confront the island's number-one political problem: the hegemonic colonial control of the island by the United States.

The Puerto Rico Emergency Relief Administration (1933–1935)

The Puerto Rico Emergency Relief Administration was created in August 1933 as an extension of the Federal Emergency Relief Agency (FERA)— which was part of Roosevelt's so-called First Hundred Days when many important First New Deal initiatives were launched. FERA was designed to provide direct financial relief to state and local governments that were unable to deliver emergency support due to the collapse of tax revenues since the start of the Depression nearly four years earlier. Through a combination of work programs and direct financial relief, FERA operated by giving grants to states and territories. When FERA funds were made available to the U.S. territories of Alaska, Hawaii, Puerto Rico, and the Virgin Islands, the majority of the money was allocated to Puerto Rico—which had the largest population by far of any of the colonial territories. In fact, nearly 75 percent of all territorial FERA funds were expended in Puerto Rico and administered through PRERA, with about 20 percent spent in Hawaii and the rest divided between Alaska and the Virgin Islands. The Puerto Rican Chamber of Commerce and other trade organizations lobbied for FERA funds, which were critical to the island's economy because the decline of insular tax revenues had limited the local government's capacity to borrow money or receive loans from the Hoover administration's Reconstruction Finance Corporation.[2]

As Manuel Rodríguez has demonstrated, the PRERA provided much more than emergency relief and had an underappreciated role in the political history of Puerto Rico in the 1930s. The agency, which was far more than a precursor to the PRRA, embarked on an array of economic development measures that responded to the environmental and economic destruction of the hurricanes and Great Depression. The PRERA was also significant as the first on-the-ground relief agency established by the federal government to make direct interventions into the daily lives of Puerto Rican citizens. In doing so, Rodríguez argues, the PRERA expanded but eased U.S. colonial domination over the island. Through its efforts to move beyond relief, the PRERA refashioned the federal government's relationship with Puerto Rican workers by offering the hope of both immediate recovery and eventual prosperity. The PRERA's representation of itself as a vehicle for modernization began the process of "transforming the former image of a distant colonial power to a regulative state concerned with the daily problems of a population deeply stricken by the Depression and widespread poverty."[3]

The governor of Puerto Rico at the time, Robert H. Gore, had taken office in July 1933. He was a terrible selection, appointed by Roosevelt at the request of James A. Farley, the powerful postmaster general and chair of the Democratic National Committee, who hoped to build a larger base for the Democratic Party on the island. Gore's tenure as governor has been rightly lambasted in the historical literature; Raymond Carr, for example, colorfully describes the Florida business leader as a "gum-chewing tycoon with the manners of an insurance salesman who confessed that he did not even know the geographic location of the colony he was to govern."[4] While all local political parties were skeptical of Gore, Coalition leaders worked with him in hopes of controlling new federal dollars coming to the island through PRERA. In October 1933, Rafael Martínez Nadal organized a parade of nearly eight thousand supporters in Viejo San Juan carrying banners that pledged support to "Roosevelt y el Nuevo Trato!" and declaring to Roosevelt, "1,500,000 Puerto Ricans Support You!" When the procession arrived at La Fortaleza (the governor's mansion), Martínez Nadal gave a "spirited speech" to the crowd before enveloping Gore "in a typical Puerto Rican embrace." This kind of public demonstration had its desired effect: Gore grounded his short time as governor on the support of the Coalition and distanced himself from the Liberal Party—even working to remove several party members from positions at the University of Puerto Rico, including Muna Lee, the wife of newly elected senator Luis Muñoz Marín.[5]

The honeymoon was short-lived, however, and as the tide rose against Gore that winter, Roosevelt replaced him with Blanton Winship, a sixty-three-year-old retired judge advocate and major general who had served in the Cuban-Spanish-American War and the First World War. In contrast to Gore, Winship was initially supported across most of the political spectrum, as both the Coalition and Liberal Party lauded the new governor as impartial to insular partisan politics. While today we can see that Winship's appointment in January 1934 took place in the context of the island-wide strike wave and that his tenure until 1939 was marked by police repression against workers and nationalists, political leaders at the time understood that close ties to the governor would be necessary to influence the direction of the PRERA.[6] Interestingly, the Coalition and Liberal Party each saw the PRERA as a pathway to opposite political outcomes on the colonial status question. Whereas Muñoz Marín and the Liberals believed that effective hurricane relief and forward-looking economic development could enhance the case for colonial reform and independence, Coalition leaders trusted that close ties to the New Deal would foster a path toward statehood—which had, after all, been part of the Democratic Party's official platform in 1932.[7] Like Gore, Winship allied himself with the Coalition for the most part, particularly Martínez Nadal and the Republican Party. When he began to lose their support in 1935, Winship faced calls for his removal from all sides. Clippings of articles attacking the governor from a variety of newspapers such as *El Imparcial* and *La Corresondencia de Puerto Rico* were sent from Muñoz Marín to Harold Ickes, who had translated typescripts sent directly to Roosevelt and his advisors in the White House.[8]

To lead the PRERA, Roosevelt appointed James R. Bourne as director, although the agency was in fact coheaded by his wife, Dorothy Bourne. Unlike Gore and Winship, James and Dorothy Bourne were actively engaged with Puerto Rican affairs. They had lived on the island since 1929 when James became manager of two fruit canneries and Dorothy began studying local socioeconomic conditions. Between 1930 and 1932, Dorothy worked with the University of Puerto Rico (UPR) and the insular Department of Education on a broad survey of rural life on the island. Following this project, Commissioner of Education José Padín asked her to supervise social work for the island's Second Unit vocational schools; by the time James was appointed to lead the PRERA, Dorothy was the founding director of the UPR School of Social Work. Under their leadership, the PRERA attacked a wide array of social and economic issues ranging from health and education to worker housing, "slum clearance," and population control. With approval from the War Department (which still had jurisdiction over Puerto Rico at this time), the PRERA operated with a bureaucratic structure that divided the agency into four basic departments: the Bureau of Social Services and the Divisions of Engineering, Education, and Agriculture, which were supported by a variety of other departments and subdivisions.[9]

Over its entire twenty-five-month existence from August 1933 to September 1935, the PRERA spent $20.7 million (about $469 million today) in funds allocated from FERA, along with $70,201 (about $1.59 million) provided by the insular legislature. In addition, PRERA received $118,000 (about $2.6 million) in cash and construction materials from Puerto Rican municipal governments, $1.6 million ($36 million) in nonperishable food supplies, and about $900,000 ($20.3 million) in clothing from the Federal Surplus Relief Corporation; the food and clothing were purchased by FERA and distributed by the PRERA. Other relief supplies, particularly children's clothing, were made by workers employed by the PRERA's innovative Women's Work Division. Between 1933 and 1935, an estimated 84 percent of the population applied for direct aid or work relief from the agency.[10]

Influenced by Dorothy Bourne, the Bureau of Social Services was central to the PRERA's goal of providing direct relief to those who could not work and identifying individuals who could be recommended for work relief in various other New Deal agencies such as the Civilian Conservation Corps or Public Works Administration. The PRERA's work reached nearly all neighborhoods and municipalities through a complex hierarchical structure based on Puerto Rican senatorial districts. Dividing the island into eleven regions, the agency established local offices in each municipality that sent at least one representative to each neighborhood. While this system was in part a legacy of the Spanish and U.S. military relief distribution models, the PRERA's organization was more complex, bureaucratic, and efficient, allowing New Deal officials to study and classify Puerto Ricans at the local level in all social sectors.[11]

The Engineering and Education Divisions contributed to the process of quantifying the island's most pressing economic problems even though they were often beset by inadequate funding and conflicting directives. The Education Division, for example, was structurally dependent on the insular legislature and, primarily due to a lack of funds, unable to fully address the needs of the 370,000 children who had not returned to school since San Ciprián made landfall a year earlier. Nevertheless, PRERA workers made an impact on education by distributing educational materials, establishing vocational and adult education programs, launching nurseries and preschools for infants and younger children, bulking up physical education, and devising plans for the construction of schools and hiring of teachers. Similarly, the Engineering Division did not have the budget to provide the large-scale construction projects needed to address the infrastructural and public health crises that were worsening month by month. The need for aid was so great that often the PRERA was reduced to solely distributing emergency supplies. Between August 1933 and September 1935, the agency received 339,125 applications for aid. Despite limitations, substantial quantities of aid were delivered, including 120,000 pounds of surplus pork and over $3 million (almost $68 million today) in milk distribution. Each family received about one dollar ($22 today) worth of foodstuffs and medicine; if a healthy man was part of the family, that man would be given work through the Civil Works Administration (CWA), a short-lived jobs program run by FERA that lasted from 1933 to 1934. Like many other New Deal programs, the CWA largely excluded women from relief jobs. Neither the PRERA nor CWA had the budget to employ all of the estimated 200,000 unemployed heads of household, and, by 1934, they were only able to find work for 40,000 men—barely 20 percent of the total number of unemployed.[12]

From Relief to Reconstruction · 43

Without direct funding, the PRERA was perhaps doomed from the start. Despite its widespread popular support, the agency could not fully realize its plans for larger development projects, and its focus on relief reflected long-standing traditions of waiting for aid from above. Also dooming the PRERA was opposition from both Winship and the Coalition, as each had each grown frustrated that the budget, payroll, and popularity of the agency were eclipsing their own. Worse, they were concerned that James and Dorothy Bourne were becoming too close to Muñoz Marín and the Liberal Party. By spring of 1935, the Coalition moved to stall PRERA projects and publicly called for the Bournes' dismissal from the agency. In March, the Coalition passed a resolution that James Bourne was a public enemy of the people of Puerto Rico; later that summer, he was arrested for slandering the legislature and was the victim of arson when his house was burned on two occasions (the family was in Connecticut at the time). The Coalition's opposition culminated in a final break with the agency when it learned of the PRERA's attempt to establish an autonomous Rural Rehabilitation Corporation of Puerto Rico that would be initially funded with start-up money from FERA. While the Coalition attempted to form its own reconstruction program, neither the PRERA plan nor the Coalition plan came to pass, as neither actually had the resources to proceed. Plus, although no one knew it at the time, FERA itself was ended shortly after the passage of the Social Security Act in August 1935.[13]

Like the Coalition, Winship sought greater control of New Deal dollars and larger influence over the direction of the PRERA, which he, echoing Martínez Nadal, accused of giving relief work to Liberals on a partisan basis. During the Gore administration, when PRERA offices were located inside the insular capitol building, the PRERA's payroll records were stolen and given to Martínez Nadal, who forwarded them to the governor with annotations marking Liberal Party members. But the accusations of bias toward the Liberal Party were in some ways a self-fulfilling prophecy: with persistent opposition from the governor and leaders of the legislature, the PRERA (and later, the PRRA) came to rely even more heavily on Liberal Party members, who eventually ran almost all relief and reconstruction operations without input from the Coalition.[14]

During its existence, the PRERA made lasting contributions in direct and indirect ways. By hiring and training nearly five thousand white-collar workers, for example, future generations of Puerto Ricans were prepared to staff the insular and corporate bureaucracies that formed during the years of rapid industrialization after World War II. This included a professional labor force of accountants, architects, bookkeepers, chemists, clerks, doctors, engineers, foremen, nurses, pharmacists, photographers, printers, publicists, and typists. Likewise, the Bureau of Social Services trained an extraordinary number of social workers, men and women who gained experience and acquired expertise in identifying and quantifying the island's most critical problems. Through these workers, the PRERA spread scientific and empirical knowledge on the island and a faith in the modernizing, progressive discourse of the New Deal. From putting tens of thousands of unemployed men to work to administering medicine to 51,000 malaria patients to funding the island's first squad of trained lifeguards on the public beaches, the PRERA undertook programs that improved daily life and altered the way many Puerto Ricans thought about the federal government. Its relief programs and development initiatives were highly popular on the island, and its bureaucratic structure influenced the ways in which the largest New Deal intervention on the island, the PRRA, operated.[15]

The Chardón Plan

As the PRERA carried out its work on the island, an influential group of civil servants and intellectuals associated with the insular government and the UPR began formulating a plan for long-range economic recovery based on locally grown ideas and strategies. The group, whose larger orbit included some of the island's leading scientists, agronomists, educators, engineers, urban planners, and other technocrats, shared ideas that had been developed over time. This was significant because even though the PRERA represented a new federal interest in the island's well-being, there was widespread ignorance in Washington about social, economic, and environmental conditions in Puerto Rico. The group included Carlos Chardón, a mycologist who graduated from Cornell University in 1921 and was the chancellor of UPR; Rafael Menéndez Ramos, an agronomist at UPR and the Agricultural Experiment Station (AES); and Rafael Fernández García, an agricultural chemist specializing in sugar agronomy who had a degree from the University of California Berkeley and served as the insular commissioner of agriculture. The Chardón group, as they came to be known, can be seen consummate insiders—privileged sons of the Puerto Rican elite whose technocratic faith in colonial reform and economic modernization reflected their own professional class ambitions. They can also be seen as perennial outsiders—ivory tower scientists and academics who were unable to make substantive contributions while insular and federal politicians fought for control of New Deal jobs and funding.[16]

The Chardón group's primary goals were to find a solution to the so-called sugar question and to resurrect the declining coffee, tobacco, and citrus industries. As they met in Río Piedras on the half-built campus of UPR, the group knew that the rehabilitation of the island's agricultural industries was dependent on land reform. They also knew that any plan to redistribute corporate-owned sugar land to farmers and workers would be sharply contested by the Republican wing of the Coalition. Although Puerto Rico had the 500-Acre Law in place, the law that ostensibly prohibited corporate ownership of land in excess of five hundred acres had never been enforced. Worse, while the Liberal Party wanted to begin enforcing the law, Republicans in the legislature sought to have it overturned.

The release of the so-called Chardón Plan in 1934 coincided with a flurry of competing development plans on the island by the Coalition and in Washington by other members of the Roosevelt administration. Throughout 1933 and 1934, high-profile tours of Puerto Rico were conducted by Eleanor Roosevelt, Rex Tugwell, Harold Ickes, James A. Dickey (head of the AAA), and even Franklin Roosevelt himself. Accompanied by the press, these tours provided detailed reports on the island's socioeconomic conditions to a wider public in the continental United States.[17] Upon arrival in Mayagüez, for example, Franklin Roosevelt was driven to Ponce and San Juan, where he remarked, "One thing that seemed to be very clear was that your problems here on the island are very much the same kind of problems that we have in many other parts of the United States. They are social problems and economic problems, and the same methods that we use to solve them in other parts of the country will be applied here in Puerto Rico." Continuing, he noted, "We cannot accomplish everything in one year. In fact, we must look ahead for a great many years, and that is why we have all come to an agreement in principle for the rehabilitation of Puerto Rico. That plan," he concluded, alluding to the Chardón group's work, "will take a great many years to accomplish, but I hope and I am confident that all of you will do your part in making the plan a success."[18]

Suddenly, as never before, officials such as Oscar Chapman (assistant secretary of the interior), Jacob Baker (assistant administrator of FERA), and William I. Meyers (head of the Farm Credit Administration) began forming their own plans for the island's rehabilitation or collaborating with planning groups on the island. While many of these New Dealers would play prominent roles in Puerto Rico in the years to come, the Chardón group (with Muñoz Marín serving as an unofficial member) carried the most influence with the Puerto Rican public and press, and, eventually, key figures in the Roosevelt administration. The Chardón Plan resulted in the formation of the PRRA in 1935, which was organized to carry out the objectives presented by Chardón, Menéndez Ramos, and Fernández García. As Juan Giusti has argued, Fernández García was most likely the Chardón Plan's primary author, particularly on the sugar question.[19]

The Chardón Plan offered a rationale for long-range economic reform and outlined clear steps for how to begin. It took a comprehensive approach to the island's most pressing problems and addressed the ways in which the sugar question, collapse of agricultural prices, and hurricane damages combined and reinforced one another. The key provision of the plan was to break up corporate-owned sugar plantations through the enforcement of the 500-Acre Law and divide the lands into parcels for landless workers and their families. While some outside advisors, including Tugwell, suggested including housing construction projects in the plan, Chardón believed that "nothing substantial can be accomplished here until we face the ever-absorbing sugar interests."[20] In addition to the sugar question, however, the plan addressed a multitude of socioeconomic subjects, including coffee, citrus fruit, and tobacco rehabilitation; development of coconut, sea island cotton, and freshwater fish industries; creation of subsistence farms and extension of agricultural credit; eradication of the cattle tick and bovine tuberculosis; forestry and soil erosion control; tax and public debt reduction; hurricane research and cooperative hurricane insurance; razing of undesirable arrabales and barriadas obreras (called at the time "slum clearance"); industrial development including transportation infrastructure and the canning industry; increased crop, price, and statistical reporting; and development of the tourism industry. Along with these initiatives, the Chardón group also recommended several smaller initiatives, such as the cultivation of garlic for local consumption, medicinal and military uses, and export to the continental United States, which was currently importing 14 million tons from Chile and Spain.[21]

Martínez Nadal and the Republican Party emerged as the strongest critics of the Chardón Plan, but others were against it as well. Due to the prominence of Liberals in the group and their ties to the progressive wing of the New Deal in Washington, Republicans, Socialists, and Nationalists all viewed the Chardón Plan as a larger problem than the PRERA. In April 1935, the Coalition adjourned the legislative session in protest of mounting popular support for the plan. Unsurprisingly, Muñoz Marín and other Liberals denounced the Coalition's protest as a means to stall implementation of the Chardón Plan and ward off enforcement of the 500-Acre Law. In the press, Muñoz dismissed the event as a stunt dressed up in "pseudo-patriotic camouflage to protect sugar interests in large land holdings."[22]

The following day, Republicans accused Muñoz, Chardón, and other Liberals of trying to overturn local elections by usurping power from the Coalition. Attacking Chardón directly, Martínez Nadal called him "the worst kind of island politician masquerading under the non-partisan guise of a New Dealer." The entire Liberal Party, he continued, was from the "old ruling caste ousted in the last election but who, as New Dealers, with Washington's aid, hope to regain control of the island's affairs." In contrast, he claimed that Coalition leaders only wanted "a square deal with the New Deal for which the people of Puerto Rico and the United States voted at the last election. We want equal opportunity and fair treatment for all citizens."[23] As with his stance against the PRERA, however, it is unclear who Martínez Nadal sought to align with in Washington as the Chardón Plan had the support of Roosevelt's closest advisors—Eleanor Roosevelt, Rex Tugwell, and Harold Ickes included—all of whom viewed the New Deal as an opportunity to rein in big business and redistribute economic power to the working classes.

The following month, Roosevelt created the PRRA to circumvent the Coalition's resistance to the Chardón Plan. Unlike the PRERA, the new agency would not be administered by the appointed governor or insular legislature. Instead, Roosevelt was convinced that the Chardón Plan could only move forward as an independent agency within the Department of the Interior. This view, which was robustly supported by Muñoz and the Liberal Party, demonstrated a shift in Roosevelt's thinking about the island. Whereas his own choice of governors, Robert Gore and Blanton Winship, were not New Dealers, he was now ready to move forward with a new agency designed by members of the Liberal Party and overseen by Ickes. While the creation of a New Deal agency by executive order was seen by progressives as the Roosevelt administration's largest contribution to establishing a reformed social safety net on the island, the PRRA was met with a tepid response from the plan's own creators, including Chardón, who originally wanted the plan enacted through the insular legislature. As

Coalition opposition grew, however, Chardón and other Puerto Rican New Dealers pragmatically agreed that the PRRA could and should be run independently from the local government.[24]

The Puerto Rico Reconstruction Administration, 1935–1955

The PRRA was created by Executive Order 7057 on May 28, 1935, to reorient recovery efforts away from a paradigm of emergency relief toward one of permanent reconstruction. Based on the findings of the Chardón Plan, the agency was dedicated to agricultural rehabilitation, land reform, and the construction of a new public health infrastructure including new public drinking water and sewer systems, rural electrification, and the building of affordable hurricane-proof houses. From its creation in 1935 until its liquidation in 1955, the PRRA became the engine of most Second New Deal activity on the island, particularly in the areas of public works and public health. By continuing and expanding PRERA initiatives with more direct funding and greater political support from within the cabinet, the PRRA attempted to confront widespread poverty, landlessness, unemployment, and ill health in all parts of the island.[25]

Unlike the PRERA, the PRRA was designed to report directly to Harold Ickes, who had advised Roosevelt to move Puerto Rico from the authority of the War Department to the Department of the Interior in 1934. Several others, including Chardón, Muñoz, and Tugwell, had informed Roosevelt that the Coalition wanted to halt the enforcement of the 500-Acre Law and harness federal dollars into a local patronage machine to enhance their own electoral power. Ickes created the Division of Territories and Island Possessions and chose Ernest Gruening to be its first director. Even prior to the creation of the PRRA, Gruening had won the support of some of the island's coffee growers and other small landowners when he introduced a plan to cancel over $5 million (about $115 million today) in debt incurred from hurricane relief loans. Miles Fairbank, an agricultural loan administrator from the Federal Land Bank of Baltimore who had recently relocated to Puerto Rico, was instrumental in designing the plan to relieve the agricultural debt.[26] Fairbank's efforts were appreciated by the island's small farmers, who supported his promotion within the PRRA just a few years later.

Funding for the PRRA was made in accordance with the Emergency Relief Appropriation Act of April 8, 1935, and the first allocations were made in August and September of that year. In contrast to the PRERA, Congress funded the PRRA through a series of additional emergency appropriations through 1938 and set aside all money allocated to Puerto Rico in a special fund for use through June 30, 1940; any proceeds derived from PRRA projects were held in a revolving fund for use on the island. This model of funding allowed the PRRA to move rapidly on many fronts, including quickly hiring large numbers of unemployed workers even as its leaders initially slowed the planning process, altering "the tempo of its activities to make a more analytical approach to many problems which experience indicated needed reconsideration, and to plan . . . a sounder reconstruction program."[27]

From its inception, one of the PRRA's primary goals was to launch a program of public works in rural and urban areas that would establish a foundation for long-term social and economic growth. The PRRA's leadership believed that diverse programs like farm worker resettlement, soil conservation, and forestry management needed to be interwoven with building the island's first cement plant, the hurricane-proof housing program, and rural electrification. Rather than take these projects on individually, PRRA officials viewed them as mutually dependent on one another: locally produced cement and renewable sources of energy, for example, were cheaper and stronger building materials for other construction projects on the island.

Although it was initially headquartered in Washington, the PRRA was a Puerto Rican–designed and staffed federal agency. Speaking about the PRRA in August 1935, Roosevelt commented that the new agency intended "not merely immediate relief but permanent reconstruction for the Island," while highlighting the Chardón Plan's bold vision of combining agricultural rehabilitation and land redistribution with "cheap and available electric power, good roads, reforestation, and adequate housing." Concluding that the "primary need for Puerto Ricans is not a direct dole-like service from the federal government, but a carefully developed economy," Roosevelt explained that the PRRA would build lasting public works "upon which in years to come the people can erect a stable trade and draw therefrom a measure of self-sufficiency."[28] These ambitions, which represented a significant shift from previous colonial policy, were dependent on substantial outlays of taxpayer funds from the federal government, local expertise and labor, and popular support.

Harold Ickes appointed Ernest Gruening to serve as administrator, Carlos Chardón as assistant administrator, and Benigno Fernández García as regional administrator. Rafael Fernández García, one of the authors of the

Chardón Plan, was named director of the Rural Rehabilitation Division. While Gruening was officially in charge, nearly all day-to-day functions were overseen by Chardón and Benigno Fernández García, who drafted all plans and policies of the agency and reported to Gruening's office in Washington. This leadership structure was designed to handle the scope of the PRRA's rehabilitation work and address the many logistical and political complexities involved, as the PRRA was intended to manage all of its own programs and tasked with consolidating many other New Deal functions in Puerto Rico as well.[29]

As for capital, the PRRA spent over $82 million (about $1.7 billion today) between 1935 and February 15, 1955, when the agency was formally dissolved. The bulk of this money was used between 1935 and 1943 and about half was spent on labor and personnel. Direct employment by the PRRA reached a peak of 58,238 in July 1937, and as of October 31, 1938, the PRRA had completed nearly 109 million man-hours of work. Like many New Deal programs, the PRRA was officially designed as a job creator tasked with attacking the unemployment crisis, which Roosevelt and Congress agreed was the most pressing problem of the Depression. The PRRA's oversized role in the Puerto Rican labor market, however, was somewhat short-lived, and by 1940 its payroll was slashed by more than 50 percent to 23,258 total employees.[30]

In nearly all cases, the PRRA's projects were conceived, designed, and supervised by Puerto Ricans, and in October 1935, Gruening officially outlawed the hiring of non–Puerto Ricans. Puerto Rican men and women worked in positions ranging from unskilled laborers to engineers, architects, agronomists, doctors, nurses, social workers, laboratory technicians, lawyers, skilled clerical and office workers, and administrators. Between 1935 and 1943, at least 90 percent of all administrative, supervisory, and clerical personnel and 99.9 percent of all other workers were native-born Puerto Ricans. In all, roughly 98 percent of the entire PRRA payroll was Puerto Rican. Without overemphasizing the point, it remains remarkable that a federal agency operated in an unincorporated territory with an essentially all–Puerto Rican staff. While most bureaucratic paperwork was done in English, nearly all interactions with the public, including social services, contracts, bills of sale, surveys, education, and medical appointments, were conducted in Spanish.[31]

After payroll, the majority of the $1.7 billion was spent on capital-intensive projects constructed by the Engineering Division. As part of a broader New Deal strategy to displace corporate monopolies in electric power and water utilities *and* remove the control of public works from local partisan interference, major large-scale projects were administered by publicly owned authorities and corporations. Public investments, which included land acquisitions as well as projects in infrastructure, utilities, roads, sewers, and buildings, accounted for $32.6 million (over $691 million today) or approximately 40 percent of the PRRA's total budget.[32] Through these works, PRRA engineers sought to make lasting contributions to personal and collective well-being in Puerto Rico.

While the extension of public works to unincorporated territories has been little explored in the historiography of the New Deal, the $691 million spent on capital investments in Puerto Rico warrants closer examination. Between 1935 and 1955, the federal government allocated, spent, and transferred ownership to Puerto Rico projects that totaled $9.24 million ($196 million today) in rural electrification; $3.41 million ($72.3 million) in reforestation, particularly in the Maricao State Forest and Luquillo National Forest (which is today's El Yunque National Forest); $3 million ($63.6 million) on primary, secondary, and vocational school construction; $2.87 million ($60.8 million) in the construction of the University of Puerto Rico and School of Tropical Medicine; $2.37 million ($50.3 million) on roads, streets, and highways; $1.89 million ($40 million) on hospitals, clinics, and other health care facilities; $1.75 million ($37 million) on eliminating the cattle tick, which had plagued and depleted Puerto Rican livestock for decades; $1.74 million ($36.9 million) on infrastructural malaria control, including mangrove removal, landfill, and "swamp drainage"; $1.67 million ($35.4 million) on soil conservation; $1.45 million ($30.7 million) on the construction of the Cataño cement plant; $825,000 ($17.5 million) on public utilities; $757,000 ($16 million) on public buildings; $400,000 ($8.4 million) on the construction of a new Home for Orphans; $200,000 ($4.2 million) on the construction of sewing, canning, and agricultural produce marketing centers; $125,000 ($2.65 million) on eradicating coconut bud rot; $81,000 ($1.7 million) for a new irrigation canal in Isabela; and over $63,000 ($1.3 million) on homes for the aged and poor in San Juan and Ponce.[33]

The first task of the PRRA was to continue and expand the work of the PRERA. The discursive and physical shift from relief to reconstruction was closely followed in the local press. In 1935, for example, *El Día: El periódico de Ponce* called for direct action to address the growing public health crisis in Ponce, where workers and the unemployed who lived in arrabales near the Mameyes swamp adjacent to the Ponce Aqueduct had relocated following the 1928 and 1932 hurricanes. Seeking access to new federal resources, the newspaper called for the PRRA to hire a team of competent engineers and allocate money for the rehabilitation of Ponce's working-class neighborhoods through the construction of new housing and modern sanitation infrastructure.[34]

But not everyone was happy, and the PRRA was attacked from all sides. While Pedro Albizu Campos and the Nationalist Party saw the PRRA as a tool of imperial control, the agency was viewed by some in Washington as a potential threat to U.S. rule in Puerto Rico. To make matters worse, the PRRA was beset with internal struggles and went through several administrative changes in its first few years that limited, hindered, and delayed its programs from taking full effect. For one thing, Gruening and Chardón never saw eye to eye. Part of this was based on Gruening's paternalistic attitude toward his insular political opponents, which echoed prevailing racist stereotypes about their childish nature, lack of education, and poor work ethic. Following an August 1935 tour of San Juan, Ponce, and Mayagüez, for example, Gruening wrote to superiors in Washington that he had grown tired of listening to local political leaders describe existing conditions. "The expansive Latin race," he explained, "loves to make flowery speeches. Of course, it would be far better if they would work more and talk less. In general, they are real children."[35] Such talk would not have shocked Chardón or other Puerto Rican elites at the time, many of whom shared similarly racist or class-based assumptions about Puerto Rican workers, jíbaros, and farmers. The differences between Gruening and Chardón, however, went beyond personal conflicts or xenophobic memoranda, and they never fully agreed on the purpose and direction of the PRRA's actual work. Whereas Chardón, Benigno Fernández García, and Rafael Fernández García were committed to using the PRRA as a weapon against large landowners that violated the 500-Acre Law and undertaking widespread land redistribution and agricultural resettlement, Gruening remained convinced that the PRRA was, at its core, a colonial reform project and showcase for American democracy in Latin America.

Gruening's belief in the diplomatic potential of the PRRA was not superficial but rather an outgrowth of his long career as a journalist and de facto diplomat in the region. His interest in colonial reform in Puerto Rico stemmed from his vocal criticism of U.S. foreign policy in Latin America.

Combining a critical analysis of imperialism with a deep interest in utilities regulation, Gruening saw the PRRA as essential to both of these causes. The agency, he expressed, would be the leading case for a "bold . . . alternative to the political and economic nationalism adopted by many other Latin American states during the Depression."[36] Roosevelt, for his part, hoped Gruening could fulfill multiple objectives at once by turning the PRRA into a formidable economic reform project *and* a notable showcase for hemispheric foreign policy. Under Gruening, however, the PRRA was often stalled by its inability to move in these two separate directions at the same time, which often put the administrator at odds with Ickes, his superior. Plus, by aligning the PRRA with Liberals like Chardón and Muñoz, Gruening faced heightened opposition from Winship, Iglesias, and Martínez Nadal—who launched a campaign in the press against what he called Gruening's despotic and arbitrary leadership.[37]

Gruening's time at the PRRA lasted less than two years, and his short-lived tenure as the agency's lead administrator was over by 1937. These years were filled with national tragedy and political chaos that engulfed all of Puerto Rican society, sparked by concurrent waves of violent nationalist uprising and brutal police repression. Just a few years earlier, as he was helping lead the strike of sugar workers, Albizu Campos's rhetoric became increasingly vehement as he positioned himself and the young cadets of the Nationalist Party as future martyrs to the cause of independence. By 1936, Albizu was openly advocating for armed struggle against the insular and colonial governments, and his speeches drew increased attention from local and federal police agencies, who also began surveilling the party's private meetings and public demonstrations such as its marches, parades, and paramilitary drills. Although some political observers viewed the violent rhetoric as a sensational sideshow to the more official partisan struggle between the Liberal Party and the Coalition, the dangerous reality of Albizu's words became clear when a series of bombs exploded in San Juan in the summer of 1935. The targets were both federal and insular buildings: on July 4, 1935, the headquarters of the PRRA in Puerta de Tierra were dynamited; a few weeks later, the Federal Court Building in Puerta de Tierra; in August, a police station in Barrio Obrero in Santurce.[38] While no one was hurt in these explosions, a gun battle with the police in October 1935 resulted in the death of four nationalists and one bystander in the Río Piedras massacre. The confrontation, which began when nationalists attempted to disrupt an anti–Nationalist Party rally by students at the UPR, marked the beginning of two years of sporadic but escalating violence, confusion, and bloodshed.

On Sunday, February 23, 1936, Colonel E. Francis Riggs, the appointed police commissioner of Puerto Rico, was assassinated by Hiram Rosado and Elías Beauchamp, two young nationalists who were subsequently detained and killed by police while in custody.[39] After leaving church in a convertible Packard, Riggs and his driver, police officer Ángel Alvarez, stopped Rosado's car. Alvarez got out of the car, leaving Riggs alone. At this point, according to newspaper accounts, Beauchamp killed Riggs with at least three shots from a .38 caliber pistol—hitting him in the head, hand, and chest. In custody, Beauchamp supposedly told police that Riggs's death was revenge for the murder of the four nationalists in Río Piedras. A few hours later, Francisco Vélez Ortiz, the district police chief in Utuado, was shot four times in a separate attack.[40]

In justifying their murders, insular police offered the feeble claim that Rosado and Beauchamp reached for rifles in a storage closet and tried to escape. While nationalists asserted that the assassination of Riggs was retaliation for the Río Piedras massacre, Albizu Campos had interpreted the appointment of Riggs and Winship as the return of direct military rule on the island.[41] Placing armed guards outside his house in Aguas Buenas, near Caguas, Albizu argued that Puerto Rico was governed by tyrants who were "only interested in crushing the nationalism of the invaded country" and that insular police powered a "government by murder." Speaking at the funeral of Rosado and Beauchamp, Albizu sought to inspire the crowd of young cadets. Mixing Catholic imagery with fatalistic militant discourse, he declared that there was "only one gateway to immortality: the gateway of valor, which leads to sacrifice for a sacred cause. We must sacrifice ourselves for the independence of our country."[42] Arguing that the "Yankees seek to intimidate us with murder," Albizu vowed that for every nationalist killed by police, an American or Puerto Rican working for the colonial government would be killed—specifying Chardón, Benigno Fernández García, and other leaders of the PRRA as potential targets. He later characterized university students as colonial collaborators, effeminate sissies, drunkards, and prostitutes.[43] Transforming himself into symbol and martyr, Albizu told the crowd that "they can kill Albizu Campos. They can kill 10,000 Nationalists. [But] a million Puerto Ricans will rise up" to avenge their deaths and defend the honor of the Puerto Rican fatherland.[44]

News of the Riggs assassination exploded across Puerto Rico and Washington. On the island, Winship placed a temporary ban on all public demonstrations and eulogized Riggs as "a kind, cultured man, fluent in Spanish and sincerely interested in Puerto Rico's needs and aspirations," whose murder was "an irreparable tragedy."[45] The insular police raided the Nationalist Party's headquarters and the homes of several of its leaders in search of evidence, apparently uncovering military equipment, homemade bombs, and other weapons. Meanwhile, the FBI and attorney general built a case against Albizu who, in March 1936, was charged with conspiring to overthrow the insular government.[46] While on bond, Albizu denounced "Yankee imperialism and despotism" and remarked that nationalists were ready to "seal our words with blood."[47] In June, after a jury composed of seven Puerto Ricans and five Americans acquitted him of the conspiracy charges, district court judge Robert A. Cooper ordered a new trial. A month later, with a jury composed of two Puerto Ricans and ten Americans, Albizu was convicted and sentenced to ten years in federal prison.[48] After a federal appeals court in Boston upheld the verdict, the forty-five-year-old nationalist leader was transferred to Atlanta Federal Penitentiary, one of the most secure and notorious in the federal system. Political violence against U.S. and Puerto Rican officials continued to escalate, however, and Winship, Cooper, and Iglesias all survived assassination attempts.

In Washington, Millard Tydings (D-MD), who was the chair of the Senate Committee on Territories and Insular Affairs, responded to the assassination of Riggs by calling for the island's immediate independence. The so-called Tydings Bill, which was actually written by lawyers for the Department of the Interior in consultation with Gruening, was introduced two months after Riggs's death. As written, the punitive and vindictive bill threatened to destroy the Puerto Rican economy by abruptly ending all federal aid and tariff protections.[49] Rightly seen as a seminal event of the 1930s, the bill has received considerable attention in the historiography of Puerto Rico and has come to be understood as part of a personal vendetta by Tydings against Albizu Campos and the rebellious nationalist movement of the decade; like many contemporary press accounts, most historians have focused on Tydings's friendship with Riggs.[50]

Their arguments are convincing, particularly in the context of the friendlier Philippine Independence Act, which Tydings cosponsored in 1934 and established a gradual process designed to ease the economic burdens of abrupt independence. Nevertheless, the personal dimensions of the Tydings Bill have obscured the fact that Tydings had grown into one of the loudest critics of the New Deal in the continental United States. By the time of the Riggs assassination, conservative Democrats like Tydings

56 · The Puerto Rico Reconstruction Administration

sought to curtail what they saw as unnecessary spending on progressive policies and spoke with increasing fervor against Tugwell, Ickes, and other members of the administration, including Roosevelt himself. The grudge between Roosevelt and Tydings was so strong that, according to Ickes, Roosevelt once threatened to punch Tydings in the face and—in a gruesome aside—privately hoped Ickes would "take Tydings' hide off and rub salt in."[51]

Ickes later wrote that if Tydings "seems bent on smearing us all he can, we ought to fight back day by day through the newspapers, which is the only means available to us to meet the vague charges that are being produced" by his numerous complaints.[52] While the incidents Ickes was referring to were not solely about Puerto Rico, they illustrate the need to place the Tydings Bill into broader perspective. By 1936, Tydings was one of the most strident critics of the New Deal in the United States *and* one of the most vocal opponents of the New Deal in Puerto Rico. In addition to opposing the National Recovery Administration, Tennessee Valley Authority, National Labor Relations Act, and Social Security Act, Tydings also criticized escalating federal expenditures in Puerto Rico and opposed both the PRERA and the PRRA. He was considered the second most conservative Democrat in the Senate and voted against the Roosevelt administration at least 77 percent of the time, earning the ire of Roosevelt as the "betrayer of the New Deal."[53] In light of this, the Tydings Bill should also be seen as a move to eliminate federal spending on the island by way of offering Puerto Rico its complete and immediate independence; it was an attack on the New Deal and the violent rebellion of the Nationalist Party at the same time.

By the end of 1937, nationalism lost some of its viability as a mass political movement. The terms of the Tydings Bill drew the practicality of immediate independence, as advocated for by Albizu, into relief for all but the most unyielding nationalists. While the party had refused to participate in the 1936 elections, the movement's turn toward political assassination, terrorism, and bombings resulted in swift and aggressive repression from federal and insular authorities. As its cause became ever more narrowly focused on Albizu, the movement drifted farther and farther away from the aims and aspirations of a broad swath of Puerto Rican society. Although the Tydings Bill was not adopted by Congress, it opened a serious debate over the merits of abrupt political independence without a period of economic transition. With Albizu imprisoned in Atlanta, the nationalist movement ceased to be an option for lasting social and economic reform on the island for the rest of the 1930s.

As for Gruening, his role in drafting the Tydings Bill ruined what was left of his relationship with Chardón, Muñoz, and other leaders of the Liberal Party and, by the end of 1936, forced him to seek a lukewarm alliance with Winship and Martínez Nadal.[54] Astutely aware that any alliance with the Coalition would undercut the PRRA's efforts to enforce the 500-Acre Law and develop its land redistribution program, Ickes, Chardón, and Fernández García all turned against Gruening. On November 14, 1936, Roosevelt signed Executive Order 7493 placing the operations of the PRRA under the direct control of Ickes.[55] That same month, Chardón announced his intention to leave the PRRA, which created a public relations disaster for the agency since Chardón was its most widely respected leader. When Ickes learned that Gruening had accepted the resignations of Chardón and Fernández García without informing him, he interpreted the move as personal insubordination and a direct attack against the PRRA. Following his resignation, Chardón resumed academic research and traveled to Colombia to further investigate scientific agriculture; after he had left the agency, Chardón told *El Mundo* that Gruening had "discredited" his position.[56] In January 1937, Ickes reached an agreement for Gruening's own resignation, although it was not made official until after months of delay, as Gruening clung to the job until spring.

On Sunday, March 21, 1937, Puerto Rico was again thrown into political upheaval when insular police shot into a crowd of unarmed nationalist demonstrators and bystanders in Ponce, the island's second largest urban area and the capital of the nationalist movement. In this incident known as the Ponce massacre, police killed nineteen people (including two of their own officers) and wounded hundreds of onlookers. The confrontation was precipitated when Winship and Colonel Enrique de Orbeta, the new insular chief of police, revoked the Nationalist Party's permit to demonstrate that had been previously granted by city officials in Ponce.[57] In Washington, Ickes recognized the Ponce massacre as "a cold-blooded shooting by the Ponce police and that those who were killed were shot by policemen themselves." He blamed Winship and Gruening for not acknowledging the reality of the situation, noting that "of course [they] have been on the other side."[58] The massacre also furthered the divisions within the Liberal Party and effectively ended its ability to win elections or exert substantial influence over Puerto Rican politics. After immediately calling for an investiga-

58 · The Puerto Rico Reconstruction Administration

tion of the massacre, Liberals quickly divided over what position to take in its aftermath—with a split crystallizing around the party's two leaders, Antonio Barceló and Muñoz Marín. While the elder Barceló tempered his anger over the police murders in Ponce while investigations were under way, Muñoz took a much more direct approach in his criticism of Winship, Gruening, and nearly all other colonial officials in San Juan—effectively ending his direct influence within the PRRA.[59]

Seizing the chance to regain control of the Liberal Party, Barceló blamed Muñoz for the party's deteriorating relationship with the Roosevelt administration and the New Deal. In the first few days after the Ponce massacre, Barceló reaffirmed the party's faith in the original tenets of the Union Party. By highlighting its origins as the party of cultural independence and political autonomy, Barceló attempted to contrast the younger Muñoz Marín with his own father, Muñoz Rivera.[60] In May 1937, Barceló looked to permanently undercut Muñoz's standing within the party by associating him with Albizu Campos and the nationalists in the minds of voters. Displaying a brand of cautious politics that was quickly becoming outdated, Barceló and the party's other elder statesmen were, according to Pedro Cabán, becoming "anxious to demonstrate [their] loyalty to the colonial regime" and, by the end of the month, officially expelled Muñoz Marín and other advocates of independence from the ranks of the Liberal Party.[61]

By this time, most of the Puerto Rican leadership of the PRRA was disillusioned. In an eighteen-page letter to Ickes, several key personnel expressed that the "organizational set up of the PRRA is basically wrong" as the assistant and regional administrator—the highest-ranking local officials—did not have ultimate authority within the agency. Important offices such as legal, finance, and personnel were in fact outside of the regional administrator's control, they argued, even though the regional administrator was "charged with the duty of executing all projects approved." They called for more clearly defined hierarchies within the PRRA and less control by Washington. The letter was signed by several top administrators, including Guillermo Esteves (assistant regional administrator), Rafael Carmoaga (lead architect), Luis Raul Esteves (head of personnel), Manuel Egozcue (head of the "Slum Clearance" Division), Eduardo J. Saldana (executive secretary), Pablo Morales Otero (head of the Health Division), Rafael A. Gonzalez (head of the planning committee), and José Benítez (leader of the engineering section of the Rural Rehabilitation Division).[62] Muñoz Marín, the agency's most important political ally on the island, agreed, writing to Ruby Black that the "PRRA functions like a madhouse because Ernest [Gruening], who does not know how to exercise authority, also does not know how to delegate it."[63]

In June 1937, Ickes officially replaced Gruening as administrator. For the island's engineers, the elevation of Ickes allowed them to reimagine the PRRA as a robust public works agency. Although public works had been part of the PRRA since its inception—and part of PRERA and the insular government before that—Ickes's stewardship sparked the most active and energetic period of its infrastructural modernization program. Between 1937 and 1943, construction proceeded at a vigorous pace in areas that most clearly impacted the daily lives of Puerto Rican citizens and most directly relied on their participation. During this time, the Engineering Division embodied a combination of the prime-the-pump indirect hiring of Ickes's PWA and the direct hiring of Harry Hopkins's WPA in the continental United States.[64] The most important decision Ickes made was to cut the size and influence of the Washington office and transfer nearly all decision-making power to San Juan, a move that transformed the PRRA into one of the most locally run of all New Deal programs. The move also shielded the agency from growing political tensions in Washington, as Ickes's primary concern was to get the PRRA moving with as little interference from Tydings and other adversaries of the New Deal as possible.[65]

Simultaneously, Ickes promoted Miles Fairbank from regional to assistant administrator and named Guillermo Esteves Volkers as regional administrator. Fairbank (who had earlier replaced Rafael Fernández García as director of the Rural Rehabilitation Division) and Esteves (who had served as assistant regional administrator under Chardón) were now tasked with managing the PRRA's daily operations and coordinating its long-term planning. The unlikely duo, who exemplified the close relationship between Puerto Rican– and American-born New Dealers, accepted their new positions on the condition that the Washington headquarters of the PRRA be closed and moved to Puerto Rico, which aligned with Ickes's own plans.[66]

Fairbank, who was born on a Maryland farm in 1888, had first come to the island in January 1934. That year, inspired by Roosevelt's first year in office, he traded in various positions in the Maryland Farm Bureau to join the New Deal as head of the Puerto Rican branch of the Productive Credit Corporation of Baltimore (which was operated via the Land Bank of Baltimore). The Roosevelt administration had created the Productive

Credit Corporation and Banks for Cooperatives in 1933 as part of the Farm Credit Act and Federal Farm Loan Act, which were designed to facilitate federal lending to farmers. Fairbank moved with his wife and two elementary school–aged children to San Juan. After two years with the Productive Credit Corporation, Fairbank was hired to lead the PRRA's Rural Rehabilitation Division. Upon Chardón's resignation in November 1936, he was named regional administrator under Gruening and confirmed by the Senate in January 1937; by mid-year he was the assistant administrator reporting directly to Ickes.[67]

That spring, *El Mundo* reported that the rumor among political circles in San Juan was that Fairbank was being considered by Roosevelt to replace Winship as governor.[68] Outraged, Martínez Nadal swore that if Fairbank "tried to be governor, I will open up a bombardment that will make even the ears of Secretary Ickes turn red." Fairbank, he argued, was too close to the Liberal Party and, as a progressive New Dealer, possessed "neither the efficiency nor the impartiality to qualify him for the confidence of the majority of the Puerto Rican Legislature" (i.e., the Coalition). Worse, Fairbank ran the PRRA like a "political machine" and "appointed only liberals and anti-Americans to official positions, ignoring conservatives who are working for statehood on the island."[69] Strangely, Martínez Nadal also claimed that Fairbank should have checked with the Coalition before unwisely spending PRRA money building "unnecessary" CCC camps, since the "inherent psychology" of Puerto Ricans rebelled at any form of regimentation and that Puerto Rican men would rather "starve than live in camps." The PRRA was in fact now tearing down CCC camps and reusing or selling the lumber, plumbing, and electrical fixtures to private citizens. Martínez Nadal curiously ended his observation by asserting that "no Puerto Rican will ever consent to regimentation in a camp—we leave that to Boy Scouts and others who enjoy that sort of thing."[70]

Despite opposition from the Coalition, Fairbank had a surprising amount of local support. In a banner headline announcing his promotion, *El Mundo* projected optimism for the shift in direction of the PRRA toward public works and found Fairbank to be a qualified and efficient administrator who, as head of the Rural Rehabilitation Division, was already respected by small farm owners and farmworkers on the island. More importantly, Carlos Chardón was supportive as well, expressing that Fairbank was committed to the mission of the Chardón Plan and remarking that he was both well qualified and adequately experienced for his new job.[71] Fairbank also received support from Cayetano Coll y Cuchí, an influential lawyer and former representative, and the official historian of Puerto Rico. A leading voice for independence, Coll y Cuchí personally wrote to Ickes to express his approval of Fairbank as the assistant administrator of the PRRA.[72]

As one of the most important figures in Puerto Rican civil engineering, Guillermo Esteves could not have offered a bigger contrast to Fairbank. Esteves was born in Aguadilla, educated at Tufts University, and had served in a variety of government positions since the 1910s, including head engineer of municipal works, superintendent of public works, and commissioner of the insular Department of the Interior.[73] The promotion of Esteves proved to be highly significant, as he oversaw the agency during its most intensive period of public works construction. Together with Fairbank, Esteves helped numerous Puerto Rican engineers, teachers, doctors, nurses, social workers, and other professionals make a substantial difference in the public health of the island, which had a positive effect in people's daily lives for decades to come. Ickes deferred to Fairbank and Esteves because he was far too busy with other projects to focus on Puerto Rico; consumed with running the PWA and the Department of the Interior, Ickes broke from his reputation as a hands-on administrator and delegated the work of the PRRA to his subordinates.

Fairbank and Esteves proved adept at negotiating with Congress, testifying several times before the House and Senate. In August 1938, Fairbank hosted a series of intragovernmental conferences to foster greater cooperation between various parts of the federal and insular governments. In October 1938, he established the PRRA's Program of Coordinated Activity, which included the commissioners of the insular Department of Agriculture and Department of Commerce, the directors of the Agricultural Extension Service and Agricultural Experimental Station, the dean of the College of Agriculture and Mechanic Arts, the vocational director of the insular Department of Education, the director of the Tobacco Institute, and the director of the U.S. Department of Agriculture's Experiment Station. Notably, none of these were Coalition-controlled positions. The PRRA used this increased cooperation with insular institutions to expand a variety of already-existing projects aimed at increasing productivity and improving the quality of life in the agrarian countryside, including soil conservation, commercial and subsistence crop development, livestock and poultry farming, the spread of 4-H Clubs, and farm management education and organization programs.[74]

When Fairbank retired from the agency in 1941, Esteves was appointed to replace him as assistant administrator even though the PRRA budget had shrunk to about $4 million (roughly $84 million today). His tenure largely involved the management of existing programs, and Esteves oversaw the completion of every single engineering project under way. By the time of its liquidation in 1955, the PRRA had invested over $1.7 billion and directly transferred at least $691 million to Puerto Rico in the form of completed public works projects and public authorities. It also left with a balanced budget. As we will see in the following chapters, the PRRA's most far-reaching accomplishments were the construction of hurricane-proof houses, schools, hospitals, roads, and sanitation systems and the completion of the capital-intensive rural hydro-electrification projects.[75]

3

Para Permanencia

The first cement plant in Puerto Rico began operations on the humid morning of August 22, 1938, crushing magnesium-rich Puerto Rican limestone and mixing it into high-quality Portland cement. The opening of the Cataño cement plant, which occurred just three weeks shy of the ten-year anniversary of San Felipe, was a long-standing dream for the island's geologists and civil engineers who had conceived of, studied, and planned for such an undertaking for years. It was, for them, one of the most significant events of the decade. For us, the plant's inauguration should be seen as one of the most critical and lasting legacies of the Puerto Rican New Deal.[1]

Locally produced cement was a symbol for Puerto Rican engineers who, like their counterparts in other circum-Caribbean countries, envisioned future possibilities of development with modern, hurricane-proof building materials. Such visions demonstrated their faith in science and technology and their belief that Puerto Rico could enter an era of productivity, development, and economic modernity. This belief was reflective of their training and education during the Progressive era, when many of the island's leading engineers entered the insular civil service after completing graduate degrees at elite universities in the continental United States. While the island's postwar industrialization program, known as Operation Bootstrap, continues to receive deserving attention in the historical literature, this chapter will focus on the ways in which Puerto Rican engineers and civil servants aligned with their American-born counterparts in the PRRA to put their plans in motion, examining both the construction of the cement plant and the related programs of "swamp drainage," which included the destruction of coastal mangroves, and the razing of arrabales and barriadas obreras, which PRRA planners called "slum clearance." While not all of the PRRA's "swamp drainage" and "slum clearance" programs involved the destruction of active mangrove ecosystems, much of the marginal land outside of cities where arrabales and barriadas were located had been previously filled during the Spanish era and by the insular government during the first thirty years of U.S. rule.[2]

As we will see, the Cataño cement plant was designed as a response to growing public health crises on the island and to meet future possibilities of industrialization. While U.S.-trained engineers like Guillermo Esteves and Manuel Font knew that constructing an all-weather infrastructure was essential to protecting their fellow Puerto Ricans from the fury of future hurricanes, they also believed in their own ability to reimagine and reshape the island's future. In the decades to come, these technocratic engineers would have no doubt felt vindicated to see that the cement plant was instrumental to the defense of the Caribbean during World War II and central to the island's postwar industrialization program.[3]

The Cataño plant was located between the low hills and marshy bay shore of Guaynabo, about ten miles southwest of San Juan near the military base called Camp Buchanan. It was funded by a series of federal allocations between 1936 and 1938 for a total cost of approximately $1.45 million (about $30.7 million today). It was built rapidly and expertly and was completed nearly $22,000 (over $463,000 today) under budget.[4] From an engineering perspective, the plant was perhaps the most important accomplishment of the PRRA as its high-quality cement products became central to nearly all of the New Deal's other development goals and construction projects. The plant also fostered new private investment in hurricane-proof construction and matched federal money with Puerto Rican experts, planners, and architects who sought an increased role in the island's reconstruction. In addition, the PRRA's ability to operate outside of the Coalition-controlled legislature meant that funding could not be derailed by insular partisan politics. The need for the plant had been articulated in the Chardón Plan, which had argued in 1934 that "under our exacting climatic conditions, concrete is the only durable and . . . socially economical construction material."[5] To PRRA engineers, building with lesser materials would be a waste of the island's limited relief dollars.

Reinforced concrete made from Portland cement played a role in the modernization of Puerto Rican architecture. Prior building materials, including hydraulic cement tiles and hollow cement blocks, had been proven as unsound for the tropical environment as wood, brick, or terra-cotta. As Beatriz Del Cueto has explained, hydraulic mortars made by mixing lime, water, and sand had been used in Puerto Rico since the mid-sixteenth century, when Spanish colonizers introduced the method and permanently changed building practices in the Caribbean. Evidence exists of crushed-brick mortars being used in some of the earliest Spanish-built fortifications, city walls, and religious structures in Puerto Rico.[6] By the end of the nineteenth century, Puerto Rican builders relied on a combination of hydraulic tiles and imported Portland cement. Hydraulic tiles, known locally as *losas criollas*, were originally imported from Barcelona; after 1909, they began to be manufactured on the island by Gumersindo Lluch and Severiano Ramírez in Cabo Rojo and by Porto Rico Mosaics in Yauco. In contrast, all Portland cement was imported—primarily from Germany, Denmark, Belgium, England, France, and, later, the continental United States. Imported cement was expensive to ship, and the heavy barrels were usually unloaded in Saint Thomas before being refreighted to the ports of San Juan, Ponce, Mayagüez, and Arecibo or to other parts of the Caribbean and West Indies.[7]

In the early twentieth century, Puerto Rican builders began using prefabricated concrete blocks, which were developed by a number of manufacturers and, within a few years, sold by Sears, Roebuck & Co. and other large mail-order companies. Around the same time, metal molds for hollow concrete blocks were brought to the island by Protestant missionaries to help expedite the construction of schools, hospitals, churches, and other religious-themed buildings. Imported Portland cement and locally constructed concrete blocks were used by the U.S. military and early colonial governments to build roads, bridges, schools, and other basic infrastructure. Upon its creation, the insular Department of Interior likewise relied on a combination of materials in their public works program.[8]

While these methods provided some security against the heavy winds, rain, and floods of tropical storms and hurricanes, they proved disastrously incapable of withstanding the periodic earthquakes that also tremor throughout the region. On October 11, 1918, a 7.3-magnitude earthquake devastated the Mayagüez and Añasco area, leveling buildings and leaving the western coast of Puerto Rico in ruins. Following the quake, the insular Department of the Interior undertook an extensive study of building materials. They found that buildings constructed with reinforced concrete made from imported Portland cement were relatively undamaged, while those built with wood, brick, stone, cement block, or unreinforced concrete all failed. Of these, wooden structures actually proved strongest against earthquakes but of course remained the most vulnerable to hurricanes, flooding, mold, and rot.[9] Even though the 1918 earthquake convinced the island's civil engineers of the necessity of using reinforced Portland cement from a public health and safety standpoint, many builders continued to use weaker construction materials because the high cost of importing cement from Europe and the continental United States was virtually prohibitive.

The inauguration of the Cataño plant in 1938, when viewed from the perspective of the island's civil engineers who understood this long history, was overdue. It was built during the peak crisis years in Puerto Rican politics, when the Riggs assassination, Tydings Bill, and Ponce massacre dominated public discourse. It was a time of heightened anxiety and uncertainty, when the island's political parties and alliances reformulated themselves or collapsed under the weight of their internal contradictions and disagreements. As one of the first major projects completed under the leadership team of Miles Fairbank and Guillermo Esteves, Cataño was a landmark achievement that tangibly demonstrated the PRRA's commitment to building a new public health infrastructure in Puerto Rico. Although it is never mentioned in broader studies of the New Deal, the Cataño plant's construction should be seen as a purely Puerto Rican undertaking of local, national, and regional significance.

It was designed by Colonel Manuel Font Jiménez, leader of the PRRA Engineering Division, who had served in the Porto Rico Regiment of Infantry during the First World War. Like others in the Porto Rico Regiment, Font was a member of the elite from the end of the Spanish era. Born in 1888, he graduated from the Massachusetts Institute of Technology in 1913 and, after the war, served as an assistant engineer in the insular Division of Sanitation and as assistant chief engineer of the Puerto Rico Irrigation Service. By 1933, Font had been named president of the Puerto Rico Section of the American Society of Engineers. He oversaw all aspects of Cataño's construction and assigned daily management to head foreman Arturo Cordova Infante. Font was an interesting figure. Between 1940 and 1942, he served as the second president of the Professional College of Engineers and Land Surveyors of Puerto Rico and was one of the few members of the Liberal Party in the PRRA that did not follow Luis Muñoz Marín to the Popular Democratic Party (PPD). Instead, Font ran for resident commissioner in 1944 on the newly re-formed Coalition ticket, which now included Republicans, Socialists, and Liberals. He lost to Jesús T. Piñero of the PPD who, two years later, became the last appointed governor of the island.[10]

The Cataño/Guaynabo area was one of three sites that Font surveyed for the plant. According to *El Mundo*, which ran an interview between Font and Antonio Cruz y Nieves, head of the PRRA's information and research section, the other sites scouted for the cement plant were on the southern coast in Tallaboa, located just west of Ponce, and on the northwestern coast in the Victoria neighborhood of Aguadilla. All three offered ideal geological conditions with plentiful natural resources and were located near the sea, with access to internal transportation routes, including paved roads, highways, and railroad lines. Similarly, all three provided access to potential consumers in the most populous metropolitan regions of the island: Cataño to San Juan/Santurce, Tallaboa to Ponce, and Aguadilla to Mayagüez. Guaynabo had an additional advantage because it was closer to PRRA headquarters in Viejo San Juan and was ultimately chosen by Font in consultation with geologist Edwin Eckel. Eckel, who worked for the TVA, had visited the island in 1934 to conduct a survey of local conditions for the production of cement with geologists and students at the UPR. Combined with local studies of the economic viability of markets and transportation, Eckel's reports on the island's karst topography and abundant raw materials such as limestone and clay were influential to securing congressional funding for the plant.[11]

In touring the island, Eckel benefited from the work of Puerto Rican geologists and engineers who had previously researched the construction of a local cement plant but lacked the private or public capital to complete the project. These engineers included Tulio Larrínaga y Torres Vallejo, the dean of Puerto Rican civil engineers who, before his political career, began construction of a cement plant in the late nineteenth century. Others who fomented the idea of the cement plant were engineer and lawyer Antonio Romero Moreno in the insular Office of Sanitary Engineering and Rafael A. González, the head of the PRRA Planning Division.[12]

Eckel's report noted what these engineers and contractors knew well: that since all cement was currently imported from Europe and the mainland United States, the construction of a local plant would drastically lower prices for cement and reduce the cost of urban and rural housing construction. In addition, Eckel argued that the utilization of island resources could stimulate new industries in glass and bottle manufacturing, paint pigment, and salt making, among other possibilities, some of which were later tried during the Bootstrap era. Like cement, salt was mostly imported to Puerto Rico at the time; schooners arrived from Nova Scotia with loads of salted cod but left the island with empty hulls.[13] Eckel's report echoed the findings of Albert W. Buel, a member of the American Society of Civil Engineers who had first advocated on behalf of building a cement plant in Puerto Rico in 1900. Buel argued that a local cement plant "should prove very profitable." Sounding like a protégé of Frederick Taylor, the leading Progressive-era proponent of scientific management, Buel noted that the higher cost of fuel to power the plant would be offset by the lower cost of labor on the island. Surmising an increased role for Puerto Rico in intra-Caribbean trade, he speculated on the cost savings of being able to internally transport the product in bags, rather than barrels, and suggested that it was "quite probable that a well-managed Porto Rican Portland-cement mill could eventually supply a large part of the demand . . . in the West Indies, Central America, and the northern part of South America, and could sell all it could possibly make when the [Panama Canal] is constructed."[14]

Puerto Rican civil engineers had similar notions. Before working for the PRRA, Guillermo Esteves had been the commissioner of the interior in 1926 when the insular government funded the construction of the Puerto Rico Island Penitentiary in Río Piedras. The prison, later called the Río Piedras State Penitentiary but known colloquially as Oso Blanco (or the White Bear), was one of the largest construction projects of the 1920s. Designed by architect Francisco Roldán and built by Armando Vivoni, the superintendent of insular public works, and Rafael Carmoega, the director of the insular government's Division of Public Buildings and later an architect with the PRRA, the Art Deco–inspired Oso Blanco was designed to resist the dangers of fire, hurricane, and earthquake. This meant that when the prison opened in 1933 its foundations, walls, floor slabs, girders, beams, columns, and stairwells were all constructed with reinforced concrete made from imported Portland cement.[15] But Oso Blanco (which closed in 2004) was an exception, and most buildings in the 1920s were not made to the same architectural standards. A decade later, however, engineers like Esteves and Font secured new federal financing for public works and seized on the opportunity to complete projects like Cataño that had been impossible to build prior to the New Deal coming to Puerto Rico.

The Puerto Rico Cement Corporation

At 12:01 a.m. on January 16, 1939, about five months after its opening, Guillermo Esteves transferred the full ownership and operations of the Cataño plant to the Puerto Rico Cement Corporation (PRCC), a newly created, nonpartisan, and publicly owned company administered by technocrats in the local government.[16] Although the corporation's legal objective was to "act as an agency of and for the People of Puerto Rico, and, in furtherance thereof, to establish, maintain, and operate an industrial enterprise for the manufacture, transportation, and sale of cement and its by-products," transferring Cataño to local control also ensured that its operations would be managed by the same PRRA engineers and administrators who designed and built the plant. While the initial leadership structure included a mix of American- and Puerto Rican–born government officials, by 1943 the PRCC featured an all–Puerto Rican board of directors, including Esteves as president, Antonio Lucchetti as vice president, Agustín M. Andino as secretary, Jorge Font Saldana as treasurer, Vicente Medina as director, Manuel Font as general administrator (though currently on active duty serving in World War II), David S. Ramírez as acting general administrator, José R. Benítez as comptroller, and Mariano H. Ramírez Bages as undersecretary and legal assessor.[17] Upon the transfer to the PRCC, Font estimated that the plant would produce between 300,000 and 350,000 barrels of cement per year, adequately serving both the insular government and the island's private contractors.[18]

Local cement production was a crucial weapon against epidemic disease and protection against hurricanes, and the PRCC aided Puerto Rican efforts to improve public health while creating greater stability and security. Though the Cataño plant is sometimes noted as one of several small-scale industrialization projects built by the PRRA, no theoretical attention has been given to its public health context.[19] By examining the cement plant from a public health perspective, however, we see that Puerto Rican public works paralleled the New Deal's emphasis on building a lasting public health infrastructure while at the same time expanding a new vision of economic security for all U.S. citizens. As Michael Grey has written, the New Deal did not have a singular health program. Instead, as evidenced by its wide-ranging concern for disease control, nutrition, nurse and physician training programs, constructing new water and sanitation systems, and extensive hospital building, the New Deal used the combined resources of many federal agencies working in cooperation with local and state governments to radically improve the nation's long-term public health.[20] Public works construction played a central role in many New Deal public health initiatives whether built by the PWA and WPA in the continental United States or the PRRA in Puerto Rico.

The Cataño plant and PRCC were thus part of a larger New Deal strategy to improve public health through the construction of clean drinking water and sanitation systems that worked in tandem with other health initiatives.[21] In Puerto Rico, PRRA-built water and sanitation systems complemented the agency's efforts to provide direct medical care. In a series of 23,180 medical and dental clinics held between 1935 and 1938, doctors and nurses working for the PRRA treated 541,435 patients, which equated to roughly 30 percent of the total population at the time. Such an investment in medical clinics would have been shortsighted without the long-term commitment to clean drinking water and a new public health infrastructure.[22]

While the cost of the Cataño plant had been financially impossible for the insular legislature to provide, it was also politically difficult to get funding from a Congress that was growing increasingly hostile to the idea of unlimited New Deal spending. In fact, during 1935 and 1936, the future of the New Deal was very much in doubt despite its widespread popularity with both rural and urban Americans. As the Supreme Court struck down some of the First New Deal's major initiatives, administration policy came under increased scrutiny from Democrats and Republicans alike. Examination of the PRRA's budget should be placed in a wider context that considers the growing resistance to the entire New Deal after 1935.

As with nearly all other New Deal programs, funding for the Cataño plant and other public works had to be politically framed around their role in providing relief jobs, even as PRRA engineers looked toward long-term reconstruction. Administrators used whatever access they had—such as writing annual reports, speaking to the press, or testifying before Congress—to highlight Cataño's appeal as both a direct job creator through the plant's 150 full-time positions and $20,000 (about $421,000 today) monthly payroll, and as an indirect job creator through the expansion of the local construction industry. The PRRA lobbied for and obtained the original $850,000 (about $18.7 million today) for the plant through the Emergency Relief Appropriation Act of December 1935 and received four more allotments totaling $616,500 ($13 million) between 1936 and 1938. Job creation was the only reasoning that worked, even though the cement plant's long-term value was substantially more important than the number of jobs it created.[23]

While the costs were high, the price of importing cement was even higher, as it fluctuated according to volatile global economic conditions that impacted supply, demand, and transport. Prior to Cataño's completion, PRRA engineers and private contractors made numerous complaints about the changing price of imported cement and the lack of stable transportation costs that had rippling effects across a range of construction activities on the island which put added pressure on already strained budgets. In 1936, Chardón protested to Gruening that while prices for materials such as lumber and cement had remained steady in continental building markets, the cost of ocean freight had risen considerably and led to overcharges from original construction budgets.[24]

Likewise, Fairbank and Esteves worried about the fluctuating prices of imported cement, such as when the 1938 dockworkers' strike curtailed the PRRA's ability to receive shipments of cement from the continental United States. The strike, which was won by dockworkers with the support of the Puerto Rico Communist Party and the Congress of Industrial Organizations (CIO), played a pivotal role in bringing industrial unionization to the island. The strike also points to the contradictory nature of the New Deal in Puerto Rico. Despite the concerns of Fairbank and Esteves about obtaining imported cement, Puerto Rican workers benefited from the application of the Wagner Act and other New Deal policies that enhanced the power of organized labor. On the island, the dockworkers' strike was an important step toward the formation of the Confederación General de Trabajadores (General Confederation of Workers or CGT) in 1940, a homegrown industrial alternative to the Free Federation of Laborers that was affiliated with the CIO.[25]

The Cataño plant was significant to other parts of the Caribbean and West Indies as well, and its construction made Puerto Rico just the second regional nation or territory with a cement plant. The other was Cuba, which had had two cement plants. The first, Fábrica Cuba, opened in 1895 under Spanish jurisdiction and closed in 1910. The second, El Morro, was built with private capital from the United States in 1916 and run by the Compaña Cubana de Cemento Portland but in fact controlled by the Texas-based Lone Star Cement Corporation.[26] Word of Puerto Rico's high-quality cement quickly spread, and soon after Cataño's opening in 1938, the PRRA, the insular government, and the U.S. State Department began receiving letters from Latin American and Caribbean neighbors inquiring about purchasing cement products. Letters and telegrams arrived from Haiti, the Dominican Republic, Colombia, the Virgin Islands, Jamaica, Curaçao, and (even) Denmark and Norway, which still had private interests in the formerly called Danish Virgin Islands.[27] A few years later, impressed with the operations of the PRCC, Rafael Trujillo Molina, the president-turned-dictator of the Dominican Republic, became determined to build his own cement plant. Writing to the PRRA, Trujillo's government requested blueprints and assistance from Puerto Rican engineers. The first Dominican cement plant, Fábrica Dominicana de Cemento, opened ten years after Cataño in 1947.[28]

Locally, part of the excitement about the opening of the Cataño plant was that it was a job creator that provided economic stimulus through direct and indirect hiring. The Cataño plant brought benefits to Puerto Rican workers who were hired directly by the PRCC or indirectly in other industries in multiple ways. As in the continental United States, even limited New Deal–related hiring led to improved living conditions at a time of unprecedented unemployment. Additionally, PRCC jobs were celebrated in the press for providing benefits completely new to island workers. In a banner headline, *El Mundo* announced an agreement signed between the PRCC and Juan Saez Corals, secretary-general of the CGT, that provided Puerto Rican cement workers with paid leave, sick pay, Christmas bonuses, retirement pay, and increased salaries.[29] Sitting on opposite sides of the negotiating table, the PRCC and CGT were in their own ways major developments of the 1930s, each influenced by but not solely products of the New Deal. It should not be construed that only working-class men experienced these changes. For married and single women alike, the PRRA offered well-paying work in its offices across the island, from social workers, census takers, secretaries and other office workers to teachers, nurses, social workers, and assistants.[30]

The Cataño plant was filling demand and creating new markets for cement products across the island. After just one year of operations, demand had risen so fast that Cataño was shipping over two thousand barrels of cement per day, twice the plant's original capacity. While engineers had originally estimated that the federal government would not see a return on its investment for three decades, the plant had fully paid for itself by 1943. In these five years, the PRCC was producing over a thousand tons of concrete per year that was sold to at least fifty-nine Puerto Rican–owned small businesses, along with larger government, corporate, and international customers as well.[31] In all, the Cataño plant was doing over $168,000 per month (about $3.6 million today) in commerce with private and government contractors and held deposits in both U.S. and Puerto Rican banks, including Chase National Bank, Banco de Ponce, Banco Crédito y Ahorro Ponceño, and Banco Popular de Puerto Rico. This was exactly the type of federal spending that Ickes and other New Deal leaders used to spur private investment in the continental United States. In Puerto Rico, the response by local contractors was so strong that the PRRA had to scale back its advertising to once per week in just one newspaper in San Juan and Ponce. Originally, not knowing what the response from private contractors would be, the PRRA had advertised in a wider range of daily, weekly, and monthly newspapers and journals.[32]

In addition to increasing demand for its own cement, the PRCC also encouraged private local investment—a historically difficult task throughout Latin America and the Caribbean. In 1939, José Ferré began an exchange of letters with the board of directors of the PRCC asking for authorization and technical assistance to build a cement plant in Ponce. Ferré calculated that the newly created Ponce Cement Corporation would aim to produce a thousand barrels of cement per day for southern contractors in addition to the PRCC's two-thousand-per-day output from Guaynabo. The company was so new that the name PONCE CEMENT CORPORATION was hand-written in ink over the crossed-out ~~PUERTO RICO IRON WORKS~~ on Ferré company stationery.[33] The PRCC responded with enthusiasm to Ferré, expressing that the PRRA encouraged investment from the island's private capital and that Puerto Rican demand for cement could easily handle another thousand barrels per day, particularly on the southern and western coasts.[34] During the Puerto Rican postwar development boom, the Ponce Cement Company became one of the largest private corporations on the island. By the 1950s, as the Cold War replaced the collective spirit of the New Deal, the head of Operation Bootstrap, Teodoro Moscoso, convinced Governor Muñoz Marín to privatize the cement plant and divest the insular government of the cost of its operations. Ironically, the PRCC and its Cataño plant were sold to Ferré—whose first foray into cement works had been assisted by the PRRA over a decade earlier.[35]

Moscoso aptly embodies the shifting priorities but continuous links between the New Deal and Cold War in Puerto Rico. Whereas he once entered public service to work for the Ponce Housing Authority after its creation in 1937, Moscoso became the architect of the island's postwar development program as the head of the Puerto Rico Industrial Development Company (Compañía de Fomento Industrial de Puerto Rico), called Fomento on the island. After the Cuban Revolution, as Washington looked to solidify alliances with anti-communist leaders throughout the Americas by distributing millions of dollars for housing and public works in exchange for their loyalty, John F. Kennedy tapped Moscoso to coordinate these efforts as head of the Alliance for Progress. In choosing Moscoso, Kennedy was making an explicit connection between PRRA's arrabales-razing and housing construction programs, the work of the Puerto Rico Housing Authority, and the island's rapid postwar industrialization during Operation

74 · The Puerto Rico Reconstruction Administration

Bootstrap. Using the Puerto Rican New Deal as a showcase for Cold War policy in Latin America, however, was complicated by the island's colonial status and its ambiguous relationship to the rest of Latin America and the Caribbean.[36]

"Swamp Drainage" and "Slum Clearance"

The PRCC represented the Second New Deal's shift toward permanent reconstruction through the construction of public works *para permanencia* (for permanence), which was the company's official slogan, and its locally produced cement was seen by Puerto Rican engineers as central to the agency's public health initiatives. Puerto Rican New Dealers viewed hurricane relief, homelessness, and communicable disease as intertwined issues that could be ameliorated by programs of what they called "swamp drainage" and "slum clearance." Not only were hundreds of thousands of Puerto Rican men and women still homeless as a result of the 1928 and 1932 hurricanes, but housing relief strategies undertaken before the PRRA had actually made public health worse. Many of the wood-framed relief houses built by the Red Cross, PRERA, and insular government, for example, were already in disrepair due to local environmental conditions. Working with insular health officials, PRRA engineers understood that the island's precarious housing situation was contributing to an increase in the four deadliest public health crises confronting the island in the 1930s: malaria, uncinariasis/hookworm, malnutrition, and a variety of life-threatening gastrointestinal disorders such as chronic diarrhea and enteritis.[37]

The increase in these deadly health threats was primarily caused by the spread of working-class arrabales and barriadas on marshy land surrounding urban areas, many of which featured makeshift houses built above standing water on wooden stilts and without access to indoor plumbing, electricity, sanitation systems, or garbage disposal networks. Such houses were vulnerable to wind and rain, prone to flooding and fire, and vectors of infectious diseases such as pneumonia, bronchitis, typhoid fever, dysentery, influenza, diphtheria, syphilis, chicken pox, measles, whooping cough, and scarlet fever. During the early years of the Depression, this form of housing worsened a public health crisis that municipalities and the insular government, already stretched to fiscal limits with relief-related debt, were powerless to curtail. As Miles Fairbank testified before Congress, the "borrowing capacity of the local government was not sufficient to permit widespread reconstruction."[38]

The PRRA saw the Cataño plant as a public health necessity that could assist in the construction of modern, hurricane-proof houses and apartments. Before embarking on housing construction, however, PRRA engineers developed an island-wide plan of "swamp drainage" and undertook a massive survey of barriada residents to quantify the number of people impacted by substandard housing and identify the needs and desires of residents. Viewed by Puerto Rican New Dealers as the best weapon against the spread of malaria, draining the swamps on which many barriadas were built was considered the first step in a plan that also included mosquito abatement, cement housing construction, and connection to public utilities and services.

By June 1939, Guillermo Esteves and Manuel Font had overseen thirty-nine such drainage projects around coastal regions of the island. This work was funded by $1.75 million in federal dollars ($37.1 million today) and conducted in four primary methods: hydraulic fill, dry fill, canalization, and tile drainage. The mosquito-breeding eradication program that complemented the projects was led by researchers from the UPR in consultation with the PRRA.[39] Some of the drainage projects were slowed by political opposition. In 1938, for example, Fairbank complained that Martínez Nadal interfered with drainage projects because Félix Benítez Rexach, one of the leading engineers contracted by the PRRA, was an advocate of Puerto Rican independence. Benítez Rexach, who had recently dredged the port of Santo Domingo in the Dominican Republic (called Ciudad Trujillo between 1936 to 1961 during the dictatorship of Rafael Trujillo), owned his own diesel-electric dredging equipment and had lobbied the insular government for work in Puerto Rico. Despite the Coalition's opposition, the PRRA's approach to drainage, mosquito eradication, and concrete construction attracted the attention of neighboring Latin American and Caribbean countries, which sent students, teachers, and health professionals to Puerto Rico to exchange ideas and information and learn more about New Deal programs.[40]

The PRRA's "slum clearance" program was a subunit of the Engineering Division and a precursor to most of the agency's other urban housing projects in Puerto Rico. Led by Manuel Egozcue, an engineer who had worked in the insular Department of the Interior and was one of the highest-ranking Republicans in the PRRA, the program was a project in social and economic modernization. While it is tempting to see such development programs through the eyes of the island's engineers at the time, it is important to understand that the "slums" being "cleared" by these

76 · The Puerto Rico Reconstruction Administration

technocrats were in fact neighborhoods of working men and women and their families that were subject to be demolished and discarded. As Jorell Meléndez-Badillo has written, terms such as "slum" or "shantytown" do not adequately capture the reality of daily life in these neighborhoods. With houses often made from improvised materials and unconnected to basic public health infrastructure, these neighborhoods were home to Puerto Rican workers who lived precariously at the very "margins of power." When discussing the neighborhoods themselves, this book has adopted the Spanish terms arrabales and barriadas (or barriadas obreras) to describe workers' communities with improvised houses and few public services, which Meléndez-Badillo explains are "not merely physical spaces but also . . . the social worlds its dwellers forged."[41] At other times, when referencing the ideas and official documents of the Puerto Rican– and American-born engineers who worked for the PRRA, this book uses the terms "slum," "slum clearance," and "swamp drainage" in quotation marks. While this book does not take the engineer's perspective as its own, it is important to understand the degree to which the ideas of Puerto Rican engineers and administrators aligned with their U.S.-born counterparts since this shared vision of developmental modernization, including a faith in science and technology, united them. Their shared faith in progress undergirded the entire PRRA public works program and influenced the ways in which colonialism was reconstructed on the island.

The construction of improvised houses and worker communities on the outskirts of cities was not new. While some arrabales had existed in Puerto Rico since at least the nineteenth century, there was a considerable increase in quantity and scale after San Felipe and San Ciprián. Some were built in existing mangrove ecosystems; others were built on flooded or marginal land that had been filled by previous works projects. The increased rate of improvised housing construction in existing barriadas was no doubt caused by the uprooting of highland communities in the Cordillera Central in the wake of the environmental damage of the storms and the ongoing economic decline of the Depression. As elsewhere, there were also internal pulls to the urbanization process, such as the continued expansion of the formal and informal market economy in which wages were paid for work and the spread of social services such as education and health care in urban areas.[42]

Examining the island, PRRA engineers saw that improvised housing had multiplied in nearly all municipal areas. In many workers' neighborhoods, makeshift wooden houses were often balanced over brackish and swampy waters polluted by food scraps, household trash, and human waste. Workers' neighborhoods such as those along the Martín Peña Canal and the San José Lagoon lacked all basic clean water, sanitation, and electricity services.[43] PRERA director James Bourne had earlier noted that some arrabales displayed environmental characteristics that went beyond overcrowding and poverty. Writing to Joseph Hyde Pratt, an Atlanta-based engineer who worked with FERA, Bourne explained that many impoverished neighborhoods were built on marshy terrain or adjacent to swamps and lagoons; contained standing water and lacked proper drainage; were composed of makeshift houses made from pieces of wallboard, tin, scrap wood, or cardboard; averaged four occupants per room; and featured extremely unsanitary conditions such as latrines built over "mudholes" that were "literally no more than a shed set in an open cesspool through which the users have to pass to get into the shed itself."[44]

While initial observations made by New Deal insiders like Bourne, Eleanor Roosevelt, and Rex Tugwell focused on the "shocking" and "unbelievable" conditions of Puerto Rican barriadas, the PRRA attempted to define and quantify the scope of the problem. This was important because, even as they proliferated, the total extent of these neighborhoods was previously unknown since neither the insular legislature or federal government had ever fully investigated barriada housing conditions.[45] Between 1936 and 1939, the PRRA conducted door-to-door surveys of residents of these neighborhoods. Organized by Egozcue and Agustín M. de Andino, assistant head of the Rural Rehabilitation Division, the survey project hired a large number of women as both office workers and field researchers. Conducted in Spanish, the surveys demonstrated that such neighborhoods had been built on flooded swampland outside of all seventy-six municipalities on the island. Not confined to the large San Juan/Santurce region, they were multiplying on semi-urban and suburban marshlands across the island, with those in Arecibo, Ponce, and Mayagüez singled out as particularly dangerous and unhealthy.[46]

The surveyors offered the first demographic analysis of the island's housing crisis, introduced long-range policy suggestions, and commented on the combination of natural disaster, economic recession, and political atrophy that had plagued previous relief efforts in Puerto Rico. Their report, *Problems in Connection with Slum Clearance in Puerto Rico, with Special Reference to the San Juan Area*, was written in a typically Progressive-era style that mixed a desire for social reform with biased moral, racial, and class-based assumptions. Written in 1939, two decades before the more famous Culture of Poverty thesis, the unpublished report victimized uneducated, working-class Puerto Ricans by lamenting their "acceptance of low social standards" and declaring that it was "not surprising that the low-income group is satisfied to seek improvised shelter."[47] At the same time, however, the report found that due to the high cost of rent and lack of well-paying jobs, there were no viable alternatives in urban areas for displaced internal migrants than to build their own houses in the ever-expanding barriadas.

Looking beyond the biases of its authors, the report offered a grim picture of everyday life in the workers' neighborhoods of San Juan/Santurce, the island's largest metropolitan area. Surveyors in 1936 had found that 9,345 families lived in thirteen San Juan–area barriadas. These included large neighborhoods such as Miranda in Puerta de Tierra, La Perla just outside the gates of Old San Juan, and Tras Talleres, La Zona, and Melilla in Santurce. They also included much smaller barriadas like Marina, Merhoff, Miraflores, Mosquito, Roosevelt, San Ciprián (1), San Ciprián (2), and Shanghai. The report noted that many soldiers of the Sixty-Fifth U.S. Infantry Regiment lived with their families in La Perla and other barriadas. A follow-up survey in 1939 found that the total number of residents had increased by 25 percent to nearly 11,500 families—which equates to roughly 57,500 people if family units in Puerto Rico are considered to average five persons per family, which they were at the time.[48]

In Ponce, barriadas were likewise found in swampy areas near canals and inlets and featured poor sanitary conditions without running water or human refuse removal systems. These included the Mameys and Saint Thomas neighborhoods along the reservoir canal; Machuelito on the eastern shore of the flood-prone Portugués River, which periodically washed away houses and caused many deaths in the areas; the Berlin, Loma del Viento, and aptly named Peligro neighborhoods along the western shore of the Portugués River; the Hoya del Castillo, which was a small neighborhood in the city itself, located in front of the district court, athletic park, Castillo School, and "homes of the better class," and composed of fifty-seven houses, all of them in very poor condition; the small Brooklyn neighborhood located on Road No. 1 outside of the city; Cuartro Calles, which bordered the estate of Fernando Toro; and the Salitral and Tablazo barriadas of Ponce Playa, on the beach near the mouth of the Portugués River with houses that were "in deplorable conditions" and "continuously threatened by floods."[49]

Conditions in these neighborhoods were made worse by previous relief efforts. During the Coolidge and Hoover administrations and the First New Deal, hurricane relief efforts had created new barriadas by constructing temporary, wood-framed houses and *tormenteras* (hurricane relief shelters) that did not meet existing local health or building codes. Relief houses and storm shelters that were built by the American Red Cross, PRERA, and the insular government were often an inadequate short-term solution to a problem that was guaranteed to repeat itself, given the annual recurrence of hurricanes in the western Atlantic and Caribbean. Temporary houses were also built by private companies such as the Fajardo Sugar Company, which constructed approximately five hundred relief houses after San Ciprián. Like the publicly built houses, however, these only lasted a few years before falling apart. "Experience has shown," PRRA engineers argued, "that it is a waste of money to build cheap wooden houses in most parts of the island. The insular government is at the present time building a number of wooden houses on partly reclaimed land at the 'Tras Talleres' in Santurce, where they are moving families from the Miranda slum." Explaining that this is a "marshy area that is overflooded at high tide," they concluded that "such a project can hardly be justified, since without question the new settlement will become another slum area within a few years" or get blown away in another hurricane. Furthermore, Miranda was a considerable distance (about an hour's walk) from the location of the new housing in Tras Talleres, placing a burden on residents who most likely worked in Puerta de Tierra or Viejo San Juan. Aside from flooding, the most immediate dangers of building wooden relief houses in these areas were communicable disease, mold, termites, dry rot, and fire.[50]

From the perspective of PRRA engineers, social workers, and planners, the inadequate housing structures in these neighborhoods were not simply the product of governmental neglect but rather seemed to be "legalized" by the insular government. They explained that houses were usually built on land that was acquired in one of two ways: either the resident rented land from a private landowner in a semiofficial arrangement, usually without a lease or contract; or the resident squatted on public land owned by the municipal or insular government, sometimes with usufruct rights. In both cases, residents owned their improvised houses even if they did not own the land where the house was built; some residents even sold their improvised houses when they moved out of the neighborhood. While there were important benefits for the poorest citizens to obtain legal or usufruct rights in housing, PRRA engineers saw these laws and customs as problematically sanctioning unsanitary living conditions. The report makes clear that PRRA engineers believed that "private persons who lease plots on a 'ground rent' basis . . . [have] under Puerto Rican law, a degree of legal title" to any dwelling they build on that land. Although the local government had sufficient laws and regulations in place to ensure the safety and health of all residents, it lacked the ability to enforce existing insular health codes and did not have the planning resources to deal with the large number of families who would be dispossessed by any program of razing arrabales in the name of "slum clearance." By surveying residents, PRRA engineers and public health workers sought to record the extent of the problem and devise a plan to use public resources to decrease controllable and preventable diseases.[51]

Social workers used the survey to quantify the poverty that stalked barriada residents who lacked surplus money for clothing, amusements, insurance, books, school supplies, or other quality-of-life amenities. Residents living in La Perla and Miranda had greater average incomes than residents of the thirteen Ponce neighborhoods. According to the report, over two-thirds of La Perla's families lived on an income of between $11 and $30 per month ($238 to $650 today), while 8 percent made under $10 per month ($216 today), 4 percent subsided on public charity and/or family support, 14 percent made between $31 and $50 per month ($672 to $1,083 today), and 8 percent made over $51 per month ($1,105 today). Similarly, about 55 percent of Miranda's families had incomes between $11 and $30 per month, while 10 percent lived on less than $10 per month, 4 percent on charity and family support, 15 percent between $31 and $50 per month, and 16 percent over $51 per month. In contrast, residents in Ponce's barriadas made substantially less per month on average. Surveys in Ponce found that families here were three to five times more likely to live on less than $10 per month, and that between 55 and 80 percent of all families lived on less than $20 per month (about $433 today).[52]

Surveys conducted in smaller towns near tobacco, coffee, and citrus farms or sugar mills and plantations found that most residents preferred to be resettled in the mountains near their places of work. Conversely, surveys in urban neighborhoods firmly established that urban families did not desire resettlement in rural areas. In San Juan and Santurce, most residents were deeply engrained in urban life and worked for wages as street vendors, domestic workers, and dock and factory workers. As the report noted, "any abrupt change in their location would bring about considerable [economic and emotional] hardship."[53] Indeed, many urban residents did not want to move from their current housing even when it was possible to stay in the same immediate area. A door-to-door survey of 1,100 of the 1,325 families living in La Perla was conducted in 1937. According to this survey, approximately 64 percent of families were willing to sell or otherwise leave their houses in exchange for a newly built house or apartment, but roughly 36 percent were unwilling to move from their current homes.[54]

Viewing temporary housing on or adjacent to swamps, mangroves, and marshes as cross-sections of poverty, malnutrition, and disease, the 1939 report made ten recommendations about what future "slum clearance" programs should be predicated upon:

(1) All housing should be built with reinforced concrete to protect against future hurricanes, but be simply designed and of low cost. To help reduce the cost of building with concrete, public housing would use locally produced cement purchased from the PRCC.
(2) All families should be resettled as close as possible to where they already live and work.
(3) Based on the monthly income of residents, rents should begin at $1.50 ($32.50 today) per month, and the average rent should not exceed $5 ($108 today) per month.
(4) To help alleviate overcrowding in other areas of San Juan, public housing should be built at rents ranging from $10 ($216 today) to $15 ($325 today) per month.
(5) Electricity, clean water, and (perhaps) gas should be provided at public expense to all low-income and working-class housing residents.
(6) Public housing in La Perla and Miranda should be based on the type already constructed by the PRRA, but should be built from a cheaper design.
(7) Insular government-owned lands adjoining swamps and lagoons in the San Juan/Santurce area should be drained and filled to provide building sites for public housing.
(8) Approximately $10 million (about $212 million today) would be required to raze the barriadas of the San Juan/Santurce area, not including the costs of land acquisition.
(9) Acquiring land for barriada removal and public housing construction would only be necessary in the island's three largest metropolitan areas: San Juan/Santurce, Ponce, and Mayagüez. In smaller municipalities and towns, where the housing crisis was less acute and many

residents worked on farms, a semirural type of housing project would be constructed.

(10) All public housing must include social services, maintenance, and care of the property at the public's expense and provide enhanced community recreation areas such as access to schools, playgrounds, and community centers.[55]

Problems in Connection with Slum Clearance in Puerto Rico was the first report of its kind in Puerto Rico and the most comprehensive examination of living conditions in the barriadas of the island or elsewhere in the Caribbean. Like the construction of the Cataño cement plant, the report was viewed by PRRA engineers, public health officials, and social workers as a major contribution to colonial reform via the modernization of Puerto Rican society. Viewing themselves as planners of progress and development, Puerto Rican New Dealers used the report to enact improvements in the daily lives of working-class residents. Locally produced cement offered PRRA workers a newfound means of contributing to social and physical mobility through an expansion of economic opportunity, advances in public health conditions, and the ability to construct hurricane-proof houses, schools, hospitals, roads, waterworks, sewers, storm drains, and other public works out of locally quarried limestone and clay. As public health workers argued, cement construction was an effective weapon against the multiple vectors of disease and poverty that were increasing on the island during the Great Depression. Access to local cement assisted public health workers and civil engineers in the transition from temporary relief to a more permanent reconstruction.

Figure 1. Cataño cement plant under construction, Guaynabo. Puerto Rico Reconstruction Administration, 1936–37. Puerto Rico Reconstruction Administration Collection. Photo courtesy of the Biblioteca Digital Puertorriqueña, Universidad de Puerto Rico, Recinto de Río Piedras.

Figure 2. Model house and subsistence garden for rural workers and homesteaders, Arroyo. Puerto Rico Reconstruction Administration, 193-. Puerto Rico Reconstruction Administration Collection. Photo courtesy of the Biblioteca Digital Puertorriqueña, Universidad de Puerto Rico, Recinto de Río Piedras.

Figure 3. PRRA employee baseball team. Puerto Rico Reconstruction Administration, 193-. Puerto Rico Reconstruction Administration Collection. Photo courtesy of the Biblioteca Digital Puertorriqueña, Universidad de Puerto Rico, Recinto de Río Piedras.

Figure 4. Directors of El Falansterio Cooperative. Puerto Rico Reconstruction Administration, 1939. PRRA Collection. Photo courtesy of the Archivo de Arquitectura y Construcción, Universidad de Puerto Rico, Recinto de Río Piedras.

Figure 5. Members of the Puerto Rico Rug Cooperative. Puerto Rico Reconstruction Administration, 1937. PRRA Collection. Photo courtesy of the Archivo de Arquitectura y Construcción, Universidad de Puerto Rico, Recinto de Río Piedras.

Figure 6. Inauguration of the Lafayette Cooperative, Arroyo. Miles Fairbank is seated second from the right as Rafael Menéndez Ramos addresses the crowd. Puerto Rico Reconstruction Administration, 1937. PRRA Collection. Photo courtesy of the Archivo de Arquitectura y Construcción, Universidad de Puerto Rico, Recinto de Río Piedras.

Figure 7. PRRA officials inspecting the construction of brick houses in Castañer. Guillermo Esteves is standing on the far left next to workers, foremen, and other officials. Puerto Rico Reconstruction Administration, 1937. PRRA Collection. Photo courtesy of the Archivo de Arquitectura y Construcción, Universidad de Puerto Rico, Recinto de Río Piedras.

Figure 8. Central plaza with American flag and concrete houses at the Caserío La Granja, Caguas. Puerto Rico Reconstruction Administration, 1937. PRRA Collection. Photo courtesy of the Archivo de Arquitectura y Construcción, Universidad de Puerto Rico, Recinto de Río Piedras.

Figure 9. Distribution of fertilizer to resettled farmers from workers in the Rural Rehabilitation Section of the Engineering Division. Puerto Rico Reconstruction Administration, 1937. PRRA Collection. Photo courtesy of the Archivo de Arquitectura y Construcción, Universidad de Puerto Rico, Recinto de Río Piedras.

Figure 10. Delivery of keys to resettled farmworkers in the coffee zone. Representing the PRRA is Francisco Méndez. Puerto Rico Reconstruction Administration, 1937. PRRA Collection. Photo courtesy of the Archivo de Arquitectura y Construcción, Universidad de Puerto Rico, Recinto de Río Piedras.

Figure 11. Recently completed construction of the main library and teachers college of the University of Puerto Rico, Río Piedras. Puerto Rico Reconstruction Administration, 1937. PRRA Collection. Photo courtesy of the Archivo de Arquitectura y Construcción, Universidad de Puerto Rico, Recinto de Río Piedras.

Figure 12. Vegetable planting at a PRRA farm near Cayey. Electric wires can be seen in the rear, along with wooden houses and unfinished telegraph towers. Puerto Rico Reconstruction Administration, 1939. PRRA Collection. Photo courtesy of the Archivo de Arquitectura y Construcción, Universidad de Puerto Rico, Recinto de Río Piedras.

4

The Road to Modernization

The road to modernization depended on building hurricane-proof public works. The PRRA's efforts to modernize the island's public health infrastructure were central to its plans for improving life expectancy, economic opportunity, and physical mobility on an unprecedented scale in Puerto Rico or elsewhere in the Caribbean region. Before the arrival of the New Deal, large parts of Puerto Rico's infrastructure were virtually unchanged since before the U.S. invasion of 1898. In rural areas, the absence of water and sanitation systems taxed public health, while the lack of paved roads and sturdy bridges made even the most basic daily activities more burdensome. Written in 1894, Manuel Zeno Gandía's *La Charca* vividly illustrates the lack of basic infrastructure in the coffee region of the rural interior mountains. Remarking on the daily commute of workers, the novel informs us: "To get there, it was necessary to descend a slope, cross the river by hopping from stone to stone, and then climb a steep hill. The narrow trail was heavily pocked by the footsteps of travelers on the muddy, mountainous terrains. Dense woods covered the paths, and one could virtually be sure that the direct rays of the sun had never bathed the earth there."[1] Through a regeneration of the built environment, PRRA engineers aimed to improve social and physical mobility, halt the advance of several interrelated disease threats, buffer the island against the effects of tropical storms, and secure a lasting and permanent recovery from the Great Depression. If reinforced concrete was a modern tool to meet these aims, locally made cement from the Cataño plant pointed to a new form of Puerto Rican modernity. After 1939, the PRRA purchased cement products directly from the Puerto Rican Cement Corporation to build thousands of public roads, schools, hospitals, health clinics, sports and recreation centers, agricultural experiment stations, municipal buildings, cooperative storehouses, sewers, storm drains, drinking water systems, reservoirs, and houses.

Long-term reconstruction was a group effort between the various parts of the PRRA, including its health unit, which worked with insular officials and contributed labor and capital to ongoing projects whenever possible. Because the insular Department of Health was primarily focused on urban areas, the PRRA health unit was designed to operate in the agrarian sectors, bringing modern health services to some parts of the rural population for the first time. The work, which was carried out almost entirely by Puerto Rican doctors, nurses, and other health professionals, was coordinated with the University of Puerto Rico and the School of Tropical Medicine. The health unit was divided into five basic parts: the rural medical service; the rural sanitation service; the workers' camps medical section; the social service section (which also provided medical service to PRRA workers and their families); and the statistics section, which compiled, analyzed, and interpreted scientific and demographic data. All laboratory work was performed by the insular Department of Health's biological laboratory, with funding, personnel, and supplies provided by the PRRA.[2]

The work of the health unit was intertwined with that of the Engineering Division. While the PRRA's health workers provided immediate care and researched solutions for long-term recovery, its engineers acted upon health-based recommendations to build permanent structures. Physically embodying the shift from relief to reconstruction, Puerto Rican engineers replaced temporary wood-based relief housing with lasting cement-based construction and supplemented new houses with an array of public works and services. In urban areas, public housing construction was based on the removal of arrabales and barriadas that, as we saw in the previous chapter, were viewed as unhealthy, unhygienic, and unconnected to the modern world.

In rural areas, PRRA housing design combined cement, brick, and packed-earth housing construction with numerous integrative rehabilitation programs, including forestry, soil conservation, agricultural diversification, seed and fertilizer distribution, road building, support for family farming cooperatives, education, and rural electrification. Large-scale vegetable farming was accelerated by the introduction of new seeds, crops, and fertilizers designed to improve the diet of rural residents, including cabbage, beans, carrots, okra, squash, beets, onions, potatoes, radishes, and turnips. As a result of soil conservation and scientific farming, PRRA agronomists enhanced the production of Puerto Rican staples such as plantains and bananas, pigeon peas, yams and sweet potatoes, pumpkins,

92 · The Puerto Rico Reconstruction Administration

rice, and cassava or yuca root. Between 1935 and 1943, the PRRA spent over $16 million (over $339 million today) on urban and rural hurricane-proof housing projects, an unparalleled investment in the permanent stability, economic security, and social mobility of the island.[3]

Hospitals and Rural Health Services

Puerto Rican New Dealers, even more acutely than their American-born counterparts, viewed the improvised housing of the barriadas and the previously built hurricane relief houses as intersections of malnutrition and disease. Deaths from malaria, tuberculosis, uncinariasis, and various gastrointestinal diseases made up over 40 percent of all mortalities in Puerto Rico during the Great Depression. Reports filed by the School of Tropical Medicine, Rockefeller Foundation, insular Department of Health, and PRRA found that nearly 90 percent of the rural population and 40 percent of the urban population had uncinariasis (the disease caused by hookworm), and between 25 and 50 percent of the coastal residents were infected with the malaria parasite. Based on these assessments, the PRRA concluded that malaria control was vital to the island's reconstruction and looked to partner directly with existing insular health agencies.[4] The spread of malaria occurred in the island's four major mosquito-breeding zones: mangrove ecosystems in lowland coastal areas covered with mangrove trees; rivers, ravines, and man-made drainage channels; higher lands in the rainy areas where water pools after periods of rain; and irrigated sugar lands.[5] Deaths from malaria had increased by almost 50 percent between 1929 and 1934—largely due to the severe flooding of the major hurricanes and the construction of temporary or makeshift housing on flooded land. By 1935, deaths from malaria averaged nearly 2,800 per year, or more than 7.5 deaths per day.[6] Similarly, hookworm and undernourishment overwhelmed the impoverished residents in working-class neighborhoods, sapping children and pregnant women of the energy and nutrition needed at the most critical moments of physical and mental development. Residents in the poorest areas lived in conditions of "slow starvation" where meat and milk were luxuries; PRRA health officials concluded that daily per capita intake could only be measured by "ounces and spoonful's." The PRRA noted that while the insular Department of Health had good public health planning and sound laws to address these health crises, it lacked the necessary funding and support to properly address them.[7]

By forging alliances with Puerto Rican doctors, nurses, and public health planners who were already working to ameliorate the effects of these diseases, the PRRA was able to provide some of the required capital, equipment, infrastructure, and staff to address the intertwined health crises. This alliance was particularly well timed since many of the insular government's existing health programs, particularly the anti-hookworm program, had been halted after San Felipe and San Ciprián. Worse, the hurricanes had destroyed about 50 percent of the sanitary latrines that had been previously built to fight the spread of hookworm. Likewise, the PRRA's anti-tuberculosis efforts were based on earlier collaborations between insular and U.S.-based health workers. In 1935, for example, the School of Tropical Medicine received funding from the PRERA and collaborated with the insular Department of Health and Rockefeller Foundation to produce a report on tuberculosis in urban areas. The team was led by doctor and professor Pablo Morales Otero of the School of Tropical Medicine, who would later direct the PRRA sanitation program. Focusing on the Barrio Obrero and Bayamón neighborhoods of San Juan, the surveyors visited 866 homes and found 4,877 inhabitants, equating to 5.6 persons per family unit and 2.4 persons per room. The closeness of shared living quarters is particularly important knowledge in combatting tuberculosis, a bacterial infection of the lungs that spreads rapidly through the air when an infected person speaks or coughs. Among the 4,039 inhabitants that consented to the survey (about 83 percent of the total), the team learned the family history with tuberculosis and conducted tests and X-rays of those suspected of having tuberculosis and provided or arranged for care of those who were infected.[8]

Doctors like José Rodríguez Pastor and Eduardo Garrido Morales, the commissioner of the insular Department of Health, assisted Morales Otero's anti-tuberculosis campaign and advised the PRRA on the construction of eight tuberculosis hospitals: four major ones in Cayey, Guayama, Mayagüez, and Ponce, and four smaller ones in Aguadilla, Arecibo, Bayamón, and Fajardo. These hospitals enabled the expansion of the local health department's anti-tuberculosis work that had divided the island into thirty-one public health unit districts and featured extensive educational campaigns in San Juan and other areas.[9] Garrido Morales, the island's leading epidemiologist, cofounded the Puerto Rico Public Health Association in September 1941. He is an interesting figure. Unlike Morales Otero, who was a member of the Liberal Party (and later the Popular Democratic

Party) and worked directly for the PRRA, Garrido Morales consulted with the PRRA but remained opposed to many facets of the Puerto Rican New Deal. The reason was political: as a Republican, he was a staunch supporter of the Coalition and viewed New Deal public health policy as a threat to established insular institutions. He later claimed that the PRRA was an undemocratic "political organization" created by the Liberal Party to crush the "majority parties" of Puerto Rico that comprised the Coalition.[10]

The PRRA's public health efforts included an explicit attempt to connect Puerto Rican doctors, nurses, and health scientists with professionals in other areas of Latin America and the Caribbean. The intra-Caribbean exchange of public health information during this era helped establish permanent and intellectual relationships between Puerto Rico and other parts of the region. In December 1940, for example, the School of Tropical Medicine hosted the first Inter-American Institute for Hospital Administrators at UPR, Río Piedras. The two-week conference provided both intellectual and physical space for hospital organizations to meet with representatives from across the region. Organized by Félix Lámela (who helped incorporate the Association of Puerto Rican Hospitals in 1942), the conference had 183 registered attendees who "represented a sizable cross section of hospital service personnel, principally from the Caribbean area, twenty-seven of whom were from outside Puerto Rico." The university's ability to host the conference was made possible by the extensive expansion of the UPR library, research centers, and other buildings that had recently been completed by the PRRA.[11]

The Engineering Division also expanded the island's public health infrastructure by building hurricane-proof hospitals and health centers in both rural and urban areas. In 1936, the PRRA reported that there were only 1,520 general-use hospital beds on the island. By the end of 1937, the PRRA had completed 64 of its 107 planned rural health centers in the interior of the island, built nineteen health centers in smaller semi-urban towns, and opened a major hospital at Lafayette.[12] These were of fundamental importance for rural Puerto Ricans since existing insular health units were located in thirty-one larger cities and towns. By 1944, the PRRA had spent $1.89 million ($40.1 million today) on a variety of hospitals, health clinics, and medical facilities, including a two-story sanitarium in Río Piedras; a new concrete school for the blind and a venereal disease clinic in Santurce; and major repairs to the leper asylum in Trujillo Alto, which had been damaged in the San Felipe hurricane.[13] In addition, rural medical centers were built for the first time in many areas across the island, including Aguada, Arecibo, Barceloneta, Isabela, Juana Díaz, Las Marías, Loiza, Manatí, Moca, Morovia, Sabana Grande, San Germán, San Sebastian, Utuado, Villalba, and Yabucoa.[14] According to Morales Otero and Manuel A. Pérez, the "nutritional and educational work initiated by the rural dispensaries and the workers' camps" was designed to substantially lower the "morbidity and mortality from gastro-intestinal disorders" while the "construction of sanitary privies in the resettlers' [houses] and other low-cost houses built by the PRRA will be instrumental in the prevention of soil and water pollution."[15]

The PRRA health unit also treated rural patients for typhoid fever, smallpox, and various dental health conditions. By the summer of 1938, when the health unit was transferred to the insular government, the PRRA had directly treated 510,435 patients at 23,180 medical clinics held in all parts of the island. The agency's Puerto Rican– and American-born doctors and nurses conducted an extraordinary number of medical examinations and treatments between 1935 and 1938, including 22,060 physical exams, 27,792 malaria treatments, 91,550 intestinal parasite treatments (hookworm and other), 97,411 typhoid fever treatments, 212,622 laboratory examinations, and 26,021 smallpox vaccinations. In addition, dentists and dental nurses working for the PRRA conducted 48,499 dental exams, which included 10,513 preventative cleanings, 169,330 tooth extractions, and at least 3,627 other miscellaneous treatments.[16]

Urban Housing Construction

Cement-based urban housing construction was an integral part of PRRA efforts to provide permanent protection against future hurricanes and curb the increase of preventable diseases. According to J. C. Hitchman of the Engineering Division, the agency's primary aim was to "provide a hurricane-proof house, and for that reason our construction work has gone largely to the building of concrete houses."[17] Due to concrete's longevity, Hitchman argued that the cost of durable concrete construction would be less than wood when considered over a thirty-year period. By 1938, Puerto Rican architects and engineers were building thousands of affordable concrete houses with electricity and indoor plumbing in urban areas that were either on top of or adjacent to former swampland barriadas.[18]

According to Rafael A. González, chair of the PRRA's planning committee, the size and scale of the island's housing program was unprecedented. Surveying the available literature on low-cost housing in other areas of the world, González reported to Carlos Chardón and Manuel Font that "we have not found another instance in which an objective as ambitious as ours has been attempted. The development of one or more types of houses made of local materials and fulfilling satisfactory conditions of permanency, comfort, and of hygienic and social requirements at a cost in the neighborhood of $500 is, indeed, a difficult task" (about $10,000 today).[19] Interestingly, the suburban resettlement program of the Resettlement Administration (RA) was simultaneously embarking on a program of "greenbelt town" development in the continental United States. Under the supervision of Rex Tugwell, the RA constructed thousands of working-class homes in the newly planned developments of Greenbelt, Maryland, Greendale, Wisconsin, and Greenhills, Ohio. Modeled on the urban planning ideas of Ebenezer Howard, who developed the concept of the garden city in Hertfordshire, England, at the turn of the century, the RA also drew inspiration from housing developments in Sweden, Germany, and the Netherlands to integrate urban and rural areas and replace the growing number of "slums" and tenements across the country.[20]

One of the first PRRA housing projects to open on the island was the majestic El Falansterio, a group of three-story art deco buildings in Puerta de Tierra comprising 216 apartments of reinforced concrete designed to withstand earthquakes, hurricanes, and fires. Completed in 1937, El Falansterio replaced the Miranda barriada and featured single-family apartments for up to a thousand people that rented for $2.00 to $4.25 per week (approximately $42 to $90 today). Apartments included two bedrooms, an indoor bathroom with a shower, an indoor kitchen, and clean drinking water; featured access to an interior patio, a community building, a kindergarten, and a small library; and provided maintenance and janitorial services. The PRRA also built storm sewers, curbed sidewalks, and an improved water supply system in the surrounding neighborhood.[21]

The construction of El Falansterio was overseen by Manuel Egozcue and designed by lead architect Jorge Ramírez de Arellano at a cost of $679,000 ($14.4 million today). Still occupied today, the building was converted into a cooperative in the 1940s, offering tenants the option of purchasing their own apartments.[22] The initial tenants of El Falansterio came from a cross-section of Puerto Rican workers including office workers, nurses, plumbers, teachers, secretaries, conductors, policemen, and small business owners—it was not designed to house the unemployed or deeply impoverished. While El Falansterio was a benefit to working-class Puerto Ricans in terms of affordability, aesthetic design, and geographic location, it should be remembered that ordinary Puerto Ricans were not consulted by the PR-RA's architects and planners, and many residents complained about certain aspects of apartment living, including the noise from the courtyard.[23]

Between 1937 and 1942, the PRRA also completed major new housing developments such as the Eleanor Roosevelt in Hato Rey; the Mirapalmeras in Barrio Obrero, Santurce; and the Juan Morel Campos at Barrio Cañas, Ponce (named for the famous Ponce-born composer who died at a young age in 1896).[24] Like El Falansterio, the Eleanor Roosevelt and Juan Morel Campos developments were designed by Ramírez de Arellano. Apartments in these reinforced-concrete structures each had two or three bedrooms, indoor plumbing, electricity, and indoor kitchens; were bordered by paved streets, cement sidewalks, sanitary and storm drain sewers, and public water systems; and were located near public schools and local police stations.[25] Designed to contain approximately two thousand low-cost houses organized around a central plaza, the suburban-styled Eleanor Roosevelt development was among the largest of all New Deal housing projects on the island. Rents ranged in these developments from $6 to $12 per month ($127 to $254 today) at the Eleanor Roosevelt to $5 to $9 per month ($106 to $190 today) at the Morel Campos. Compared to the wooden relief structures built by the local government and the increasing construction of improvised housing, PRRA housing opened worlds of opportunities for working-class Puerto Ricans that were unforeseen just years before. In the Ponce area, the PRRA located nine parcels of land to purchase in Ponce and two in Ponce Playa, and began construction on 4,290 concrete houses in the area. Designed to house over 21,000 people, the PRRA also constructed concrete storm sewers, a new water supply system, a nearby incinerating plant, and temporary workingmen's residencies for PRRA construction workers in the southern city.[26]

Urban housing construction was eventually transferred from the PRRA to the Puerto Rican Housing Authority (PRHA) after it was created in 1938 following the passage of the Wagner-Steagall Housing Act (which had created the U.S. Housing Authority). The PRHA established five local offices in Arecibo, Mayagüez, Ponce, Río Piedras, and San Juan. By 1950, the San Juan office took over the Arecibo and Río Piedras offices, leaving only three local authorities to administer public housing needs on the island. Due to the increased pace of urbanization, PRRA efforts at resettling urban workers from barriadas to hurricane-proof public housing had failed to completely solve the housing problem in Puerto Rico. By 1950, the PRHA estimated that the number of new arrabales had nearly doubled since 1940,

98 · The Puerto Rico Reconstruction Administration

with approximately 40,000 new improvised houses constructed during that time. In all, there were over 95,000 such dwellings across the island, housing up to 500,000 people. Of the 35,000 such houses in San Juan, nearly 70 percent were owner-occupied and 30 percent were rented. As Zaire Dinzey-Flores has argued, although the PRHA viewed public housing as a temporary stepping stone toward private homeownership, publicly built houses in fact became permanent communities. After World War II, the PRHA focused largely on arrabales-razing projects and the construction of large low-income housing projects.[27]

Rural Rehabilitation and Rural Housing Construction

Hurricane-proof houses were also built in rural areas of the island. Headed by Rafael Fernández García and Francisco A. López Domínguez, the Rural Rehabilitation Division spent $26.5 million ($562.2 million today) on the resettlement of thousands of small farmers and landless workers to newly constructed houses and a variety of projects to enrich life in the agrarian countryside. According to Guillermo Esteves, the Rural Rehabilitation Division supplied resettled farmers with coffee, tobacco, and fruit seeds and fertilizers to help "rehabilitate their farms, which had been seriously devastated by the cyclones of 1928 and 1932" and which still "suffered seriously" from overproduction and "the economic depression that followed the First World War."[28] The rural housing program was led by engineer José Benitez Gautier, architect Gérman Ramírez de Arellano (brother of Jorge Ramírez de Arellano), and engineers Heliodoro Blanco and Emilio Serra Colón. By December 1937, they had built 1,268 concrete houses as a core part of its broader agrarian rehabilitation and land tenure program. As of 1944, the PRRA had spent $12.8 million ($271.5 million today) on the construction of cement-based rural houses that were "earthquake-proof, hurricane-proof, insect [and] pest-proof, fire-proof, cool, and sanitary, and that will require very little maintenance, if any."[29] When administrators in Washington inquired about the use of less expensive brick materials, Puerto Rican engineers argued that reinforced concrete was more assuredly earthquake- and hurricane-proof and thus a more sound financial investment.[30] To keep costs down, the PRRA redesigned rural houses to eliminate provisions that were specific for the urban houses. For example, the PRRA concluded that foundations in rural areas did not need to be two feet underground, as was the case in urban areas to protect against rats and possible outbreak of bubonic plague. In rural areas, Puerto Rican engineers advised, rats find shelter in trees, not under buildings, and thus a shallower foundation would lower costs.[31]

The Rural Rehabilitation Division also took over the construction of flood relief houses started by FERA and the PRERA in 1933. By January 1937, the PRRA was constructing hurricane- and flood-relief houses in Gurabo, Humacao, Juncos, San Lorenzo, and Yabucoa. With shared funding from the insular legislature, the PRRA expanded its rural flood-relief program into a more comprehensive project that addressed community concerns such as repairing damaged school buildings and constructing entirely new schoolrooms, roads, waterworks, electrical systems, and sewers. By 1939, the PRRA had acquired 4,674 parcels of land and had built 667 houses that were occupied by resettled farmers and farmworkers.[32]

Housing construction was part of a larger plan of rural rehabilitation. Between 1936 and 1944 the PRRA transformed over 40,000 acres of previously uncultivated land into small farms by acquiring it from large or absentee landowners.[33] For migrant workers and homesteaders displaced by the hurricanes, the PRRA created two- or three-acre *parcelas* (plots) in the tobacco, coffee, and citrus fruit regions, located work on neighboring farms, and built "hurricane-proof concrete, brick, or rammed-earth houses, thus creating subsistence farms where agricultural laborers have been installed as re-settlers," which were made available for rent or purchase. As of April 1944, the PRRA had moved 6,111 farmers onto parcelas with houses and 3,871 farmers onto parcelas without houses. The average rent was $2.50 per month for land with houses ($42 today), and 50 cents per month for land without houses (about $8.50 today). The cost of buying these houses was within reach for some, but not all, rural workers: the PRRA sold land with houses to 3,101 settlers at a rate of $1.75 per month ($30 today) for twenty-five years and land without houses to 520 settlers at a rate of 35 cents per month ($6 today) for ten years.[34]

Mariano Marí, who headed the fruit zone unit of the Rural Rehabilitation Division, was later pivotal in the distribution of rural houses and gardens as head of the division's land utilization section. The plots enhanced access to subsistence farming in the tobacco and coffee regions by offering ownership of the land rather than reliance on traditional usufruct rights alone. Access to these plots usually involved a legal contract of conditional usufruct rights between the PRRA and the tenant. In Patillas, on the southeastern coast, for example, the Rural Rehabilitation Division signed a contract of usufruct rights to Anselmo Ruiz and his wife Basilia Delgado, who rented a newly constructed house on five acres of land from the PRRA.

The house, which was located in Barrio Jagual, was made of galvanized iron with wooden interior walls and stood approximately 20 feet by 20 feet in size. Ruiz and Delgado agreed to pay $1 per month (about $21 today) for the first year of the contract, $2 per month the second year, and $3 per month after that. Written in Spanish, the contract stipulated that the tenants would use the land for agricultural purposes. Like other areas of Patillas, the homestead was enhanced by the construction of a new water line and a bridge over the Patillas Canal.[35]

Housing projects in the semi-urban countryside were desirable and popular. The municipality of Caguas, in the eastern highlands, was a tobacco- and sugar-growing region with 48,585 residents across the Caguas Valley in 1935. The island's fourth largest city, Caguas had grown from 5,450 residents in 1899 to 22,599 residents in 1935. The PRRA's housing project there, called the Caserío La Granja, welcomed its first homeowners in December 1937. A year later, residents displayed their popular support for the project with day-long festivities to celebrate the neighborhood's one-year anniversary. Funded by the PRRA and an assortment of local sponsors who sought to be associated with the New Deal public housing program, the celebration featured music, games, a motor parade to the inauguration of the "Ayuso" bridge, speeches, worker exhibits, lunch, volleyball, a boxing exhibition, a dance, and songs—including the premiere of the "Hymn of Caserío La Granja," dedicated to Franklin Roosevelt. Headed by Angel Socorro and Jorge Muñiz Rivera, the president and vice president of the La Granja Benefit and Recreation Society and supported by Vicente Morales and Irma Martínez Aponte, the secretary and treasurer, the festivities included words from Miles Fairbank and other PRRA administrators. Sponsors included Caguas-based businesses such as the New York Dress Company, El Encanto, Los Díaz Comerciantes, La Mallorquina, Muebleria Universal, the Caguas Bus Line, El Borinquen laundry, La Greca café, Merino Rodríguez & Hermanos contractors of San Juan, the Porto Rican Leaf Tobacco American Supplies, Inc., and a variety of beer and rum producers, including Ron Superior, Ron Gioconda, Boca Chica, Kofresi, Cerveza India of Mayagüez, Pabst, and Corona of Santurce (aka "La Cerveza Puertorriqueña").[36]

Rural rehabilitation projects also involved agricultural pest eradication, reforestation, and soil erosion control. Two of the most harmful pests in Puerto Rico were the cattle tick and the rhinoceros beetle (also known as the coconut beetle). Cattle ticks, which plagued the island's rich pastureland, spread bovine babesiosis, called cattle tick fever or the "Texas fever" at the time, which is a highly fatal disease that attacks the red blood cells of infected animals.[37] Cattle tick treatment and eradication were major concerns of the cattle industry of Texas, Chihuahua, and other parts of northern Mexico from the 1860s through the 1940s. In Puerto Rico, the Rural Rehabilitation Division constructed 991 dipping tanks throughout rural areas so that owners of cattle, horses, mules, and other livestock could get them dipped as part of an island-wide cattle tick elimination program. Though the costs were high—by 1944 the PRRA had spent $1.75 million ($37.1 million today) on cattle tick eradication—the number of animals treated was impressive: in the western third of the island, where 315 dipping tanks were built, the PRRA treated 115,863 cattle, 18,776 horses and mules, and 79,688 goats and sheep in the first year alone. In all, multiple hundreds of thousands of animals were treated, with all labor, chemicals, and other supplies paid for by the PRRA. As in Mexico and the continental United States, quarantine districts were set up in the island to control the movement of infected animals. During the mid-1940s, the island was declared cattle tick–free.[38] Similarly, the PRRA worked to eliminate the rhinoceros beetle, which had been a major destructive factor in the island's coconut groves. Rhinoceros beetle elimination and the coconut rehabilitation program resulted in the hiring of thousands of Puerto Rican workers on coconut plantations, cleaning up debris on over 30,000 acres and planting more than 95,000 trees. Without these kinds of projects, which revitalized local farms and created jobs, new houses would have been useless in rural areas. Other projects did not work out. Among the pastoral failures of the Rural Rehabilitation Division was the importation of forty Nubian and Toggenburg goats from North Africa and Switzerland for breeding. As Miles Fairbank explained, the introduction of these "splendid little animals made quite an impression on the countryside, but they soon fell prey to tropical parasites" and the program was discontinued.[39]

Workers in the Rural Rehabilitation and Forestry Divisions coordinated reforestation and soil erosion projects in cooperative agreements with the CCC, PWA, Puerto Rico Forest Service, and Federal Forest Service on publicly protected lands such as the Luquillo National Forest, Toro Negro State Forest, and Maricao State Forest. Reforestation was not limited to these national and state forests, however, and the PRRA built worker camps in several areas of Puerto Rico, including Mayagüez, Isabela, Patillas, Caguas, Cayey, Sabana Grande, Río Grande, Canóvanas, and Mona Island. Some PRRA-built camps, such as Guajataca in San Sebastian and Guavate in Caguas, remain recreational areas today open to the public and used by Puerto Rican Girl Scouts and Boy Scouts. The Rural Rehabilitation Division also worked with the insular Forest Service and Federal Bureau of Fisheries to establish fish hatcheries in Luquillo and Maricao to feed the streams and reservoirs being constructed or repaired by PRRA engineers. Still open today, the Vivero de Peces de Maricao (Maricao Fish Hatchery) was built in 1937 to study the island's freshwater fish and introduce new species such as the rainbow trout and brown trout to the island—though neither took to the warm waters. Within three years, the Maricao Fish Hatchery was producing 500,000 fish a year, including largemouth bass (which was successfully introduced to Puerto Rico in 1915), improving both local recreation and diet.[40]

Working with the CCC, the PRRA Forestry Division built over a hundred miles of roads and trails in the island's forests, along with observation towers, picnic areas, campgrounds, bridges, swimming pools, parking areas, and water, sanitation, and recreational services. Aside from providing public access to sites of natural beauty and wonder, these roads allowed forest workers to plant millions of cedar, mahogany, and satinwood seedlings compiled from quick-growing native and neighboring Caribbean-area trees. Between 1933 and 1942, the CCC employed 2,400 Puerto Rican men to work on environmental infrastructural and reforestation projects in El Yunque. Unlike the stateside CCC, much of their work after 1935 was funded by the PRRA. Like their counterparts in the continental United States, however, the *Tres C's* published its own newsletter, the Spanish-language "Ecos del Yunque" (Echoes of El Yunque). Their work, particularly on El Yunque, is still a central symbol of Puerto Rican culture today. It was achieved with help from the $3.4 million investment (almost $74.8 million today) in reforestation provided by the PRRA.[41]

Agricultural Cooperatives

The PRRA Cooperative Division helped establish agricultural cooperatives through collaboration with Puerto Rican farmers and farmworkers. According to Guillermo Esteves, the agricultural rehabilitation and land tenure programs shared three intertwined goals, designed to provide both short-term relief and long-term recovery from the 1928 and 1932 hurricanes: (1) to directly aid coffee, tobacco, and fruit farmers whose land had been destroyed by the storms; (2) to provide work to thousands of unemployed agricultural workers who suffered "because of the fact that there was no work available in these farms of the highlands of Puerto Rico and the fruit growing regions along the sea coast" due to the destruction of the farms; (3) to "create subsistence and small-sized family farms and make them available to agricultural laborers and small farmers who had lost all they had, in order to offer them the facilities of permanent homesteads and improve their social and economic position."[42]

The Cooperative Division, working alongside the Rural Rehabilitation and Engineering Divisions, helped establish agricultural and commercial cooperatives in the sugar, coffee, tobacco, citrus fruit, coconut, plantain, vanilla, pork, chicken, freshwater fish, cotton, and other agricultural sectors. The division also provided seeds, stock animals, mechanical equipment, technical support, education, canning, and crop marketing services to cooperative farmers and provided over $6.25 million ($132.6 million today) in low-interest loans to small family farmers. The program, which involved the resettlement of large numbers of Puerto Rican workers who had been displaced by the storms, resulted in the replanting of over 15,000 acres of food crops and 3,000 acres of cash crops by resettled workers.[43] Two of the biggest examples of PRRA experiments in cooperative farming were the Castañer Cooperative in the northwestern coffee highlands and the Central Lafayette in the southeastern sugar region. Other cooperatives financed by the PRRA included a variety of agricultural and handcraft industries, whose worker members included both men and women from across the island. In addition to Castañer and Lafayette, which will be detailed below, the PRRA invested over $7 million (almost $150 million today) in cooperatives, including the Arecibo Fruit Growers Cooperative Association, Asociación Azucarera Cooperativa Los Caños, Bayamón Vegetable Growers Cooperative Association, Coconut Growers Cooperative Association, Cooperativa de Cosecheros de Vegetales de Río Grande, Cooperativa de Productores de Hortalizas de Jayuya, Cooperative Handcraft Incorporated, Primus Pottery Cooperative, Puerto Rico Artcraft Cooperative, Puerto Rico Rug Cooperative, Puerto Rico Tobacco Marketing Association, Sociedad Agricola Cooperativa de Puerto Rico, and the Villalba Vegetable Growers Cooperative Association.[44]

The Castañer Cooperative attempted to rehabilitate large-scale coffee farming on 1,645 acres of hurricane-ravaged land in the municipalities of Adjuntas, Lares, and Yauco. The cooperative combined a focus on soil conservation and crop diversification with large-scale land utilization and scientific management, and it was viewed as essential to the recovery of the coffee industry since coffee bushes took several years to mature. It was improbable that the coffee growers of this region, most of whom were already

104 · The Puerto Rico Reconstruction Administration

in debt, could have recovered without considerable personal investment. Nearly two hundred agricultural workers were resettled at Castañer, each provided with a one-acre homestead and a newly constructed hurricane-proof house on land purchased by the PRRA from private owners. The cooperative not only helped revive coffee but diversified the agricultural output in the region as well: of the 1,163 acres of crops and seedbeds planted at Castañer, about 63 percent were in coffee, 6 percent in sugarcane, 5 percent in vanilla beans, 2 percent in citrus, and 24 percent in bananas, eddo and tannia roots, tomatoes, and other subsistence vegetables, with a portion of those lands dedicated to seedbeds and pasture lands.[45] In 1943, the PRRA helped construct the island's first-ever rural hospital at Castañer. A joint effort by the PRRA, the Brethren Service Commission, the National Selective Service, and the insular government, the hospital provided free medical care to cooperative resettlers and other agrarian workers in the area and developed crucial education and disease prevention programs. The hospital was replaced by a larger facility in the 1950s, which is still in operation today as the Hospital General Castañer.[46]

The Central Lafayette, a cooperatively owned sugar central and mill, was the PRRA's largest experiment in cooperative agriculture. Lafayette's 9,738 acres in Arroyo, Patillas, and Maunabo were subdivided into twelve newly formed land cooperatives comprising 4,427 acres, with an additional 5,311 acres owned by the PRRA. Although it was regarded by PRRA administrators as an economic failure, the history of Central Lafayette is more complex. The establishment of a sugar mill cooperative had been an early goal of the Chardón Plan, and when the PRRA was formed in 1935, Carlos Chardón immediately tried to purchase between 15,000 and 20,000 acres of sugarcane land. The idea was buoyed by the passage of Law 47 by the Coalition-controlled legislature in 1935, which supported breaking up corporate lands of over five hundred acres.[47] Chardón and Francisco López Domínguez hired a team of five to survey and appraise potential cane lands and mills. The appraisers Luis de Celis, Francisco Colón Moret, Temístocles Díaz, Agustín M. de Andino, and José Acosta Velarde recommended several tracts of land, and the PRRA entered discussions to purchase the Central Aguirre in Salinas. When this did not come to pass, Chardón and Antonio Lucchetti led negotiations with Antonio Fantauzzi to buy Central Lafayette and nearly ten thousand acres from his family for $3.815 million in 1936 (about $82.7 million today).[48]

New owners of a large tract of sugarcane land and a sizable mill, the Cooperative Division helped form the Lafayette Cooperative Sugar Association in 1937. Workers in the area had participated in the great sugar strikes of 1933 and 1934—at least 3,000 of the 18,250 workers on strike in Patillas, Arroyo, and Maunabo were employees of the Fantauzzi family who worked at the Central Lafayette. The other striking workers were from the Los Caños, Coloso, Cambalache, Roig, Alianza, and Fajardo Sugar centrals. In January 1934, workers at the Central Lafayette had reached an agreement that regulated working hours and wages, signed by company representative Gregorio Manautou and a representation of Lafayette workers, including Pablo Pachó, Alejandro de Jesús, and Pedro G. Pérez of Arroyo; Marcos Plaud Cintrón, Miguel Freytes, and Juan M. Ramos of Patillas; and Isabelino Rodríguez, Pablo García, and Nicholás Amaro of Maunabo. The agreement was ratified by the Commission of Mediation and Conciliation, represented by Luis Villaronga, José C. Menéndez, and Gabriel Blanco, and sent to Governor James Beverly in February.[49]

In addition to financing the purchase of the mill and the construction of resettlement houses, the PRRA performed a series of engineering tests and services at Lafayette, including surveying, deep well testing, pumping for water supply, ditch cleaning, leveling, rendering, mapping, blueprinting, and constructing ten workers camp units.[50] The PRRA also loaned the cooperative $1.4 million ($29.7 million today) for operations, to be paid back over a thirty-year period. The cooperative made over $200,000 (about $4.2 million today) in profits during its first year of operations, which were distributed to small family farmers, farm workers, and the cooperative revolving fund. Despite the initially positive start, however, the problems of maintaining such a large undertaking were increasingly evident.

On one hand, the central faced political opposition from the Coalition. Miguel Ángel García, the Speaker of the House, claimed that the Lafayette Cooperative was the work of the new "dictatorship" in Puerto Rico, the likes of which had been previously "unknown in our democracy."[51] García and other Republicans were mostly concerned that cooperative farmers were mostly members of the Liberal Party. In a confidential memo to William Leahy, who had been appointed governor in 1939, Fairbank wrote that the "only thing this proves is that the farmers affiliated to [the Liberal] Party have been more interested in the cooperative movement than the others." There was "little information," he added, "to substantiate the inference that these men were selected primarily on the basis of their political affiliations or that they are using their positions for political purposes."[52]

On the other hand, the central had trouble paying workers enough to survive as cooperative farmers. While Lafayette guaranteed higher wages

106 · The Puerto Rico Reconstruction Administration

than private sugar centrals, they were accused of violating the wage and salary standards set by the Fair Labor Standards Act (FLSA) of 1938. In the fall of 1939, at least two hundred workers had met with labor lawyer Robert W. Claiborne due to wage and salary violations. Claiborne, who intended to file a lawsuit against the cooperative, had moved to Puerto Rico in 1936 from the U.S. Virgin Islands; settling in Maricao, he had purchased a former coffee farm and rededicated it to fruit, goats, and chickens while he practiced law. After being appointed as the regional attorney and acting territorial representative of the Wage and Hour Division of the U.S. Department of Labor in 1938, Claiborne had briefly served as the first FLSA administrator in Puerto Rico. As Anne Macpherson has shown, even though his appointment was originally recommended by large employers and the island's Republican Party, they soon turned on him when he tried to actually enforce the law. Accused of radicalism, Claiborne was removed from the FLSA and fought against the effort to make a colonial exception to the minimum wage in Puerto Rico. By the end of 1939, he had formed a law partnership with Victor Gutierrez Franqui and Ernesto Ramos Antonini and agitated for workers' rights against private and cooperative employers across the island.[53]

The Lafayette Cooperative, which was originally run by Rafael A. González and Salvador Antonetti of the PRRA, was eventually turned over to the board of the Lafayette Cooperative Sugar Association, which included José Alsieux, Dr. Pablo Bonelli, Juan Cervoni Massari, Andrés Moret, Mateo Navarro, Rafael Nído, Claudio Rodríguez, Agustín Torres, and Idelfonso Veglio. Capital stock was distributed by the board to cooperative members. By 1940, the PRRA liquidated its holdings in the Central Lafayette, when its farmer-owners were unable to make payments on the purchase price due to declining revenues in 1938 and 1939. Historian Gloria Tapia Rios has written that PRRA administrators believed Lafayette's falling profits could be blamed on the "individualistic nature" of sugar farmers who, despite education efforts, did not fully embrace the cooperative spirit of the program. Many did not pay rent or principal on their new homes, costing the cooperative revenue that it needed to operate the mill. Tapia Rios has also argued that external factors limited the PRRA's ability to continue managing the cooperative, especially as the gathering winds of World War II necessitated a reduction of PRRA activity on the island.[54]

While the PRRA viewed the Central Lafayette as a failure, the Lafayette Cooperative Sugar Association outlasted many sugar centrals on the island and successfully ran the mill until its closure in 1973—reflecting the longer process of agricultural decline in Puerto Rico. Lafayette produced butyl alcohol and acetone during World War II and, as at Castañer, left behind a two-story hospital for the region's families that was built by the PRRA, owned by the cooperative group, and is still in operation today.[55] Equipped with departments for X-rays and diagnostics, laboratories, a pharmacy, and a nursery, the Lafayette Hospital provided medical care for over a thousand families in the area. Designed by Jorge Ramírez de Arellano with assistance from Félix Lámela, the hospital was led by medical doctors Pablo M. Bonelli and Alberto Mejia Berrios. Among the many women who worked at the hospital, key positions were filled by Rosa H. Colón, the superintendent of nurses; Lydia Pérez, the pharmacist and head lab technician for X-rays; and Delia Soegard, the lead dietician who had previously worked for the PRRA at Castañer surveying the health and dietary conditions of rural residents.[56]

In addition to the hospital, the Central Lafayette experiment left an imprint on public health in the larger southeastern sugar region that encompasses Arroyo, Patillas, and Guaynabo. Between 1935 and 1936, the PRRA health unit funded a thorough study of rural health in the area. Working with the insular Department of Health, UPR, and the School of Tropical Medicine, Pablo Morales Otero led a team of PRRA workers to canvas eighteen thousand acres of land in Guayama, Arroyo, Patillas, Maunabo, and Yabucoa. The group of sanitary inspectors, nurses, and social workers— which included Manuel A. Pérez, R. Ramírez Santos, Rafaela Espino, Adriana Ramú, J. L. Fuster, Dolores González, and Mario Marrero—went house to house collecting data and sending doctors when encountering a sick resident. The team first surveyed eight farms comprising sixty-nine families in Colonia Lafayette before extending their work to include 860 families throughout the three primary municipalities of Arroyo, Patillas, and Maunabo that covered the lands the PRRA purchased for the Central Lafayette.[57]

The project was designed to accomplish three goals: to study public health at the time of the PRRA purchase; to create an index of the families that lived and worked in the sugar region; and to create a baseline for future studies of this region. The report, together with the mid-decade census conducted by the PRRA's Rafael B. Díaz and Conchita R. Muñoz, provides an extraordinary look at the housing conditions of the area. In 1936, there were 860 families living in the region and a total of 4,400 residents, equating to 5.1 residents per family. This figure was slightly higher or lower in some of the regions, ranging from a high of 6.4 in Colonia

108 · The Puerto Rico Reconstruction Administration

Lafayette to a low of 4.6 in Patillas. The 860 families lived in 770 houses that contained 860 dwellings; of these, 68 were adjoining quarters in which 158 families lived; 58 buildings contained two families; seven contained three families; one contained four families; one contained eight families; and one contained nine families. The report concluded that 16.7 percent of the population in these municipalities was under age five, which was higher than the island average of 14.6 percent (for comparison, about 9.3 percent of the population in the continental United States was under five at the time). There was a noticeable drop in the working-age population between the ages of 25–34, which implies migration from this area to larger urban centers.[58] Although the PRRA's inability to run Lafayette beyond 1940 reminds us of the New Deal's colonial limitations, the establishment of modern hospitals at Castañer and Lafayette suggests that the cooperative project offered increased physical security and social mobility through the construction of a new public health infrastructure.[59]

Schools

By March 1938, the PRRA had built 285 cement-based public schools in 189 towns or cities across all regions of the island, ranging from Aguas Buenas, Aguada, and Aibonito to Villalba, Yabucoa, and Yauco.[60] Although this construction had exhausted the agency's $500,000 ($10.6 million today) budget for rural school buildings, local residents, education advocates, and parents demanded more school construction. In 1938, for example, insular commissioner of education Jose Gallardo wrote to Harold Ickes to protest the limited construction budget when as much as $3 million ($63.6 million today) and then $1 million ($21.2 million) had been originally discussed or promised. Similarly, Evangelista Rosario, the local school director in the small northern coastal town of Barceloneta, wrote to Miles Fairbank requesting the PRRA's help in repairing the existing school infrastructure.[61]

In smaller towns such as Villalba, a southern coffee region, and Bajadero, a small neighborhood on the eastern bank of the Río Grande de Arecibo, parents, teachers, and other residents helped shape the New Deal's school-building program by directly contacting PRRA officials to make requests for schools in their areas. Letters came directly from parents like Santos Vega, who represented the local Asociación de Padres y Maestros (Parent-Teacher Association or PTA) for the Teodoro Alonso Criado School in Villalba and wrote to the PRRA asking for a new school. They also came from Rufino Gómez, the president of the PTA in Bajadero, who wrote asking for a new vocational school in his area. In other cases, local residents offered to do school repair work themselves if the PRRA could supply building materials and money. In the case of the eastern town of Naguabo, for example, the local PTA was given approximately $400 in supplies (almost $8,500 today) for the construction of an indoor restroom in their school.[62]

The PRRA school construction program was enhanced by the agency's ability to purchase lands from private owners and transfer the deed to municipal control. Such was the case when the PRRA bought a portion of Salvador S. Mandry's farm in Ponce in 1937 upon which they built a public school and turned the land title over to city authorities that October. Rafael B. Pérez Mercado, a lawyer from Guayama who later worked for the Puerto Rico Housing Authority, was the head administrator of the land and title section of the PRRA Legal Division. In this role he oversaw a large number of land grants made to various municipalities for schools built by the PRRA. For the years 1937 and 1938 alone, these included Carolina (including the neighborhoods of San Anton, Sabana Abajo, Hoyo Mulas, Santa Cruz, Cacao, Matin González, Barrazas #2, Barrazas #3, Canovanillas, Pueblo, Carruzos, Cangrejos, and Trujillo Bajo), Cayey, Cidra, Ponce, Rincón, and Río Piedras.[63]

The island received its first accurate count of school-aged children in 1935 as part of the special census. The total population was listed at 1,723,534, of which about 33 percent were classified as urban (563,616) and 67 percent were classified as rural (1,159,916). The PRRA found that 61 percent of school-aged children in Puerto Rico did not attend school. In some areas of the Cordillera Central the crisis in education was even worse. Of the total number of 638,728 school-aged children on the island, roughly two-thirds lived in rural areas. Of these 430,233 children, only 29 percent attended school. These percentages were almost inverted in urban areas, where 59 percent of the 208,495 children attended school. In fact, despite the fact that only one-third of the island's school-aged children lived in urban areas, nearly the same number of kids went to school as in rural areas: 124,547 in urban areas versus 125,520 rural. While 85,788 children in urban areas were not in school, a staggering 304,629 children in rural areas were not enrolled in school in 1935. Puerto Rican educators estimated that the island needed at least 1,714 more urban schoolrooms and teachers and 6,065 more rural schoolrooms and teachers to adequately address the crisis. During the 1936 and 1937 school years, the PRRA employed 1,403 elementary teachers in urban areas at a salary of $900 per year (about $19,000 today) and 2,022 teachers in rural areas at a salary of $700 per year (about $14,800 today). While this was clearly not enough to solve the crisis in elementary education, teachers and school administrators worked with the PRRA to hire, train, and pay as many teachers as possible within the limits of their budget.[64]

School construction was not a one-size-fits-all program but varied according to the size and needs of each city. In Aguada, the two PRRA-built classrooms cost an estimated $6,000 ($127,300 today) with twenty men working full-time for three months. The larger city of Ponce received 205 classrooms at an estimated cost of $615,000 ($13 million today) with 2,050 men working full-time for thirty-six months. In San Juan, by contrast, the PRRA built 448 classrooms at a cost of $1.34 million ($28.4 million today), employing 4,480 men full-time for thirty-six months. At a cost of $2,500 ($53,000 today) for hurricane- and earthquake-proof concrete rooms, $1,800 ($38,000 today) for hurricane-proof rooms, and $1,200 ($25,000 today) for standard wood-framed rooms, school construction provided a temporary boost to the local economy and made a long-term investment in public school education.[65] While relief work was not the only objective of the public-school construction program, the PRRA often had to highlight the number of jobs created by school construction to justify its funding as a relief agency. As general counsel Henry Hirshberg explained, the PRRA did so not only as a strategy to secure financing but also out of legal obligation, since most PRRA funding was allocated from congressional emergency relief funds.[66] As with New Deal agencies in the continental United States, most of the PRRA's financing hinged upon how many relief jobs it created even when its programs were designed for long-term social improvements.

New Deal financing also enlarged the University of Puerto Rico. Between 1935 and 1938, the PRRA completed eight new buildings for UPR in Río Piedras, a medical research center in Mayagüez, and a hospital for the School of Tropical Medicine in Puerta de Tierra (which is now part of the UPR School of Medicine).[67] In 1939, the PRRA allotted over $456,000 ($9.7 million today) for the UPR, $453,000 ($9.6 million) for the School of Tropical Medicine, and $386,000 ($8.2 million) for the Insular Home for Boys in Guaynabo. These projects were overseen by lead architect Rafael Carmoega Morales, who had graduated from Cornell University and worked for both the insular and federal governments prior to joining the PRRA. Assisted by Francisco Cardón, Rafael J. Hernández, Augusto R. Pilard, Gérman Ramírez de Arellano, and Eloy Ruiz, Carmoega presided over a variety of critical projects at the university, including the library and clock tower at Río Piedras; a biology laboratory for the Río Piedras Experiment Station; electrical installation in the main administration building; electricity, seats, and curtains in the auditorium; landscaping; reinforced concrete work on tennis and basketball courts; construction of a power plant and workshops for the engineering school; the construction of the Normal School and Teachers' College; and the construction of the engineering building on the Mayagüez campus.[68] By the end of 1943, the PRRA had invested $2.87 million (over $61.3 million today) toward the physical enlargement of the university, which contributed to its full accreditation by the Middle States Association of Colleges and Schools in 1946.[69] As with other public colleges and universities, the physical enlargement of UPR was not solely about how many jobs it created or whether it solved the crisis of the Depression; rather, it was designed to empower generations of Puerto Rican students to shape their own reconstruction—a notion at the very heart of public higher education.

Roads, Waterworks, and Recreation

In addition to houses, hospitals, and schools, Puerto Rican engineers constructed thousands of miles of paved roads to connect rural areas with main roads that had been built during previous periods. Between 1933 and 1938, the combined roadbuilding projects of FERA, PRERA, and the PRRA resulted in over 290,000 miles of paved insular and municipal roads that connected rural residents to health centers—and health centers to city hospitals—as never before. The PRRA spent $2.37 million ($50.3 million today) replacing dirt roads that were perpetually made muddy and impassable during rain or washed away in bigger storms. Workers leveled and subgraded roads, laid block stone, paved, graded, and cleaned side ditches, and extracted and crushed large rocks in an effort to limit future landslides. In some areas, such as on the road leading to Barrio Real in Patillas—not far from where San Felipe made landfall—the PRRA built reinforced concrete bridges to replace ones that had been previously destroyed. Public roads were also built by laying asphalt, creating shoulders, building concrete sidewalks, curbs, and gutters, laying concrete foundations for bridges, and placing concrete forms and reinforcement steel for main sewer lines.[70]

In Mayagüez, PRRA engineers confirmed that two-thirds of the city's 41,000 residents lived in neighborhoods without paved streets or public sewerage systems. "The city has some sixty-two kilometers of so-called 'streets,' mostly in deplorable condition," wrote PRRA officials, "and a great part of it consisting merely of a right of way, with no grading, paving, or other improvement. The municipal water system delivers an apparently adequate supply throughout the city, [but] no part of the city regarded by this report as 'slum' territory is provided with sewers. Night soil disposal is by septic tanks and drainage by open ditches. In the lower sections . . . the natural water level is so near the surface that water lays practically stagnant in these open drains." Mayagüez officials estimated that the construction of a new sewer system would require a loan of $1 million ($21.2 million today), but as the city had already reached the limit of its borrowing power, such a loan was impossible. In 1937, Manuel Marín, the mayor of Mayagüez, explained to Miles Fairbank that his office "has received different propositions for the purchases of lots of ground in the surroundings of the city for the purpose of housing poor people living on unsanitary sections of this city" and that "this municipality is very much interested in this project and I would appreciate your cooperation." In reply, Fairbank reassured Marín that he was anxious to get to work in Mayagüez during the second year of the "slum clearance" program but did not yet have funding even though the PRRA was committed to modernizing the public health infrastructure in the island's third largest city.[71]

As we saw with schools, public road construction drew close scrutiny from local residents who sent letters of support and complaint to PRRA offices. On one hand, Eugenio Orsini, the president of the Mayagüez chapter of the Agricultural Association's Coffee Growers Section, and Germanico Belaval of Río Piedras each sought reimbursement for damage to their property caused by PRRA trucks. On the other hand, twenty coffee farmers and marketers from the Río Prieto barrio of Yauco, who claimed to represent over three hundred other agricultural workers, petitioned the governor's office asking that highway construction be continued and not terminated in their area. Their hand-signed petition claimed that this road was essential to the entire coffee zone, as it affected their livelihood and that of their workers. In addition, the coffee farmers worried that if the work was not continued soon, progress that had already been made would be lost forever due to "las continuas lluvias de estos meses en esta zona" (the continuous rains in these months in this area). Leahy forwarded the letter to the PRRA.[72]

At first glance, these small examples may not seem as important as the decisions and actions of insular political leaders in San Juan or federal officials in Washington. But these letters, like many others buried in the archives or lost altogether, are testaments to the ways in which common people in Puerto Rico observed, considered, and influenced the sweeping changes of the times. They reveal, as Teresita Levy has argued, that Puerto Rican history has been one of "activism and participation" in shaping the empire and evidence and, as Efrén Rivera Ramos has written, that Puerto Ricans have continually expressed the "capacity for agency" while living within the U.S. colonial system.[73] By taking advantage of new opportunities, demanding further action, or seeking recompence for personal property, interactions like these demonstrate the complexity of Puerto Rican history and should be regarded as significant testimonies about the New Deal in Puerto Rico.

Puerto Ricans were equally pragmatic regarding the construction of concrete and cement drinking water systems, sewerage, and storm drains. Mayors across the interior mountains, from San Sebastian in the northwest to Cidra in the southeastern-central, wrote letters asking for help repairing or building new sewerage systems for their communities. From Adjuntas to Utuado, the PRRA repaired, modernized, and constructed fifteen municipal waterworks and built entirely new water systems and filter plants in Comerio, Isabela, Patillas, and San Lorenzo. By 1938, the agency had additionally built eight water systems for rural housing developments and eight for vocational schools, as well as constructed a new major sewer with concrete curbs and gutters in Mayagüez.[74]

New waterworks assisted in the construction of a public swimming pool in Guajataca, a barrio of Quebradillas, which was just one of several new sports and recreation centers built by the PRRA. In addition to 130 new sports fields and recreation centers in both rural and urban areas, the PRRA built a basketball court and grandstands in Yauco, constructed an assembly hall for girls in Santurce, and helped develop 4-H clubs in rural towns and municipalities. Sporting culture is strong in Puerto Rico and was in no small way assisted by the construction of schools, community centers, and recreational fields and courts for youth.[75] Such public works were a hallmark of the Puerto Rican New Deal. Local participation in these programs was not only a pragmatic response to the infrastructural and environmental destruction of the hurricanes and the growing public health crisis on the island but also evidence of Puerto Ricans' agency in contesting and shaping the New Deal as workers, supervisors, consultants, and beneficiaries.

5

Rural Electrification

Between 1935 and 1943, the PRRA Rural Electrification Division constructed seven modern hydroelectric projects in the Cordillera Central by dam-
ming or diverting small rivers to create a series of man-made lakes. These
dams were designed to generate inexpensive electric power and provide
adequate flood relief and year-round irrigation for the dry southern coast
of the island. They also, importantly, improved public health by providing
abundant reserves of clean drinking water and aided the implementation
of public sewerage for residents of the rural interior of Puerto Rico for
the first time. The concrete dams, tunnels, and reservoirs of the hydroelectric program relied on local cement produced at the Cataño plant and
purchased from the Puerto Rico Cement Corporation. The Rural Electrification Division was led by Antonio S. Lucchetti Otero, the island's most
significant electrical engineer, and it was funded through a federal investment of $9.24 million (over $196 million today) while employing a variety
of workers, managers, and engineers from the island's relief rolls. The $9.24
million investment was the largest single expense of the PRRA's $32.6 mil-
lion public works budget (about $691.6 million today) and accounted for
about 28 percent of the total PRRA budget.

Electric power is so important to modern life that, paradoxically, it is
often overlooked when examining the political history of a nation, region,
or society. This oversight can trick you into believing that the spread of
electric service during the twentieth century was an inevitable development unmoored to larger political and economic issues. The electrification
of rural Puerto Rico suggests otherwise, demonstrating that the generation and delivery of hydroelectric power in Puerto Rico was reflective of a
broader Second New Deal strategy. Rural electrification was welcomed by
Lucchetti and other engineers who had long been unable to circumvent or
dismantle the local water and power monopolies that directed public water
and electric resources to the large sugar corporations that had flourished
since the dawn of the U.S. occupation in 1898. The electrification of the

island's countryside shows how the Puerto Rican New Deal transformed hurricane relief efforts into a long-range program of colonial reform via infrastructural modernization. As part of a broader question about private versus public stewardship of natural resources, the process of rural electrification in Puerto Rico—like rural electrification in the continental United States—was shaped by changes in administration, law, and financing that emerged during the 1930s. While these policy changes began during the New Deal, they were not completed until after the Second World War.[1]

Rural Life in Puerto Rico during the Great Depression

As in the continental United States, access to electric power in rural Puerto Rico was delayed decades after its availability in urban areas. There were many reasons for this lag, including the island's colonial status, natural and geological obstacles to electrification, and the entrenched local power monopolies and insular political parties that supported them. But, spurred by the New Deal, the rural electrification of Puerto Rico occurred at nearly the exact same time as (and in some cases, years before) it did in the continental United States.[2]

Living conditions in rural Puerto Rico were similar to those in rural areas of the continental United States. In Puerto Rico, nearly all of the rural population lived entirely without electric power or indoor plumbing during the 1930s. The key difference between Puerto Rico and the continental United States at this time was that rural residents made up about 70 percent of the population in Puerto Rico and only about 44 percent in the United States. In both areas, rural life was affected by soil exhaustion, the lack of access to adequate health care, and vulnerability to natural disasters. Following San Felipe and San Ciprián, the lack of electric power and clean drinking water worsened the levels of malnutrition, overall poor health, and spread of preventable diseases among rural residents.[3]

Improvised housing and the lack of adequate building materials also impacted rural health. During the 1930s, basic design, materials, and construction methods were virtually unchanged from the nineteenth century. Most rural houses were made of wood with a thatched-palm or corrugated tin roof, raised on stilts when possible, and protected from daily flooding by a small ditch dug around the outside of the house. The kitchen, which was almost always outdoors, usually consisted of a few shelves attached to the side of the house with a nearby wood firepit or a separate standing shed about 20 or 25 feet from the main house with a wood- or charcoal-burning firepit. Such conditions were especially hazardous for women, whose back-breaking labor included retrieving water from streams or outdoor pump wells, hand-scrubbing laundry, and cooking over open fires. Poor nutrition during pregnancy also taxed women's health in the countryside as spoilage-caused dysentery lurked in perishable foods kept in creeks and streams for lack of refrigeration or regular ice delivery. The combined toil of hard labor and the lack of public health infrastructure contributed to the ill health, economic depression, and spread of chronic disease in rural areas.[4]

Life was particularly hard for rural children, who were acutely susceptible to otherwise preventable or treatable diseases such as malaria, tuberculosis, pellagra, typhoid, and hookworm. Among itinerant workers, the combination of inadequate housing and sanitation services resulted in almost inescapable levels of malnourishment as anemia and other complications of vitamin deficiency plagued men and women workers and caused infant mortality rates to soar.[5] As in rural areas of the continental United States, dirt-floor outhouses were the most common means of sanitation in rural Puerto Rico, and as a result, nearly 90 percent of the rural population had hookworm.[6] An infectious disease spread by parasites that live in damp soil and human waste, hookworm can be highly preventable through improved sanitation, plumbing, and education. Barefoot children were especially vulnerable to hookworm in rural Puerto Rico, the Appalachian Mountains, the Pacific Northwest, and the American South.[7] As the parasite sapped iron and protein in the host body, hookworm exacerbated other health threats such as malaria and tuberculosis and contributed to malnutrition, in part because 60 percent of Puerto Ricans did not have access to refrigerated milk.[8] The so-called jíbaro diet of salted cod, rice, and beans provided perhaps more protein than the "sharecropper's diet" of salted fatback, cornmeal, and molasses in the southern United States, but it lacked the essential vitamins, iron, and nutrients especially necessary during pregnancy and childhood.

In terms of rural electricity, there were two major factors limiting its development in Puerto Rico. The first was geological, as the island contains no oil or coal reserves and has a mountainous topography with hundreds of small rivers, streams, and lagoons but no natural lakes. Puerto Rico receives abundant but uneven amounts of rainfall, widely varying from between 100 and 250 inches per year in El Yunque to less than 30 inches per year on the dry southern and southwestern coasts. The lengths of the island's rivers vary from the sixty-mile Río de la Plata in the north to the seven-mile Río Cañas in the south. The net water flow of the island's rivers varies as well; although flow is perennial in the north, many rivers in the south run dry for long parts of the year.[9] All of this variation means that while hydroelectric power made the most sense for the island as a whole, its practicality and cost fluctuated greatly from region to region. While today, annual rainfall in the El Yunque can amount to 100 billion gallons and provide clean drinking water to over 800,000 people, prior to the New Deal, low-lying urban areas such as San Juan, Santurce, and Mayagüez supplied their own water via gravity-based aqueducts and steam-generated power fueled by imported oil, and were not willing or able to provide reliable drinking water to the mountainous interior.[10]

The second factor was political. As in the continental United States, private utility corporations controlled all water and electric power through regional monopolies on the island. Experimentation with electric power began during the last decade of Spanish rule, when a royal decree in 1890 established construction and installation standards for Puerto Rico and Cuba. Spanish concessions to local entrepreneurs did not grant private or corporate ownership of electric power, but rather established mercantile associations that the Crown could seize in the event of military necessity—though it is not clear that this ever occurred, even during the Cuban-Spanish-American War.[11] After the U.S. occupation of Puerto Rico in 1898, most of these mercantile associations strengthened their power by establishing legal corporate identities under U.S. law. Some, such as the Sociedad Anónima Luz Electrica of San Juan and the Compañía Anónima de la Luz Electrica of Ponce, horizontally integrated with smaller providers and formed holding companies to create regional monopolies of electric power on the island by 1904.[12] Following a decade of mergers, takeovers, and consolidations, electric and water resources were almost completely controlled by a handful of private corporations. By 1910, the three largest regional monopolies in Puerto Rico were all publicly traded in international markets. They were the Canadian-owned Porto Rico Railway, Light, and Power Company, the American-owned Ponce Electric Company, and the Puerto Rican–owned Mayagüez Light, Ice, and Power Company. Each of these private companies also controlled local water rights.[13]

These three corporations took their organizational form during the first decade of U.S. imperial rule. Colonialism alone, however, does not explain their movement toward consolidation, integration, and monopoly. Rather, the global history of industrial capitalism between 1890 and 1910 is marked by widespread corporate mergers via stock buyouts, takeovers, and consolidations into holding companies, as new forms of scientific management steered the visible hand of the market toward greater efficiency via vertical and horizontal integration. As César Ayala has demonstrated, the sugar industry in Puerto Rico was vertically integrated after 1898, following highly similar patterns as the industries in Cuba and the Dominican Republic—two nations that were not under direct colonial rule but were in fact indirectly controlled by U.S. economic policy and military power. During the first two decades of the twentieth century, U.S. policy was articulated by Progressives including Republicans like Theodore Roosevelt and William Howard Taft and Democrats such as Woodrow Wilson; each made only limited reforms to the growing mania of mergers and consolidations. While their actions marked a change from the era of complete unregulation of the late nineteenth century, they pursued only the most egregious monopolies such as the breakup of John D. Rockefeller's Standard Oil Company in 1911.[14]

Between 1890 and the 1930s, electric power in Puerto Rico was generated to benefit export-driven agricultural operations. Originally, this was in the form of small electric railways that connected urban centers to ports, such as the 4.7-mile-long track owned by the Ponce Railway and Light Company (a subsidiary of the Ponce Electric Company) that began carrying freight between Ponce and the port at Playa de Ponce in 1905. By 1907, Puerto Rico had about seventeen miles of electric railway track, nearly all of it built to transport agricultural export freight.[15] The island's water resources were also allocated toward agribusiness irrigation, especially sugar. On the dry southern side of the island, electric power was used to pump irrigation water to the sugar plantations. In 1914, the insular government issued $5 million ($149.5 million today) in bonds to construct a thirty-five-mile public irrigation system between Patillas and Juana Díaz featuring over a hundred miles of canals that distributed water to 33,000 acres of sugarcane.[16] Even though most of the major sugar and tobacco farms had their own privately generated supplies of electricity for lighting their houses and industrial operations, public water and electric resources were continuously diverted to service corporate agriculture. For example, the Puerto Rico Irrigation Service, which was established by the insular legislature in 1908, constructed four large storage reservoirs and nearly a hundred miles of canals, causeways, and distribution laterals to service the large sugar estates on the southern coast of the island.[17] The fact that these insular investments in irrigation using electric pumps contributed to the expansion of sugar planting during the first three decades of the twentieth century should not be surprising, as it will be recalled that, prior to the Jones Act, the insular government was directly controlled by Washington with the only exception being thirty-five elected members of the legislature.

The development of hydroelectric power in this early era was another by-product of agricultural irrigation. In 1915, the insular government began building hydroelectric facilities to generate power for profitable private irrigation projects rather than for residential or rural customers. When the Puerto Rico Irrigation Service began generating its own electricity, over 85 percent of its power was used to pump irrigation water to the sugar sector, leaving only 15 percent sold directly to local customers for lighting and other domestic use.[18] Reflecting an opportunistic corporate strategy, private power corporations resisted insular efforts to establish hydroelectric power but then maximized their own profits from the new publicly built systems. For example, as the demand for indoor lighting, refrigeration, and other electric products grew during the 1920s, the Ponce Electric Company declined to expand their own private power system; instead, they purchased power from the small public system at wholesale rates and resold it to their customers for a considerable profit.[19]

For most of the 1920s and 1930s, Ponce was the only area in the south of the island with reliable, although limited, electric power. As a natural monopoly, the Ponce Electric Company was the only provider. The desire of Ponce residents for greater access to electric power was articulated in the Nationalist Party's newspaper *El Nacionalista de Ponce* (later called *El Nacionalista de Puerto Rico*), which took aim not only at U.S. colonial rule but also at specific corporate targets such as the Ponce Electric Company. In 1930, Ponce native Pedro Albizu Campos called for government control of electric power, including all lighting, phone, railway, and street trolley systems, demands that were included as one of the seven primary points of the Nationalist Party's official platform.[20]

By the end of the 1930s, other groups made similar calls for public ownership of natural resources and public access to affordable utility services. In September 1939, for example, the unemployed workers' union planned a hunger march to mark the arrival of new governor William Leahy. The union of unemployed workers, which was supported by the Communist Party and the taxi drivers' union, campaigned for the extension of PRRA "slum clearance" and hydroelectric programs, demanding that "running water and electric lights, first aid stations, schools and school lunch rooms be extended to zones where most of our people live. We are against slums; we are for a program of building hygienic houses for the people."[21]

The call for public control of electric power from the Nationalist Party and unemployed workers' union was not unusual in Latin America at the time, as similar developments in Argentina, Chile, Cuba, Ecuador, Mexico, and Uruguay pointed to rising levels of economic nationalism in Latin America that targeted and criticized foreign ownership of local resources such as electric power. In Cuba, for example, calls to nationalize and regulate the power grid influenced the revolution of 1933 that brought caudillo Fulgencio Batista to power. Electric power in Cuba was nearly entirely owned and operated by General Electric (GE) through its subsidiary corporation, the American and Foreign Power Company. Between 1922 and 1924, GE had acquired most of Cuba's electrical network with the cooperation of then-president Gerardo Machado—who was ousted in 1933.[22]

Protests against the corporate control of electric power in Latin America and the Caribbean paralleled the growing pressure for public ownership of water and electric utility resources in the continental United States that was begun by Progressive reformers in the 1920s and realized by the Roosevelt administration during the 1930s. In Puerto Rico, the goal of breaking up power monopolies and bringing water and electric resources under public control was not met until electrical engineers, working with the PRRA, built the infrastructure, secured the financing, and developed new legal structures to transfer control of these natural resources to publicly owned corporations. While this work was under way, the PRRA also bankrolled the acquisition of the private power corporations, defended their work before Congress, and helped establish the Autoridad de las Fuentes Fluviales or Puerto Rico Water Resources Authority in 1941.[23]

Rural Electrification in Puerto Rico

The most important figure in the process of rural electrification was Antonio S. Lucchetti Otero, who was a forty-seven-year-old electrical engineer when he starting working with the PRRA in 1935. Like his counterpart Morris Cooke of the Rural Electrification Administration, Lucchetti believed in the ability of progressive engineers to enhance the lives of residents of the agrarian countryside through publicly generated and distributed electrification. By joining the PRRA, Lucchetti ensured that the New Deal's fight against the private monopolization of electric power was extended to Puerto Rico. During the next several years, he oversaw the construction of the necessary infrastructure, obtained the needed financing, and fought for the creation of a public authority so that the island's technocratic engineers and public servants could control the island's natural resources.

Lucchetti was born in Ponce in January 1888. After graduating from Cornell University in 1910, Lucchetti returned to the island and began a career in public service that lasted for the rest of his life. He was a central figure in civil engineering for two decades before he was asked to lead the PRRA's Rural Electrification Division, largely due to his leadership of the insular Utilización de las Fuentes Fluviales (Water Resources Utility or UFF). Initially, Ernest Gruening and Carlos Chardón had considered asking an American engineer to head the program, in part because they were not sure Lucchetti would agree to augment his work at the UFF by leading the PRRA's program. In the end, Gruening offered Lucchetti an annual salary of $4,000 (about $88,000 today) on top of his salary at UFF, and he agreed. Three years later, in 1938, the PRRA tried to renew his contract without the additional pay by arguing that the Rural Electrification Division was little more than an expansion of the UFF itself. After negotiation, his supplemental salary was set at $2,000 per year.[24]

The biggest difference between the process of rural electrification in Puerto Rico and the continental United States was the degree to which it was locally planned, administered, and constructed on the island. PRRA projects were in fact designed and built by a far more locally based staff than the TVA, which hired local laborers but relied on outside engineers, experts, and administrators who were brought into the Tennessee Valley from other regions of the country.[25] The PRRA program also faced unique challenges due to the tropical climate, the uneven water supply, and the tumultuous politics of the 1930s. In addition to his expertise in electrical engineering, Lucchetti brought a familiarity and knowledge of local politics that proved essential to weathering the political violence between 1936 and 1937 and offered stability within the rural electrification program when the PRRA went through its major organizational changes in 1937 with the resignation of Chardón, the removal of Gruening, and the introduction of Fairbank and Esteves in their place. Even more importantly, he offered continuity between the smaller hydroelectric projects undertaken by the insular government with the larger-scale projects of the PRRA. The stability and continuity embodied by Lucchetti underscores the extent to which New Deal public works were products of Puerto Rican knowledge, vision, expertise, and labor.

122 · The Puerto Rico Reconstruction Administration

The PRRA rural electrification program was the single largest public works project in the history of Puerto Rico. The staff of engineers gained essential skills and experience working for the PRRA that assured the net effect of rural electrification would outlive the New Deal years, as many later worked for the WRA. Key members of Lucchetti's staff included electromechanical engineer José R. Mera; resident engineers Pedro Colón and Horacio R. Subirá; assistant civil engineers Oscar M. Girod, Miguel A. Quiñones, Orlando R. Méndez, Félix Córdova Jr., and Harold Toro; and assistant electrical engineers Justo P. Morales, Santiago Orsini, and Ulpiano Barnés. In addition, workers were overseen by Puerto Rican managers, foremen, and supervisors, such as construction foreman Ángel Delgado and chief inspector Ernesto A. Coll.[26] The decision for these engineers to align themselves with the PRRA was a pragmatic one. As Lucchetti explained, the PRRA gave "splendid impetus to the program of rural electrification which the insular government, under the spur of public demand, had for several years been developing, contemplating its expansion to cover all the unserved areas within its territory."[27] Aligning with the PRRA provided an opportunity to expand public electric service into rural areas and continue plans that had been halted by the destructive forces of San Felipe, San Ciprián, and the Great Depression.

The Rural Electrification Division completed seven major projects between 1935 and 1942. Upon completion, the projects—including all property, constructions, and lands—were "surrendered, relinquished, and transferred" to the insular government as permanent "property belonging to and owned by The People of Puerto Rico."[28] Emphasizing the public nature of these works, Fairbank inaugurated the Toro Negro hydroelectric plant by expressing the agency's "most sincere wishes that [the] project will materially contribute to the welfare of the People of Puerto Rico and will redound to the ultimate improvement of their economic condition." Comparing hydroelectric power to use of local materials at the Cataño cement plant, he wrote that it was the PRRA's "earnest hope that this may prove to be another important step in the development of the natural resources of the Island and in the production and distribution of electric power for its inhabitants at rates that they can easily afford."[29]

The PRRA's first three projects were the enlargement of the previously built Toro Negro hydroelectric plant #1, the construction of Toro Negro #2, and the construction of Carite plant #3. Located three miles north of Villalba in the southern center of the island, Toro Negro #1 was originally constructed by the insular government in 1925 with a special five-year tax levied on island residents. Starting in 1936, the PRRA Rural Electrification Division refurbished the plant with new turbines, penstock pipes, canals, transformers, switches, and other control equipment. Like all of its projects, the enlargement of Toro Negro #1 was funded by the PRRA—not by insular taxes. Simultaneously, PRRA engineers began constructing Toro Negro #2 at the headwaters of the Río Toro Negro. The second plant greatly increased the overall capacity of hydroelectric power generation in the area. Both projects, along with Carite #3, which was located just north of Guayama, were completed during 1937.[30]

The next two hydroelectric dams built by the Rural Electrification Division were Las Garzas and Dos Bocas, which each required more complex and innovative engineering. Located on the Río Las Vacas in Adjuntas, the Garzas project consisted of constructing a reservoir, creating three river diversions, and building a hydroelectric plant.[31] The centerpiece was the creation of a 150-acre lake located 2,415 feet above sea level. It also called for one of the more remarkable accomplishments of Puerto Rican engineering. Here, working with a team of engineers that included José Benitez Gautier, Heliodoro Blanco, and Emilio Serra Colón of the Engineering Division, Lucchetti's Rural Electrification Division constructed an 11,700-foot-long tunnel to carry water from the wet northern side of Mount Guilarte to the dry southern side, creating natural falls to generate 24.5 million annual kilowatt hours of power through two 5,000 horsepower water wheels.[32] Just under 4,000 feet tall, Mount Guilarte received 98 inches of annual rainfall at the time, all of which had been previously unusable in the southern part of the island. The Garzas hydroelectric dams served dual purposes of irrigation and power generation: water was diverted and carried by gravity to Ponce and the surrounding area, and power was connected to the UFF's electric system with six 38,000-volt circuits. In addition, the PRRA built ten miles of all-weather access roads, a 3,000-foot incline railway for machinery, and a 65-foot diversion tank. The dam opened in November 1941.[33]

The engineering of the Dos Bocas hydroelectric plant in the north-central section of the island between 1937 and 1942 involved the construction of a large two-mouthed reservoir that stored 37.5 million cubic meters of water in a surface area of over 600 acres and an extended water surface of more than five miles. Supplied by Río Caonillas in the eastern mouth and Río Grande de Arecibo in the western, Lago Dos Bocas consisted of a concrete dam and two generation units directly below the lake measuring a combined 12,450 horsepower of electric power, enough to generate more than 30 million kilowatt hours per year.[34] Construction of Dos Bocas embodied the island's material and symbolic transition from an agricultural to an industrial economy: in 1938, Lucchetti wrote to Fairbank asking him to convert sugarcane cars of the American Railroad Company of Puerto Rico to transport bulk amounts of cement from Cataño to the dam site. According to Manuel Font, the American Railroad Company would give the cars to the PRRA for free but was not willing to pay for the cost of conversion, which he estimated to be about $25,000 (more than $500,000 today).[35]

The significance of the Dos Bocas dam was not lost on Puerto Rican engineers and other historical actors at the time. At the inauguration of the plant in November 1942, Esteves highlighted its public nature, remarking that Dos Bocas would be administered, maintained, and improved in the future by the people of Puerto Rico.[36] Rex Tugwell, who been appointed governor the year before, used the inauguration of hydroelectric power production at Dos Bocas to offer unusually poetic and utopian testimony to the engineers and workers of the Puerto Rican New Deal, noting that

> The sun and the waters of heaven are here made to operate for the people. This is pure gain. Here the energies of man are multiplied; here invisible, untiring public servants work for everyone to whom the transmission lines can reach. We begin something here which is a miracle and which may miraculously go on into the far future. It was built with public funds, granted with foresight and wisdom; it will be managed by a public authority. It will produce continuous values. Alongside them its costs will recede until they are hardly visible. No man will profit from it; but all Puerto Ricans will share its services. . . . It was built by them and no one shall ever take it away.[37]

While work on Las Garzas and Dos Bocas continued, engineers and workers in the Rural Electrification Division enlarged the irrigation, water filtration, and generating plant systems at Isabela and built more than a hundred miles of high-tension transmission lines and two hundred miles of distribution lines across all sections of the island, including through the Cordillera Central. In just a few short years, Lucchetti and his team had more than doubled the kilowatts generated by Puerto Rican hydroelectric plants, from 29.2 million kilowatts in 1936 to 60.2 million kilowatts in 1941.[38] Public works construction on this scale had been nothing more than an infrastructural fantasy to Puerto Rican engineers during the preceding era.

Lands Acquired for Rural Electrification Projects

As important as rural hydroelectrification was to residents of the interior mountains, it should be stressed that there were also social costs and complexities involved. One of the most complicated issues involves the lands on which the hydroelectric facilities were built. At first glance, the issue of land being transferred from local ownership to federal control may seem to support the notion that the New Deal was little more than a tool of colonial exploitation. Following this logic, one might surmise that the PRRA expropriated the ground beneath Puerto Ricans' feet by force or swindle, using eminent domain to evict small landowners and contributing to what many people believed to be a colonial plague of increased landlessness on the island. Analysis of the archival records of lands bought by the PRRA for its rural electrification program, however, suggests a more nuanced history.[39]

Lands purchased by the Rural Electrification Division represented an opportunity for Puerto Ricans to pragmatically confront, negotiate, and even profit from the creation of a new land market in the central mountains. During the first half of the Great Depression, there was virtually no market for land due in part to the global economic downturn and the environmental destruction wrought by the 1928 and 1932 hurricanes. While there were significant amounts of small private landowning, farmers and other landowners had very few means of converting their fixed capital of land into the liquid capital of money. There were also extraordinarily high levels of debt in the mountains, incurred by these farmers and landowners by loans from private U.S. and Puerto Rican banks and the federally run Puerto Rico Hurricane Relief Loan Section. In addition, landowners often borrowed money from unregulated informal lenders, some of whom were large landowners that were genuinely attempting to help their neighbors and others who, as loan sharks, were simply profiteering from the extreme financial distress of the region. By 1935, the inability to sell part or all of one's land had become a burden that underscored the problematic nature of a relief system that had long been based on charitable aid and loans instead of a coordinated and forward-looking reconstruction program.

Rural electrification created a new market for land in some areas of the island. The group of ninety-seven land purchases by the Rural Electrification Division between 1936 and 1941 demonstrates that some Puerto Ricans negotiated and benefited from the PRRA program. While a few of the sellers were members of wealthy families that owned many tracts of fallow land—either inherited or taken over from owners who were unable to pay back their private loans—other sellers were in substantial amounts of debt and had no immediate prospects of obtaining value from their land. Because land tenure is always a contested issue, it is helpful to understand how these land purchases took place.[40]

The Rural Electrification Division obtained land for its projects in two ways: either public lands were signed over from the insular government, or private lands were purchased directly from individual landowners. The PRRA owned these lands for only a short period of time, and by 1942, the agency had legally transferred all property, constructions, and lands back to the insular government. While lands acquired for rural electrification projects were not confiscated by direct force or eminent domain, there must have been indirect pressure for some residents to sell. Lucchetti began seeking title to land owned by the local government soon after the PRRA's creation in May 1935. By the end of the summer, he had drafted numerous maps marking lands required for several proposed hydroelectric projects, including Toro Negro #1, Toro Negro #2, and Carite #3, which he submitted to Carlos Chardón.[41] With over two decades of experience working in the Puerto Rican government, Lucchetti was well aware of the physical topographies and political headwinds he faced and was prepared to meet internal resistance from opponents in the Coalition. Like New Dealers in the continental United States, Lucchetti had learned to balance competing forces and desires at the state and local levels. Unlike his continental counterparts, however, the colonial system meant that he had to face partisan political forces from two separate governments. On the island, Lucchetti faced resistance from all sides, including from Coalition leaders in the insular legislature, Governor Winship's office, and other notable figures such as former director of PRERA James Bourne, who was growing critical of the PRRA. Despite this resistance, the Rural Electrification Division acquired public lands from the local government using a very narrow and specific scope. Over the next six years, lands requested for rural electrification projects were carefully surveyed and their direct use explicitly defined, whether for large construction projects or the installation of transmission lines.[42]

Land was also purchased by the Rural Electrification Division directly from individual landowners. Here, the types of lands the PRRA acquired varied considerably and can be best illustrated by a few examples. In some cases, the division negotiated for the purchase of complete parcels of land—meaning the owner would have to move. Some landowners in this situation were able to purchase more productive land back from the Rural Rehabilitation Division in what amounted to an upward exchange. In other cases, the PRRA purchased small, fallow, or partial sections of land that adjoined plots of public land already obtained from the insular government. In these cases, lands were usually acquired for the construction of power transmission lines, service roads and trails, the installation of narrow-gage tracks, or staging of construction machinery.[43] Some lands were purchased to be flooded as part of the creation of large man-made lakes such as Las Garzas or Dos Bocas. While a portion of the acquired lands were completely unusable for agriculture due to their steep slopes, deep ravines, exhausted soil, lack of irrigation, or environmental damages, others were highly productive plots planted with coffee, bananas, and other fruits for subsistence, nutritional supplement, or local markets. The PRRA paid different amounts based on the quality of the land. The minimum price paid for lands in the central mountains relating to rural electrification projects was about $100 (over $2,100 today) per cuerda (a unit of measurement used in some areas of Latin America that measures approximately 0.97 acres) and the average payment was about $190 (about $4,030 today) per cuerda. Between 1936 and 1941, the PRRA purchased 1,037 cuerdas directly from private sellers—resulting in the transfer of approximately $197,000 ($4.179 million today) in federal dollars directly to Puerto Rican landowners.[44]

The backstories of the land sellers varied as much as the type and quality of lands exchanged. Whereas some lands were owned by families who held thousands of acres, others belonged to small farmers who owned less than one cuerda. Although we do not have recorded ethnographies of these individual sellers, we can imagine their decision-making process by examining the social and economic circumstances in which they lived. While some made sizable profits from selling lands that were not in use, others were saved from desperate situations with much smaller amounts. One question we must ask is if this land was not confiscated by direct force, why would large or small individual landowners sell their land to the PRRA? A sampling of the land acquisition case files and title transfers for rural electrification projects between 1936 and 1941 provides some clues. For Norberto García Jimenez and his wife María Josefa Teresa Roig Casalduc, for example, it had to have been with immense sadness that they sold 26 cuerdas in Río Abajo, Utuado. While the $2,800 in Depression-era dollars (over $59,400 today) surely helped their financial situation, the loss of their wooden house and thatched-palm tobacco drying area to the floodwaters of the Dos Bocas dam must have been personally painful.[45] Their story must be balanced, however, with the fact that Dos Bocas was designed to produce nearly 30 million kilowatts of power per year and serve the rural residents of Utuado, Arecibo, and nearby areas with affordable electricity and fresh drinking water for decades to come.

The Oliver family also sold land to be used on the Dos Bocas project. For the extended family, including Andres Oliver, Eduardo Oliver, Isabel Bujosa Oliver, Juan and Aminta Oliver, and Juan and Hermina Oliver Maldonado, the sale of approximately 74 cuerdas in Río Arriba, Arecibo, returned over $32,000 (almost $679,000 today). If the Oliver family was not already wealthy, this was an extremely good start. This fortune may seem to overshadow the $1,063.26 (over $25,500 today) that Estafanía Martínez Ríos made from the 6.74 cuerdas she sold in Don Alonso, Utuado. But it would be a mistake to assume that the money meant any less to her. As a widow with six daughters and two sons, all of whom except the oldest daughter were minors, Martínez Ríos used the money she received to pay off a $459 (over $9,700 today) personal loan she took out from Manuel Serrano Fuentes and a $360 (over $7,600 today) loan from the Hurricane Relief Loan Section. With the remaining $244.26 (roughly $5,182 today), she was able to begin a new life with her eight children, most likely in San Juan. Her high level of indebtedness was no doubt caused by the extremely low wages for women workers in rural Puerto Rico, the high cost of importing food and other basic necessities, and the destructive force of the hurricanes that limited agricultural work in the area.[46]

Similarly, Juana Torres Candelaria sold three cuerdas in Arecibo for $700 (about $14,800 today) for the construction of Dos Bocas. With this money, she was able to move her eight children (one son and seven daughters, all but one of whom were minors) to an urban area of the island. While Domingo Vivaldi Pacheco was able to sell nearly 15 cuerdas in Saltillo, Adjuntas, for $1,800 (nearly $38,200 today) for the Garzas reservoir, José Bujosa Jaume profited over $8,000 ($169,700 today) for his 200 cuerdas in Utuado and Areciba for Dos Bocas. For Angela Torre Ortiz of Barrio Garzas, Adjuntas, the sale of 19 cuerdas returned $1,600 (almost $34,000 today) while the larger estates of Aurele M. Gatti of Saltillo, Adjuntas, and Tomas García Moya y Georgina Santoni of Rio Abajo, Utuado, netted $7,500 ($159,000 today) and $15,000 ($318,000 today), respectively.[47]

The Hurricane Relief Loan Section had been organized by the Hoover administration following San Felipe in 1928. Coffee farmers in the central highlands, where Estafanía Martínez Ríos's land was located, made up 96 percent of the 3,033 loans made by the Hurricane Relief Loan Section between 1929 and 1943. Coffee farmers, whose faced a multiyear window if they replanted coffee on lands destroyed by hurricanes, were loaned $5,209,526 ($110.5 million today) of the total of $5,673,049 ($120.4 million today) provided by the relief loans. Underscoring the difficulty of small landowners like Martínez Ríos to recultivate coffee, by 1943 only thirty-seven loans were repaid in full while over five hundred loans were rendered completely uncollectable because of foreclosures by prior lienholders, when properties failed to sell for the amount owed to the holder of the first mortgage. While over a thousand loans were successfully readjusted, the data suggest that there was no real land market in Puerto Rico during the Great Depression other than those lands sought by the PRRA for public works construction.[48] Viewed in the context of the times, the evidence indicates that the widowed Martínez Ríos would have had little chance at reentering the coffee market or escaping her accumulated debt. As with the example of Norberto García Jimenez and María Josefa Teresa Roig Casalduc, whose small house and tobacco-drying shed are most likely still at the bottom of Lago Dos Bocas today, we must balance the personal story of their individual families with the improvements in public health, communication, and quality of life experienced by the larger society in evaluating the impact of these land sales.

It is worth noting that the land sales highlighted here, like all other lands purchased by the Rural Electrification Division, were based on surveys conducted by Puerto Rican engineers, negotiated and contracted in Spanish, and notarized by Puerto Rican public notaries. Led by lawyer Rafael B. Pérez Mercado (the head of the land and title section of the PRRA's Legal Division) and overseen by insular attorney general Benigno Fernández García, the land sales were notarized by Ángel Fiol Negron, Celestino Domínguez Rubio, and the firm of Domínguez y Domínguez. The fact that the PRRA was a bilingual federal agency with a predominately Puerto Rican staff set it apart from all other New Deal agencies at the time. The land sales were conducted in Spanish, and many literate Puerto Ricans felt comfortable writing to PRRA administrators directly in Spanish or English with requests, complaints, and concerns about ongoing construction projects. Such complaints were usually taken seriously by PRRA officials, who relied on the support of the Puerto Rican people as workers and beneficiaries for the survival of their programs.[49]

Many letters referenced small damage claims, like that of Gerónimo Fontánes of Saltillo, Adjuntas, who wrote that PRRA trucks had damaged his small farm where they were building a road on the Garzas dam project.

Fontánes was not a critic of the New Deal. Rather, he also used the letter to ask for employment on the project. In many cases, such as a letter of complaint from Manuel V. Torres, which alleged that PRRA employees had twice trespassed and caused damage on his property in Peñuelas, senior officials were involved in the response. Referencing the Torres letter, Lucchetti personally wrote to Miles Fairbank and his assistant, Tomás Bernardini Palés, instructing them that while he was not familiar with Torres's name, the general area of the property in question was used to build transmission lines between Garzas and Tallaboa. Lucchetti informed Fairbank that he would investigate the matter further to better determine the exact location of the Torres property and personally survey the extent of the damages.[50]

Complaints also came in the form of hand-signed petitions arguing that PRRA public works conflicted with previously negotiated arrangements for supplying irrigation and drinking water to large farms. In August 1936, a petition signed by eighty-two merchants, industrialists, and small-scale farmers of Jagua Pasto, Guayanilla, argued that the Garzas project conflicted with previous irrigation arrangements between themselves and the insular legislature. Located sixteen miles west of Ponce on the southern slope of the island, these Guayanilla farmers and entrepreneurs had most likely been served by the Ponce Electric Company and Puerto Rico Irrigation Service. While this complaint pitted their personal interests against the collective improvement of extended rural electricity, other concerns demonstrated the long-standing legacy of environmental activism in Puerto Rico. For example, the municipal government of Peñuelas sent a letter to Fairbank on behalf of the neighbors and taxpayers of the southern town that strongly protested the pollution of the Guiana River caused by the Garzas project. Writing that the inhabitants of Peñuelas are "protesting vigorously," the letter explained that residents were "being forced to use dirty water that they fear could lead to a ruinous epidemic." The combined concern for the natural environment and public health reflected in this letter was common to many Puerto Ricans in the 1930s, who aligned with the PRRA to combat these issues yet also expressed concerns and complaints when these needs were not met, or when new health or environmental problems arose.[51]

Creating the Water Resources Authority

In the spring of 1940, Antonio Lucchetti testified before the U.S. House Committee on Insular Affairs in favor of the creation of the Puerto Rico Water Resources Authority (WRA). Calling it a matter of vital importance, Lucchetti argued that its creation was essential to preserving the capital-intensive construction projects that had already been built or were currently under construction by the PRRA. The formation of a locally owned public authority to administer the newly built rural hydroelectric facilities had been a topic of heated debate for several years in both Puerto Rico and the continental United States. As he prepared for his testimony, Lucchetti knew there was entrenched opposition to the idea in both San Juan and Washington. Speaking before members of the House, Lucchetti warned that the failure to create a "Little Tennessee Valley Authority" for Puerto Rico would risk wasting tax dollars that had already been spent on the program.[52]

When asked repeatedly by Fred L. Crawford (R-MI) and Charles Hawks Jr. (R-WI) if the true purpose of the WRA was to compete with private electrical utility corporations, Lucchetti skillfully answered that the PRRA was simply "struggling to preserve our own system" and explained that corporate interests were opposed to state-built hydroelectric plants. "Private interests have been making opposition" to us, he continued, "by opposing any legislation" to build publicly funded hydroelectric plants. When asked by Crawford if the WRA would challenge private electricity companies, Lucchetti responded with disdain, noting that concern for private companies was not the issue since existing utilities "wouldn't build a line a half a mile long to reach a farmer." Asked if he planned to extend public electricity networks into urban areas of the island, Lucchetti replied that he could not possibly know what the WRA would do in the future. When Crawford informed him that private utility rates were falling in Puerto Rico, thus negating the need for the WRA, Lucchetti testified that the drop in private rates was only due to new public competition created by the PRRA. Exasperated, Crawford exclaimed that private companies would not be able to compete with a public corporation and would almost certainly be driven out of business by the WRA. Further, the creation of the WRA would "take power out of the local legislature and remove it from local political influence." This was undemocratic and un-American.[53]

Lucchetti and other Puerto Rican New Dealers had heard these arguments before. Modeled on the New York Power Authority and the Tennessee Valley Authority, the WRA was designed to be a self-financing public authority that provided clean water and cheap electric power to the rural interior mountains of Puerto Rico. Crawford, who had made his money building, financing, and operating beet sugar mills in the continental United States during the First World War, was one of many Republican opponents of the bill.[54] As of March 1940, at least three bills to create the WRA had been defeated in the Puerto Rican Senate by the Coalition—one of which was pocket-vetoed by Winship due to unspecified reasons. In an ugly back-and-forth in the island's newspapers, Lucchetti had accused Rafael Martínez Nadal of using his elected position to advocate on behalf of the private utility companies.[55] Although the TVA had previously made the argument that it would not conflict with private power, Crawford understood that a public utility like the WRA would have a greater chance of dominating the private industry in Puerto Rico, an island much smaller than the Tennessee Valley.[56]

In May 1941, one year after Lucchetti's testimony, the Puerto Rico Electric Power Authority Act was passed by the local legislature and sent to La Fortaleza by Luis Muñoz Marín, the newly elected president of the Senate, where it was signed into law by acting governor Guy J. Swope as Insular Act Number 83. The law created the WRA as a public authority that operated as "a corporation having legal existence and personality separate and apart from that of the Government. The debts, obligations, contracts, bonds, notes, debentures, receipts, expenditures, accounts, funds, undertakings, and property of the Authority, its officers, agents, or employees shall be deemed to be those of said government-controlled corporation and not to be those of the [insular] Government or any office, bureau, department, commission, dependency, municipality, branch, agent, officer or employee thereof."[57] Antonio Lucchetti was named the first executive director of the WRA.

Lucchetti was not alone in his conviction about the WRA's importance, and influential politicians to the left of the New Deal expressed support as well. Congressman Vito Marcantonio of East Harlem, for example, expressed that the creation of the WRA would be especially good for the health of poor families. Marcantonio, who championed Puerto Rican causes both in his district and on the island, noted that the WRA would also buffer the island from further soil erosion, agricultural underperformance, and tree depletion as hygienic indoor kitchens replaced outdoor wood- and charcoal-burning firepits.[58] Even as public support increased, however, entrenched interests on the island had blocked all previous proposals to create the public authority. At the start of the 1940 hearings, the *New York Times* warned that the Committee on Insular Affairs expected a "Puerto Rican Free-For-All" at the House WRA hearings.[59] Sugar farmers and other large landowners, who, according to Lucchetti, owed their "whole existence to the [current] irrigation service" of the insular government, preferred the status quo. To these landowners, the WRA was too closely related to the enforcement of the 500-Acre Law, which was also now being discussed by Muñoz Marin and other officials in the Popular Democratic Party. Powerful landowners such as Senator Pedro Juan Serrallés were against the water resources bill. At the time, the value of Serrallés's land and property was estimated to be $10 million (about $212 million today). Arthur L. Quinn, a well-known sugar attorney for the Serrallés estate and the Puerto Rico British West Indies Sugar Association, testified against the bill. High-ranking members of the Coalition, such as Bolívar Pagán, also objected to the bill as a matter of principle, arguing that the new law would turn over the water resources of Puerto Rico to the "unbridled dictates of one man—the executive director"—which everyone knew, he left unsaid, would be Lucchetti. As a key figure in the PRRA, Lucchetti was a close ally of Pagán's political rival, Muñoz Marín.[60]

The creation of the WRA was followed in a variety of newspapers, including *El Mundo*, *El Dia*, *La Correspondencia*, *El Imparcial*, and the *New York Times*. Newspapers reported that a growing majority of Puerto Ricans embraced the idea of public works and supported the creation of the WRA, alternatively called the "Little TVA" or "Puerto Rican TVA" in the daily press. In October 1939, editors at *El Mundo* had celebrated the recent resolution of the Puerto Rican Farmers Association in support of the bill. The Farmers Association, which had not previously commented on the bill, declared that the goals of the WRA aligned with their own values and voted on an agreement, stating that "the extension of such [hydroelectric] service to all of the rural districts of the island is imperative to provide comfort, spread culture, and improve the standard of living on all the farms of Puerto Rico, which constitutes one of the principal aspirations of the organized farmers." Editors at *El Mundo* agreed that the formation of the WRA was the first step to buying out the remaining private utility companies on the island and expressed that it was "in favor of the program of nationalizing hydroelectric service . . . not only for everyday household use, but also for the industrialization of the farms."[61]

Popular support for the WRA paralleled public animosity toward the electric monopolies. As we saw above, residents of Mayagüez, Río Piedras,

Ponce, and San Juan led strikes against the Mayagüez Light, Power, and Ice Company, the Ponce Electric Company, and the Porto Rico Railway, Light, and Power Company—which was colloquially known as the Trolley Company in honor of its electric trolley cars in Santurce—as early as 1934.[62] By February 1940, *El Imparcial* declared, "There is No Excuse for Not Passing the Bill to Create the Water Resources Authority of Puerto Rico," which had the "thunderous" support of the people, who viewed the creation of the WRA as a chance to permanently extend the coordinated work of the UFF and the PRRA. For almost two years, the collaboration between the UFF and the PRRA had increased rural access to power and lowered rates across the island, as the investment in public works had forced private companies to lower their rates for the first time.[63] In August 1938, when construction of Las Garzas and Dos Bocas was just getting under way, José Enrique Colom had predicted in *El Mundo* that new public competition would drive private utility prices down. Colom, the insular commissioner of the interior, noted that the PRRA hydroelectricity projects were essential to reducing the costs of economic development across the island, as the UFF would sell electricity to the Cataño cement plant at a much lower rate than the private utilities, such as Porto Rico Railway, Light, and Power Company, which had "flatly refused" to negotiate the price of power service to the plant.[64]

The WRA was seen as a chance to make the gains of public power on the island permanent. In March 1940, *La Correspondencia* expressed hope that "the Joke Will End This Year" and that the bill would be passed, as the WRA was urgently needed and would provide a crucial service to Puerto Rican farmers by moving the control of electric power away from political forces and into professional hands.[65] Over the next year, as WRA legislation continued to stall in the local legislature, *La Correspondencia* lamented the failure to pass the WRA bill but expressed concern that the U.S. Congress might try to do so from Washington. Deeply convinced that the WRA would "greatly benefit the whole island," the editors warned that it would be wrong for the federal government to "humiliate" Puerto Rico by overriding the local legislature. Though they granted that the Coalition had some legitimate objections to the bill, *La Correspondencia* argued that many Puerto Rican politicians legislated "following the dangerous course of political passion and personal hatred," and the common good was better served by disinterested public service that was not motivated to "benefit private persons and private entities [that] injure the social interests of the country." The failure of the legislature to pass the bill had created a "caricature of a democratic system" whereby senators and representatives were attempting to govern as executives.[66]

A significant consequence of the Puerto Rican New Deal, the creation of the WRA had both immediate and long-lasting effect on the island by supplying cheap, renewable electric power for home and industry; lessening dependence on imported fuel; conserving the wood supply, which had been depleted for use as charcoal; and contributing to improvements in public health. In addition, the WRA was designed to be self-financing through the sale of revenue bonds, which allowed it to operate independently from the insular budget and/or debt limit, while not creating new burdens on local taxpayers. As one of the most politically feasible models of financing large-scale public works during the Great Depression, revenue bonds were the most common method of constructing hydroelectric power grids during in the 1930s.[67]

For Lucchetti, the creation of the WRA marked the apex of a long technocratic career in public service. Reflecting the same liberal faith in progressive engineering expressed by engineers in the Rural Electrification Administration, Lucchetti believed that the WRA could be operated as an efficient and nonpartisan agency that earned the public's trust, good will, and patronage, "irrespective of their position in party politics, religion, race, or class." Its ability to serve all areas of the island without discrimination would be essential to its success, just as the UFF was respected by the people, who, he added, "speak highly of the service it renders, want it extended, and want it to grow and to be kept functioning with economic efficiency."[68] Most of all, the WRA meant the survival of the electric system built by the PRRA's Rural Electrification Division and the millions of dollars already invested by U.S. taxpayers. Without increased expansion and coordination of the island's power supply, Lucchetti feared that hydroelectric facilities such as Las Garzas and Dos Bocas would fall into private hands within a few years.[69]

Rather than allow this privatization of public works, however, Lucchetti planned on breaking up the private power monopolies that had dominated the electric and water supply on the island for decades. As for his earlier testimony to Congress that the WRA would not compete with private electricity corporations and had no plans for taking them over, it appears to have been an adeptly disingenuous answer to the hostile Republican congressmen who were intent on protecting the "free market" and private corporate interests. Lucchetti had planned to use the WRA to put pressure on the private monopolies all along, especially after the U.S. Supreme Court

136 · The Puerto Rico Reconstruction Administration

dismissed a lawsuit against the PRRA and insular government brought by the Porto Rico Railway, Light, and Power Company, which had charged that the rural electrification program violated its own ninety-nine-year charter that had been signed in 1906. Rather than violate private company rights, however, Lucchetti moved to directly buy them out. Under his leadership, the PRRA purchased the Ponce Electric Company in 1937 but was unable to reach agreements with either the Porto Rico Railway, Light, and Power Company or the Mayagüez Light, Ice, and Power Company.[70]

During World War II, the WRA sold discounted electric power to the Cataño cement plant and contributed to the island's rapid mobilization for war. Lucchetti then used the WRA's participation in the war effort to convince Roosevelt that the War Powers Act allowed for the "temporary" expropriation of the island's remaining private power companies. Following a series of last-minute protests and appeals from the companies, the WRA purchased the Porto Rico Railway, Light, and Power Company for $10.33 million (about $177.6 million today) and the Mayagüez Light, Ice, and Power Company for $1.55 million (about $26.6 million today). The long struggle against the private ownership of natural resources, electric power, and water distribution in Puerto Rico was over.[71] For the rest of the decade, the WRA expanded the process of electrification begun by the UFF and continued by the PRRA. By 1951, more than 35,000 rural families (totaling over 175,000 people) used electricity at home for the first time.[72] Four years later, in 1955, the WRA operated nineteen hydroelectric-generating stations, four steam-generating systems, and 108 distribution stations that sent electricity across thousands of miles of transmission lines. That year, the WRA serviced 208,130 residential customers, 33,771 commercial customers, 2,700 industrial customers, and 457 listed as "other."[73]

In addition, the WRA expanded the supply of clean drinking water to all areas of the island. In 1942, just one year after its formation, the PPD-controlled Senate passed the Aqueduct Act, which was the first step in protecting the public water supply against regional drought and pollution. The act stipulated that any municipal water supply system found not meeting the health standards of the insular Health Department would be turned over to the WRA. Almost immediately, declarations were made of the water systems of San Juan, Ponce, Mayagüez, Arecibo, Caguas, Aguadilla, Cayey, Juana Díaz, and Vega Baja. When San Juan filed an injunction against the new law, the act was upheld by the Puerto Rican Supreme Court. The water supplies of San Juan and Ponce, the island's largest, were found to be "wholly inadequate, unreliable, and of inferior quality."[74] The legislature next passed the Puerto Rico Aqueduct and Sewer Authority Act, which was signed into law by Governor Rex Tugwell as Act Number 40 on May 1, 1945. The law created the Aqueduct and Sewer Authority (ASA), which took over the PRRA's public works in these areas. While 76 of 77 municipalities had public water systems in 1945 (even if many of them were unfit to drink), only 42 of 77 had public sewer systems.

Antonio Lucchetti served as executive director of the WRA from its inception until his death in 1952, ending a forty-year career dedicated to bringing hydroelectric power to the island. He was first replaced by Chief Engineer Carl A. Bock and then, in May 1955, by Sol Luis Descartes, the secretary of the Treasury under Muñoz Marin. Descartes, who was about twenty-three years younger than Lucchetti, was an engineer associated with the Agricultural Experiment Station who had worked with the PRRA on the 1935 census and published a variety of pamphlets and books with the UPR, ranging from the organization and earnings on 130 sugarcane farms to the inflation of retail food prices on the island. Like Lucchetti, Descartes was born in Ponce and graduated from Cornell University.[75]

By 1965, all Puerto Rican municipalities had clean drinking water and working sewers.[76] The creation of the WRA and ASA signaled a watershed moment for public development in Puerto Rico. These public authorities later served as models for several postwar public corporations in Puerto Rico during the Operation Bootstrap era, including the Government Development Bank, Puerto Rico Industrial Development Company, Puerto Rico Glass Company, Puerto Rico Pulp and Paper Corporation, Puerto Rico Shoe and Leather Company, and Puerto Rico Clay Products Corporation.[77]

Conclusion

From the New Deal to Today

The study of the New Deal in Puerto Rico invites comparisons with our own times. As of this writing, recovery is still incomplete from a series of recent hurricanes, the largest and most destructive of which were María and Irma in 2017 and Fiona in 2022. In addition, a large number of small- to moderate-scale earthquakes began shaking the island in late 2019, just before the onset of the global COVID-19 pandemic. Whereas San Felipe and San Ciprián contoured Puerto Rico's recovery from the Great Depression, these recent environmental events have occurred during an ongoing and severe recession that shows no sign of abating. In 2015, Governor Alejandro García Padilla declared that nearly $74 billion in debts were unpayable. The following year, Barack Obama signed the Puerto Rico Oversight, Management, and Economic Stability Act (PROMESA), which established an undemocratic financial oversight board and a process for restructuring the debt with bondholders. The Financial Oversight and Management Board, which features a mixture of Puerto Rican– and U.S.-born lawyers, financial executives, and federal regulators, has largely called for the privatization of Puerto Rico's public corporations and austerity measures common in so-called failed states elsewhere. Meanwhile, the island's population shrank by 11.8 percent between 2010 and 2020 and is now about half the size of the Puerto Rican diaspora living and working in the continental United States.[1]

These recent events have been covered by journalists and scholars on the island and in the diaspora's intellectual sector; rather than taking a deep dive into current events, this conclusion will instead sketch how the reform impulse of the Puerto Rican New Deal directly and indirectly contributed to the present-day crises.[2] While some readers may conclude that the PRRA was a colonial policy failure that had little long-term effect, others might suggest that the problem started when the federal government abandoned the progressive policies and planning of the New Deal. Although the former group most likely reached those conclusions before reading this book, the latter group, which might advocate for an updated or "new" New Deal featuring fresh waves of federal intervention using renewable energy and other local resources, is perhaps equally dogmatic. The problems of today are not the same as the problems of the Great Depression. The most durable lesson of the New Deal in Puerto Rico is that the PRRA was a locally run agency that could not have existed without the meeting of federal capital and Puerto Rican expertise. One of the most unique and underappreciated agencies of the entire New Deal, the PRRA was based on the knowledge, creativity, and labor of Puerto Ricans. The land purchases, population surveys, social work, medical care, and other essential services were conducted by Puerto Rican workers and administrators who found common cause with like-minded colleagues born in the continental United States. In doing so, the PRRA helped transform the island from an agricultural society to a modern industrial economy that reformed but strengthened the colonial system. The island's continuing colonial status also demonstrates the New Deal's limits for addressing the crises of today that, by nearly unanimous agreement, must first resolve the status question through a process of self-determination. Any solutions for Puerto Rico's interwoven crises must, as César Ayala and Rafael Bernabe have stressed, combine self-determination with social justice and economic planning. These solutions must be generated by Puerto Ricans on the island and in the diaspora.[3]

This book has argued that technocrats working for the PRRA combined economic modernization with colonial reform. Among their most impactful undertakings were rural electrification and the construction of the Cataño cement plant. Taken together, these public works accounted for about one-third of the PRRA's $691 million engineering budget and are tangible and symbolic examples of how the 1928 and 1932 hurricanes became catalysts for long-range modernization. The projects were key components of the recovery program first articulated by the Chardón Plan and had direct and indirect bearing on social and economic life in Puerto Rico for the remainder of the twentieth century and into the twenty-first. While both projects aligned with other Second New Deal public works in the continental United States, the legacies of the WRA and PRCC have diverged from other New Deal public authorities and corporations.

Today, public authorities are essential to an array of services provided by municipal, state, and federal governments that are inadequately served by

140 · The Puerto Rico Reconstruction Administration

private capital, ranging from housing and transportation to electricity and recreation. They come in many different shapes and forms. While some of the larger federally created agencies, such as the Tennessee Valley Authority, Federal Deposit Insurance Corporation, and Amtrak, are well known to their multitudes of users, most are little understood or considered unless or until something goes wrong. Supporters of modernization programs during the Depression used the public authority as a means of raising funds through revenue bonds—which are issued against future earnings rather than state taxing power—and a way around partisan politics and inflexible government regulations. As Gail Radford has shown, however, critics today warn that their embedded lack of democratic oversight, potential for incurring unsustainable levels of debt, and unseen power to transform citizens into customers pose risks to the larger economic system.[4] Whereas New Dealers lauded the public authority's ability to raise capital at a time when local and state governments (and the insular government) were unable to do so, the model in some cases has become overburdened by massive amounts of debt and a threat to the delivery of essential public services. Puerto Rico, where the sale of revenue bonds is triple-exempt from local, insular, and federal taxes—making them extra attractive to a range of investors—is a perfect example.[5]

The legacy of the Puerto Rico Water Resources Authority is a clear illustration of the dangers of over-relying on the public authority model in a colonial context. Readers of this book might wonder how the WRA—the creation of which was a breakthrough moment in generating renewable energy, delivering clean drinking water, and defeating the monopolistic private control of the island's natural resources—became the Puerto Rico Electric Power Authority (PREPA). So how did we get from the WRA and its promise of hydropower to PREPA and its near-complete reliance on fossil fuels?

As this book has shown, the creation of the WRA in 1941 occurred after a protracted legal and political struggle led by electrical engineer Antonio Lucchetti. But the WRA's commitment to renewable hydroelectricity only lasted about a decade, reaching its zenith in the early 1950s before the public utility began moving in new directions to keep up with shifts in U.S. and global practices. Operating in an unincorporated colonial possession of the United States, the WRA (and later, PREPA) had little choice but to follow U.S. power generation strategy. Following the completion of Lago Caonillas Hydroelectricity Plant #1 in Utuado in 1949, the WRA shifted away from hydroelectric power in favor of larger, petroleum-based thermoelectric power plants designed to maximize delivery to the island's ever-growing urban and suburban areas. During the 1950s, the WRA opened the San Juan Thermoelectric Plant, the Palo Seco Thermoelectric Plant in Cataño, and the Costa Sur Thermoelectric Plant in Guayanilla, just west of Ponce; in 1963, engineers installed approximately ten miles of underwater cable to connect the island of Vieques to the thermoelectric systems on the main island of Puerto Rico.[6]

By this time, the WRA had begun an experiment with nuclear power in conjunction with the U.S. Atomic Energy Commission by constructing the Boiling Nuclear Superheater (BONUS) reactor on the west coast just north of Rincón. This should have been no surprise. In 1955, the WRA's Sol Descartes had reported that "the first two of a group of young, talented engineers have been accepted for training at the School of Nuclear Studies and Engineering at the Argonne National Laboratory of the Atomic Energy Commission. More will follow."[7] The beachfront complex was the first nuclear reactor in Latin America and the second boiling-water type of nuclear superheater in the United States, joining three boron-based (BORAX) reactors built in Idaho in the 1950s. Nuclear engineers first achieved a controlled nuclear chain reaction at Rincón in April 1964 and demonstrated consistent satisfactory performance in November 1965. The WRA halted nuclear operations in 1968, however, due to technical problems and the expensive costs of maintenance and repairs, and BONUS was decommissioned by the Atomic Energy Commission. In accordance with federal policy, all nuclear materials, control rods, and other highly dangerous components were removed to the continental United States while the reactor's piping systems were flushed, exterior parts decontaminated, and all interior parts buried in concrete by 1970. The decommissioned nuclear dome is still there today. Radioactivity at the site, which is owned by PREPA, continues to be monitored by the U.S. Department of Energy.[8]

After ending its experiment with nuclear power, the WRA continued its trajectory away from hydropower and made major investments in oil-fueled generation. During 1971 and 1972, just before the onset of the global oil crisis, they added the Aguirre Thermoelectric Plant in Salinas and switched to a combined-cycle gas turbine model, designed to improve efficiency. In 1979, the WRA legally changed its name from the Water Resources Authority to PREPA. According to PREPA, the corporate rebranding was an explicit acknowledgment that river water was no longer the principal source of electricity on the island. Indeed, by the end of the 1970s imported petroleum and its derivatives accounted for 98 percent of all electricity generated in Puerto Rico while hydroelectric power represented only 2 percent. When PREPA acquired the Cayey municipal system in 1981, it had consolidated all of the island's electric grid under its control, giving itself a public monopoly on power generation and supply.[9] In 1993, Governor Pedro Rosselló signed an executive order allowing PREPA to purchase natural gas and coal from private producers. One such provider, Applied Energy Systems, opened a coal-burning plant in Guayama and began producing and selling coal-based power to the insular government in 2002 on a twenty-five-year contract. In addition to high levels of air and water pollution caused by the plant, Applied Energy Systems then marketed and sold coal ash as landfill to private contractors in Puerto Rico, causing irreparable health and environmental damage to residents of the southern coast and other parts of the island.[10]

More broadly, the fate of PREPA from the 1980s to today has been tied to the rise and fall of Puerto Rico's colonial economy. From 1976 to 1996, the island's economy enjoyed sustained growth in large part due to Section 936 of the federal tax code that granted U.S. corporations tax exemption from income generated in Puerto Rico. In 1996, however, Bill Clinton signed legislation that began a ten-year phaseout of the tax exemption law, a move supported by leaders of the island's statehood movement such as Pedro Rosselló and resident commissioner Carlos Romero Barceló of the New Progressive Party. The phaseout of Section 936 was also encouraged by the U.S. Treasury Department, which mistakenly believed that ending the exemption would result in corporate tax revenue increases from businesses located in Puerto Rico; instead, it precipitated the island's current debt crisis.[11] It is also a reminder of the precarious position of the island within the U.S. colonial system. When the end of Section 936 became final in 2006, the Puerto Rican economy was plunged into a protracted period of recession, unemployment, and outmigration that was exacerbated by the housing crisis of 2008 and the destructive hurricane season of 2017. As Irma and María made landfall that September, large sections of PREPA's transmission and distribution infrastructure were destroyed, leaving thousands of Puerto Rican citizens without power for months and years into the future. The infrastructure problems were worsened by the series of earthquakes that have occurred on the island since 2019.

While the natural disasters revealed the island's colonial status to observers who had not previously paid attention to Puerto Rican politics, they also exposed the fragility of PREPA's aging infrastructure, the dangers of the public authority model in a colonial environment, and the weakness of the Puerto Rican economy since the repeal of Section 936. Beginning in 2006, PREPA and the insular government began borrowing heavily through the sale of triple-exempt revenue bonds to continue operations, which led to massive and unpayable debts even as utility rate prices grew and service worsened. At least $4 billion of the $74 billion debt was held by PREPA, which became the leading symbol in public discourse about the failure of the Puerto Rican economy.[12] In 2020, control of PREPA was ceded to a joint venture partnership between the Canadian ATCO Energy and Quanta Services of Texas called LUMA Energy. Three years later, in 2023, a newly created subsidiary of New York's New Fortress Energy called Genera PR was awarded a ten-year contract to run the island's twelve oil-based power-generating facilities. The transfer of power generation from PREPA to LUMA Energy to Genera PR capsulizes the ongoing neoliberal transition from the New Deal to today.[13]

The PRCC, which was privatized in 1951 when Teodoro Moscoso and Luis Muñoz Marín sold it along with three other public corporations to Ferré Enterprises, had a different trajectory than the WRA. Although the reasoning behind the sale of the PRCC to José Ferré has not been adequately explained, its effects were clear: a local monopoly in cement manufacturing and distribution that became the centerpiece of the Ferré family's industrial portfolio as the island's urban and suburban built environment expanded during the Cold War. While the sale offered the PPD a chance to recoup the insular government's initial investments in industrial development without burdening it with the future costs of operations, the PRCC had in fact registered considerable profits during World War II. Its sale, in other words, was not a financial inevitability. Once celebrated by Puerto Rican engineers as a major achievement of the New Deal era, the Cataño plant was eventually shuttered by Ferré Enterprises in favor of their enlarged Ponce cement plant. In 2002, the family sold the Ponce Cement Company to CEMEX of Mexico, the world's leading supplier of ready-mix concrete. Ironically, the sale of the Cataño plant to the Ferré family generated millions of dollars in profits during the Cold War suburbanization boom, and by the 1960s, the Ferré family were among the island's largest industrialists and most noted art collectors, philanthropists, and political leaders of the resurgent statehood movement. José Ferré's brother, Luis A. Ferré, cofounded the pro-statehood New Progressive Party and was elected governor of Puerto Rico in 1968, displacing the PPD after two decades in power.[14]

During the war, however, the Cataño plant played an instrumental role in the island's mobilization as the PRCC sold discounted cement to the WPA, the War Department, the War Emergency Program, and a variety of private contractors. Shifting almost entirely to defense production, the PRCC sold 90 percent of its cement and concrete to war industries while the Ponce Cement Corporation sold roughly 99 percent of its output to the federal government. At Cataño, cement production increased over 300 percent from nearly 375,000 barrels in 1940 to over 1.1 million barrels in 1945 due to the construction of military bases, docks, and airfields such as the Borinquen Army Air Field (later called Ramey Air Force Base), the Roosevelt Roads Naval Station, and the National Guard and naval training facilities on the islands of Vieques and Culebra.[15] Just as wartime development turned U.S. cities such as Detroit and Oakland into the "arsenal of democracy," military construction helped transform Puerto Rico into, in the words of Jorge Rodríguez Beruff and José L. Bolívar, the "bulwark of the Caribbean."[16] Much of that development was aided by locally produced cement from the PRCC and discounted electric power provided by the WRA.

The PRRA also transitioned to wartime construction as its engineers and workers built defense-oriented designs such as a steel truss bridge over the Río Grande de Loíza in Trujillo Alto (along today's Highway 181); a 2,000-foot-long tunnel in Old San Juan connecting the Spanish fortifications of San Felipe del Morro, San Cristóbal, and San Gerónimo; and the construction of seven regional airfields in Dorado, Vega Baja, Arecibo, Mayagüez, Santa Isabel, Salinas, and Ponce.[17] Working with the War Department, the PRRA also embarked on a variety of aquatic internal improvements ranging from flood control on several of the island's rivers, including the Buncana and Portugués in Ponce, Chico in Patillas, Guamani in Guayama, Lapa in Cayey, and Maunabo in Maunabo, to improvements of the large harbors in San Juan and Mayagüez and smaller ones in Aguadilla, Arecibo, Fajardo, Guanica, Guayanes, Humacao, and Ponce.[18]

The rapid construction of military works brought an influx of wartime dollars into the Puerto Rican economy and turned the island into one of the largest anti-submarine commands in the world. As César Ayala and José Bolívar have estimated, per capita wartime spending in Puerto Rico outpaced the amount spent on Western Europe by the Marshall Plan.[19] Following the attack on Pearl Harbor and declaration of war against the Axis Powers, Nazi U-boats moved their deadly operations from the British Isles to the Caribbean and western Atlantic in a lethal campaign against cargo ships that supplied U.S. manufacturers with raw materials from Latin

America. The U-boat campaign inflicted substantial loss of life and property to U.S., West Indian, Latin American, and European-based cargo ships and merchant marine crew members. During 1942, for example, while the U.S. Navy focused on rebuilding the Pacific fleet at Pearl Harbor, the United States sank just one submarine for every 23.5 cargo ships sunk in the Caribbean or western Atlantic by German U-boats. Accounting for 80 percent of all Caribbean casualties and 20 percent of all Allied shipping losses during the entire war, direct attack on cargo ships brought the fear, uncertainty, and violence of the Second World War to the people of the Caribbean and West Indies.[20] Since radar was still in development at this time (and not widely used until at least 1943) Nazi submariners toyed with the crews of merchant ships from their underwater lairs, from which they launched both day- and nighttime raids, blowing holes in ships and watching them sink. Some U-boats stalked survivors so close that merchant seamen, treading water, could distinctly hear their own death orders being given to gun crews.[21]

Although its hydroelectrification and cement-based public works were instrumental to the war effort, the PRRA's attempt to revitalize the island's agricultural sector through soil conservation, bovine and fruit pest eradication, and the support of cooperative farming initiatives did not make up for the decreased food imports during the war. Indeed, the U-boat campaign had dire consequences for the people and societies of the Caribbean region. In Puerto Rico, for example, the Nazi submarine war resulted in a dramatic decrease in food and other supplies just as the island was beginning to recover from the decade-long turmoil caused by the Great Depression and San Felipe and San Ciprián hurricanes. As elsewhere, the decline in food imports, construction materials, medical supplies, and other necessities of daily life on the island was compounded by increased unemployment and threatened the fragile recovery that had begun during the New Deal. Likewise, the submarine campaign also halted exports of valuable commodities like coffee, sugar, tobacco, and tropical fruit.[22]

World War II continued and expanded New Deal efforts to maximize employment. In addition to the large number of Puerto Ricans who served in the military, others found work on PRRA, WPA, and other New Deal defense projects. Ranging from highly skilled engineers and administrators to common laborers, many of whom had job experience in the PRERA and PRRA, Puerto Rican men and women were employed in both civil and military construction across the island during the early years of the war.[23] Additionally, according to monthly civilian personnel reports, the War Department's engineering office in San Juan employed over eighteen thousand men and women workers by November 1943.[24] About one-quarter of these workers were employed on civil engineering projects, such as utilities work and river navigation projects. The remaining three-quarters were employed on military projects. While the vast majority of the construction-related jobs were held by men, nearly 50 percent of those employed in clerical and office work were women.[25] Among nonclerical work, however, only 268 of the War Department's 1,339 employees were women: one in a subprofessional grade, one in craft grade, and 266 in clerical grade. In the field, only sixteen of the Department's 11,391 skilled, semiskilled, or unskilled workers were women.[26]

The defense of the Caribbean was not a peripheral event to the history of Puerto Rico or to the broader course of World War II. Rather, defending the region against submarine attack was central to the protection of thousands of miles of coastline and natural resources in North America, Central America, South America, and the Caribbean. By the end of 1943, Allied defenses operating out of Puerto Rico and other strategic locations had eliminated the lethal threat of German torpedoes in the Western Hemisphere and helped win the Battle of the Atlantic. Doing so was a vital aspect of Allied war strategy, as it enabled the United States to gain control of ocean commerce between the Americas and Africa, Europe, and the United Kingdom. The control of the Atlantic not only resulted in the unencumbered transport of food, arms, and medical supplies from North and South American ports but was also vital to the planning and timing of the Allied invasion of Europe in June 1944, its liberation, and the eventual defeat of Nazi Germany in 1945.[27]

The PRRA's modernization program also left a large imprint on Puerto Rican politics. In doing so, the New Deal brought Puerto Rico closer in line with regional political developments—as populist political coalitions were forming in other areas of Latin America and the Caribbean—even as it strengthened the colonial bonds holding the island within the U.S. territorial system. After 1940, the PRRA's public works program and land reform agenda were continued and expanded by the Popular Democratic Party, which worked closely with the PRRA to ensure a seamless transition of its works to the insular government. In addition, many members of the PRRA leadership team went to work directly for the PPD-controlled legislature and, eventually, governor's office. While the exact form of populism led by Luis Muñoz Marín and the PPD shared many characteristics with the development of populism in other urbanizing Latin American and Caribbean nations during the 1930s and 1940s, particularly Cuba and the Dominican Republic, it differed from them by its colonial relationship with the United States.[28]

Puerto Rico's ties to other parts of the region were also fostered by an extensive public relations campaign in Latin America. Led by Antonio Cruz y Nieves and John W. Thomson, the PRRA's information and research section produced an array of Spanish-language publicity and cultural propaganda in published print media, broadcast radio, and filmed newsreels. The section's Spanish-language publicity detailed the agency's programs ranging from cattle tick elimination to rural electrification, and was printed in newspapers and magazines for distribution in Puerto Rico and throughout other areas of Latin America and the Caribbean. For example, the information and research section published educational materials designed to help farmers adapt to modern agricultural practices. One such publication, "El Granjero y su Casa" (The Farmer and His House), was written in Spanish in clear and concise language. According to Miles Fairbank, the monthly journal was well received not only by farmers, agricultural workers, schools, and cultural workers on the island but also by officials in "other Latin American countries, several of whom are on our regular mailing list."[29] In addition, the information and research section publicized its rural rehabilitation work to readers in Argentina, Bolivia, Brazil, Colombia, Chile, Costa Rica, Cuba, Dominican Republic, Ecuador, Guatemala, Mexico, Peru, Uruguay, and Venezuela. The PRRA also provided information in English and contributed to the WPA Federal Writers' Project series of state and territorial guidebooks. Reviewed and edited by leading Puerto Rican scholars and editors, *Puerto Rico: A Guide to the Island and Boriquén* featured brief essays on the island's social, political, and natural history; its architecture, industry, and commerce; and its religion, sports, and culture.[30]

The emergence of Puerto Rican populism was connected to the victory of the Popular Democratic Party in the election of 1940, when Muñoz Marín was elected to serve as president of the Puerto Rican Senate. The election marked the end of the Coalition's control of the insular legislature, which it had enjoyed since 1933. The PPD had been formed only a few years earlier from the ashes of an intraorganizational rivalry within the Liberal Party that reached its breaking point in 1937, when Muñoz was formally expelled from the party. While he remains a highly debated figure in Puerto Rican politics today, Muñoz brought a large segment of the population together, including members of diverse classes and political parties, who felt alienated from contemporary political leaders. Ranging from impoverished sugar and farm workers to bankrupt but once-prominent coffee hacendados and sugar colonos in rural areas, and from unemployed professionals, students, and intellectuals to new industrial workers in urban areas, members of the PPD included former Liberals and Socialists alike. Claiming the image of the jíbaro and the Puerto Rican countryside as its own, the PPD was able to build a New Deal–style political coalition based on party loyalty in exchange for direct government intervention in public works, land reform, employment, and rural rehabilitation.[31]

During the 1940 campaign, Muñoz was able to distance himself from the most unpopular elements of the federal government while, at the same time, skillfully presenting the PPD as the logical heir to the popular modernization and colonial reform programs of the New Deal years. Contrasting himself and his nascent party with the ousted Rafael Martínez Nadal and Coalition, Muñoz advocated for the continuation of PRRA reconstruction projects and a redoubled emphasis on land reform, instilling the future of a revived New Deal with a greater cultural nationalism.[32] He was able to do this by blurring the lines between the PRRA and the PPD in the public eye while maintaining a close relationship with key PRRA administrators, such as Guillermo Esteves and Antonio Lucchetti. Between 1941 and 1944, Muñoz kept close watch on PRRA construction projects through official and unofficial channels, taking reports from Esteves and conveying them directly to the broader Puerto Rican populace through radio and newspapers. He was so proficient on the minutiae of PRRA workings that many people were convinced that he was in charge of the programs, writing to his Senate office seeking employment in the PRRA.[33]

Muñoz's strategy was effective during the early part of the war because it was unclear who would lead the New Deal during the 1940s. As a federal relief agency tasked with helping the island's recovery from the hurricanes and Great Depression, the PRRA was not designed to be a permanent political institution. Throughout 1939 and 1940, Miles Fairbank unsuccessfully tried to generate support in Washington and San Juan for the creation of what he called the Insular Reconstruction Authority. The plan was to create a public corporation that would outlive the PRRA as a permanent credit agency for Puerto Rico and the U.S. Virgin Islands subsidized by $25 million (about $532 million today) in federal funds to assist in the industrialization of agriculture and promote increased economic self-sufficiency. Under the plan, the insular government would have had the ability to raise an additional $80 million ($1.7 billion today) through the sale of bonds.

Fairbank wrote the bill, gave addresses at Mayagüez and other locations, and garnered press attention, but the plan was never sponsored in Congress. According to Luz Marie Rodríguez, Fairbank was so committed to the plan that he had PRRA architect Germán Ramírez de Arellano design Spanish-styled offices for the Insular Reconstruction Authority to be located at the site where PRRA's offices stood—within Luis Muñoz Rivera Park in Puerta de Tierra where the Supreme Court is located today. But it was never built. In taking a shot at the insular Republican Party, Fairbank also displayed his lack of understanding about the mass mobilization of rural Puerto Ricans being undertaken by the Popular Democratic Party. "Puerto Rico has one class of leadership, largely absentee," he expressed, "that for reasons of its own will not take the initiative in such a program. Another class is intelligent, but is lacking in coordination and resources and stands by waiting for guidance. The great mass of the population is bewildered at the economic crisis."[34]

Muñoz campaigned in 1940 on land reform. As attorney general, Benigno Fernández García's actions against the sugar industry helped generate mass popular support for the PPD in the 1940 election and after.[35] Since the development of the Chardón Plan, Muñoz had consistently advocated the enforcement of the 500-Acre Law and made it the central issue of his campaign. Resistance from sugar and other landed interests in the Republican Party had thwarted nearly all legal challenges and legislative attempts to break up the large agricultural corporations, limited companies, partnerships, trusts, voluntary associations, and other private organizations, whether owned by local or absentee capital.[36] Even the limited land reform law passed by the Coalition in 1935 (Law 47) had stalled, when sugar interests tied up the legislation in court. In March 1940, however, the Supreme Court delivered corporate landholding a blow when it upheld the 1935 law. Muñoz celebrated the decision in the pages of *La Democracia*, claiming he was now liberated to write an even stronger law.[37] On April 22, 1941, the insular legislature passed the Land Law of 1941 (Law 26) and established the Puerto Rico Land Authority as a public corporation to enforce it. Building on the Supreme Court case, the new law connected the PPD with the various strains of the PRRA agricultural rehabilitation and land resettlement programs.[38]

The creation of the Land Authority allowed the PRRA to liquidate its own land resettlement and rural rehabilitation programs; the PPD-controlled legislature simply took over the work, with employees moving seamlessly from the PRRA's payroll to that of the insular government.[39]

The Land Law allowed the insular government to distribute land to landless farmworker families through settlement communities called parcelas, on which plots would be used for subsistence farming while family heads would be able to continue to work for wages. As anthropologist Ismael García-Colón has argued, the insular government intended to make land tenure more democratic through parcela distributions, which would "eliminate social relations of servitude, and settle Puerto Rico's highly mobile landless workers." To these ends, the law "stipulated that residents of the community hold only tax-free usufruct rights rather than ownership titles" and that they "could not transfer, sell, change, rent, give, or assign their rights of usufruct without losing rights to their parcels."[40] As García-Colón has shown, land reform and redistribution "facilitated migration as an escape valve for unemployment" and transformed the agrarian economy by "providing landless families with land for housing purposes and subsistence agriculture, allowing women and men to migrate for work in the manufacture and service sectors."[41]

Large sugar and other landed interests continued to fight against efforts to break up their holdings that exceeded five hundred acres through sworn testimony and by bringing lawsuits against the Land Law. The last of a day-long line of sugar interest representatives, Rafael Gonzáles, testified that breaking up large plantations would only decrease income and employment. Russell & Co., owner of the South Puerto Rico Sugar Company of New Jersey, filed a legal injunction to prevent its lands from being expropriated by the new law. Their affidavit stated that the company's lands were valued at $3 million (about $63.6 million today) and its crops at $2 million (about $42.4 million).[42] Interestingly, however, sugar's reaction to the new law only increased the PPD's standing in the mind of the public; popular support for land reform remained high. When the first land distributions began in Gándara in 1945, corporate interests sued the government to stop the expropriation and redistribution of land, as they feared the program would empower formerly landless workers and enable them to more easily leave their jobs. Despite opposition from the island's Republican Party, land reform moved forward and became, during the next two decades, one of the most popular government programs among the rural population who were the base of PPD support.[43]

On September 19, 1941, just five months after the creation of the Land Authority, Roosevelt appointed Rexford G. Tugwell to serve as the governor of Puerto Rico. Although Tugwell had been interested in Puerto Rican affairs for some time and offered advice to the Chardón group, he had never been directly involved in any New Deal activities on the island. Muñoz Marín cabled Franklin and Eleanor Roosevelt to say that Tugwell would have the full support of the Puerto Rican people. He was briefly named the chancellor of the UPR before being appointed governor.[44]

Like Muñoz, Tugwell believed that the PPD would continue the Puerto Rican New Deal into the 1940s and beyond. Upon arriving on the island, however, Tugwell had initially assumed that the Farm Security Administration (FSA) would be heir to the PRRA. He named a mixture of Puerto Rican and American officials to the board of directors of the Land Authority, including Carlos Chardón, whom he asked to return from Venezuela to run the land program and enforce the 500-Acre Law. Others include Ralph Will of the FSA, Rafael Picó and Rafael Menéndez Ramos of the UPR, and Acosta Velarde of the sugar industry. After taking office, Tugwell became convinced that the PPD was the best vehicle to revive the Puerto Rican New Deal and immediately began working to involve the Muñoz and the PPD-controlled legislature in PRRA affairs.[45]

Tugwell shared Muñoz's vision of transferring all PRRA public works to the insular government and informed Roosevelt that 90 percent of the Puerto Rican public were in favor of continuing New Deal programs. He was, in other words, confident that the PPD could hold its slim but significant majority in the insular legislature and prevent the Coalition from retuning to power. The PPD controlled the legislature by "about one vote in each house," he wrote to Roosevelt in January 1942. "But it is a well-disciplined majority. And we expect to do a lot of business [with the PPD]. I am well aware that our sugar friends and the Coalitionists have been hoping to stop the Puerto Rican New Deal with martial law."[46] Working together, Muñoz and Tugwell created nineteen public corporations and at least forty-one new insular agencies, expanding the number of bureaucratic public servants on the island from 15,000 to over 21,000, and more than doubling the insular budget from $47 million (about $893 million today) to almost $113 million (about $2.1 billion).[47]

On the cultural front, the PPD's populist program was aided by the insular Division of Community Education (DIVEDCO), established in 1949. Building on the work of the PRRA's information and research section, DIVEDCO used educational films, visual arts, and written works to educate poor and working-class Puerto Ricans—particularly jíbaros and campesinos—about modern life and, at the same time, produce works that could be internationally viewed and exhibited. While DIVEDCO was originally organized by New Dealers such as sociologist Fred Wale and photographers Edwin and Louise Rosskam and Jack and Irene Delano, it soon cultivated the work of a legendary cohort of Puerto Rican writers and visual artists such as Pedro Juan Soto, René Marques, José Luis Vivas Maldonado, Rafael Trufiño, and Lorenzo Homar. DIVEDCO films and other works were often exhibited in schools and community centers built by the PRRA in the rural countryside and explored topics such as public health, medicine, sanitation, scientific agriculture, adult literacy, housing, and consumerism.[48]

By establishing an administrative structure that allowed for the transfer of PRRA programs to the local legislature, Tugwell fortified the PPD's position and offered Muñoz control over the powerful patronage mechanisms that formed one component of its populist political coalition. Upon Tugwell's return to the continental United States in September 1946, Harry Truman appointed Jesús T. Piñero as governor of Puerto Rico. A founding member of the PPD, Piñero had been born in Carolina, Puerto Rico, in 1897 to a wealthy sugar farming family. He became close to Muñoz in the early 1930s and was elected to serve as resident commissioner in 1944.[49] Piñero's appointment—the first time a Puerto Rican had been named governor on a non-interim basis—was a product of the PPD's populist moment and should not be credited to Truman or Tugwell. During his administration, the PPD lobbied Congress for greater political autonomy within the colonial system; when Truman signed the Elective Governor's Act on August 5, 1947, Puerto Ricans were permitted to directly elect their own governor for the first time. A year later, in November 1948, Muñoz Marín swept 76 of 77 municipal districts on the island and won the election with 61 percent of the popular vote; he was sworn in as the first elected governor on January 2, 1949.[50] In office, Muñoz worked to establish the Estado Libre Asociado or Commonwealth of Puerto Rico, which was inaugurated on July 25, 1952, about three years before the liquidation of the PRRA in 1955.[51]

The successes and failures of the Commonwealth as a colonial reform project designed to transform the economy and resolve the status question are subjects of political debate that stretch beyond the limits of this book. Muñoz's populist political coalition, based in part on PRRA programs of land reform, public works, and economic modernization, dominated Puerto Rican politics until 1968, with Muñoz serving as governor until 1964 and Roberto Sánchez Vilella serving one term until 1968. That year, when Sánchez Vilella was defeated by Luis A. Ferré and the New Progressive Party, it marked a new era in Puerto Rican politics. While many PRRA engineers, planners, and experts were members of the PPD, some would have conceded that the party's populist project was in actuality less ambitious than the original designs of the Chardón Plan or the extensive public works campaigns of the New Deal years.

Shortly after its creation in 1939, the Puerto Rico Cement Corporation adopted the phrase PARA PERMANENCIA as its company slogan. As found on its stationery, packaging, complimentary matchbooks, and other advertisements, this motto served as a kind of mantra for the work of the PRRA and a symbol for the entire Puerto Rican New Deal. The hurricane-proof houses, schools, hospitals, drinking water and sewerage systems, and other vital public health infrastructure constructed by Puerto Rican workers with locally made cement became lasting components of the island's built environment. While some engineers and workers sought to provide lasting recovery from the effects of San Felipe, San Ciprián, and the Great Depression, others sought to regenerate social conditions by transforming the island's economy from one built around agriculture to one based on industry. The slogan, which was continued to be used by Ferré Enterprises after they acquired the PRCC, can also be seen today as a prescient comment on the ways in which the PRRA's increased intervention into daily life enhanced the U.S. colonial control of Puerto Rico during the New Deal and into our times.

NOTES

Introduction

1 Although Puerto Rico is an archipelago, this book uses "Puerto Rico" and the colloquial phrase "the island" interchangeably. Similarly, while it is by law an unincorporated territory, this book refers to Puerto Rico as a colonial possession of the United States. All dollar amounts in this book have been adjusted for inflation to 2023 dollars using the Bureau of Labor Statistics inflation calculator, located at https://www.bls.gov/data/inflation_calculator.htm. For example, the total expenditures of the PRRA were $82 million in Depression-era dollars, which equates to $1.739 billion today. Of this amount, $69.7 million ($1.478 billion) was appropriated from Congress and $12.3 million ($260.9 million) came from a PRRA-generated revolving fund.

2 On the study of natural disasters, see Louis A. Pérez Jr., *Winds of Change: Hurricanes and the Transformation of Nineteenth-Century Cuba* (Chapel Hill: University of North Carolina Press, 2001); Mike Davis, *Late Victorian Holocausts: El Niño Famines and the Making of the Third World* (London: Verso, 2002); Ted Steinberg, *Acts of God: The Unnatural History of Natural Disasters* (New York: Oxford University Press, 2006); Mark Healey, *The Ruins of the New Argentina: Peronism and the Remaking of San Juan after the 1944 Earthquake* (Durham, NC: Duke University Press, 2011); Sherry Johnson, *Climate and Catastrophe in Cuba and the Atlantic World in the Age of Revolution* (Chapel Hill: University of North Carolina Press, 2011); Stuart B. Schwartz, *Sea of Storms: A History of Hurricanes in the Greater Caribbean from Columbus to Katrina* (Princeton, NJ: Princeton University Press, 2015); June Carolyn Erlick, *Natural Disasters in Latin America and the Caribbean: Coping with Calamity* (New York: Taylor & Francis, 2021); Magdalena Gil, "Disasters as Critical Junctures: State Building and Industrialization in Chile after the Chillán Earthquake of 1939," *Latin American Research Review* 57 (2022): 775–793.

3 Over the last two decades, several studies have examined the global reaches of U.S. domestic policy, including David Ekbladh, "'Mr. TVA': Grass-Roots Development, David Lilienthal, and the Rise and Fall of the Tennessee Valley Authority as a Symbol for U.S. Overseas Development, 1933–1973," *Diplomatic History* 26, no. 3 (Summer 2002): 335–374; Elizabeth Borgwardt, *A New Deal for the World: America's Vision for Human Rights* (Cambridge, MA: Belknap Press, 2007); David Ekbladh, *The*

156 · Notes to Pages 3–6

Great American Mission: Modernization and the Construction of an American World Order (Princeton, NJ: Princeton University Press, 2011); Kiran Klaus Patel, *The New Deal: A Global History* (Princeton, NJ: Princeton University Press, 2017); Tore Olsson, *Agrarian Crossings: Reformers and the Remaking of the U.S. and Mexican Countryside* (Princeton, NJ: Princeton University Press, 2017); Geoff G. Burrows, "Rural Hydro-Electrification and the Colonial New Deal: Modernization, Experts, and Rural Life in Puerto Rico, 1935–1942," *Agricultural History* 91, no. 3 (Summer 2017): 239–319; Daniel Immerwahr, *How to Hide an Empire: A History of the Greater United States* (New York: Farrar, Strauss & Giroux, 2019); Amy Offner, *Sorting Out the Mixed Economy: The Rise and Fall of Welfare and Developmental States in the Americas* (Princeton, NJ: Princeton University Press, 2019).

4 On the New Deal as a holding operation, see Anthony J. Badger, *The New Deal: The Depression Years, 1933–1940* (Chicago: Ivan R. Dee, 1989), 3–10.

5 For example, see Gaylord T. M. Kelshall, *The U-Boat War in the Caribbean* (1988; repr., Annapolis, MD: Naval Institute Press, 1994), 8; Fitzroy André Baptiste, *War, Cooperation and Conflict: The European Possessions in the Caribbean, 1939–1945* (New York: Greenwood, 1988), 79–81, 160.

6 Schwartz, *Sea of Storms*, 227, 252. According to Schwartz, the decade between 1925 and 1935 experienced more Atlantic hurricanes than any time in the previous five hundred years, partly due to El Niño conditions in the Pacific Ocean, which were also a leading cause of the Dust Bowl. On the environmental impact of the Depression years, see Sarah T. Phillips, *This Land, This Nation: Conservation, Rural America, and the New Deal* (New York: Cambridge University Press, 2007); Timothy Egan, *The Worst Hard Time* (New York: Mariner, 2006).

7 After the Treaty of Paris, Puerto Rico and Guam were ceded to U.S. military control, Cuba became independent of Spain, and the United States purchased control of the Philippines for $20 million (over $600 million today). Hawaii was annexed to the United States in the same year. While France had begun building an isthmus canal in the 1880s, the United States acquired the site in 1903 and completed the Panama Canal in 1914—control of which offered great influence over oceanic trade for the rest of the century. For more on the Cuban-Spanish-American War and the Philippine-Spanish-American War, see Louis A. Pérez Jr., *The War of 1898: The United States and Cuba in History and Historiography* (Chapel Hill: University of North Carolina Press, 1998); Paul Kramer, *The Blood of Government: Race, Empire, the United States and the Philippines* (Chapel Hill: University of North Carolina Press, 2006); Antonio Gaztambide-Géigel, *Tan Lejos de Dios . . . Ensayos sobre las relaciones del Caribe con Estados Unidos* (San Juan: Ediciones Callejón, 2006); Julian Go, *American Empire and the Politics of Meaning: Elite Political Cultures in the Philippines and Puerto Rico during U.S. Colonialism* (Durham, NC: Duke University Press, 2008); Alfred W. McCoy and Francisco A. Scarano, eds., *Colonial Crucible: Empire and the Making of the Modern American State* (Madison: University of Wisconsin Press, 2009); Paul Kramer, "How Not to Write the History of U.S. Empire," *Diplomatic History* 42, no. 5 (2018): 911–931.

Notes to Pages 6–7 · 157

8 Christina Duffy Burnett and Burke Marshall, "Between the Foreign and Domestic: The Doctrine of Territorial Incorporation, Invented and Reinvented," in Duffy Burnett and Marshall, eds., *Foreign in a Domestic Sense: Puerto Rico, American Expansion, and the Constitution* (Durham, NC: Duke University Press, 2002), 1–2, 13; Efrén Rivera Ramos, "Deconstructing Colonialism: The 'Unincorporated Territory' as a Category of Domination," in *Foreign in a Domestic Sense*, 113. For racist language, see text of *Downes v. Bidwell*, 182 U.S. 244 (1901). For the makeup of the Supreme Court in 1901, see José Trías Monge, *Puerto Rico: The Trials of the Oldest Colony in the World* (New Haven, CT: Yale University Press, 1997); Bartholomew Sparrow, *The Insular Cases and the Emergence of American Empire* (Lawrence: University Press of Kansas, 2006). Puerto Rico's unincorporated status remains in place today as it does in Guam, the Northern Marianas, and the U.S. Virgin Islands, whose residents are also birthright U.S. citizens. American Samoa is also an unincorporated territory, but its population are U.S. nationals rather than citizens. As recently as April 2022, the Insular Cases have been used as precedent for the unequal legal protection of Puerto Ricans living on the island: in an 8–1 decision, the court decided in favor of the United States in the case of *U.S. v. Vaello Madero*, with Sonya Sotomayor providing the lone dissent. In a separate opinion, Neil Gorsuch noted that the Insular Cases should be overturned as they "rest on racial stereotypes" and "deserve no place in our law." See "High Court Rules Congress Can Exclude Puerto Ricans from Aid Program," *Washington Post*, April 21, 2022. See also Supreme Court decisions in *Sánchez Valle v. Puerto Rico* (2016) and *Puerto Rico v. Franklin California Tax-Free Trust* (2016). On the legal difference between incorporated and unincorporated territories, I have consulted "Definitions of Insular Area Political Organizations," Office of Insular Affairs, U.S. Department of the Interior, https://www.doi.gov/oia/islands/politicatypes.

9 On the dichotomy between U.S. citizenship and colonial subjectivity, see Ismael García-Colón, "'We Like Mexican Laborers Better': Citizenship and Immigration Policies in the Formation of Puerto Rican Farm Labor in the United States," *Centro Journal* 29, no. 2 (Summer 2017): 134–171. The Jones-Shafroth Act was written by representative William Atkinson Jones (D-VA) and senator John Shafroth (D-CO), the chairs of the House Committee on Insular Affairs and Senate Committee on Pacific Islands and Puerto Rico, respectively. For Wilson, the law was an extension of progressivism to the territories that provided a dramatic contrast to the policies of his political opponents from the Republican and Progressive Parties, especially former presidents Theodore Roosevelt and William Howard Taft. The law was also part of Wilson's vision of an era of New Freedom and had global implications beyond Puerto Rico. It was passed at the same time that Wilson sought to build moral consent for U.S. entry into the Great War by arguing that the United States must make the world "safe for democracy," just two months before the Selective Service Act, which permitted the drafting of U.S. citizens into military service. Approximately 20,000 Puerto Ricans served in World War I. Historian Harry Franqui-Rivera has disproven the misnomer that citizenship was extended to Puerto Ricans in order to

158 · Notes to Pages 9–10

draft them into the war. Rather, Puerto Ricans were seen by military leadership as undesirable and inadequate for combat. See Harry Franqui-Rivera, *Soldiers of the Nation: Military Service and Modern Puerto Rico, 1868–1952* (Lincoln: University of Nebraska Press, 2018).

10 Marlene Park and Gerald E. Markowitz, *Democratic Vistas: Post Offices and Public Art in the New Deal* (Philadelphia: Temple University Press, 1984), 3. This more democratic understanding of economic citizenship was sharply constrained along racial and gender lines and was often stifled by regional (i.e., southern) politics. See James T. Patterson, *Congressional Conservatism and the New Deal: The Growth of the Conservative Coalition in Congress, 1933–1939* (Lexington: University Press of Kentucky, 1967); Ira Katznelson, *When Affirmative Action Was White: An Untold History of Racial Inequality in Twentieth-Century America* (New York: Norton, 2005); Ira Katznelson, *Fear Itself: The New Deal and the Origins of Our Time* (New York: Norton, 2013).

11 Morton Keller, ed., *The New Deal: What Was It?* (New York: Holt, Rinehart & Winston, 1964), 1–2. See also Badger, *New Deal*, 2.

12 On the AAA in Puerto Rico, see Rafael Bernabe, "Prehistory of the Partido Popular Democrático: Muñoz Marin, the Partido Liberal and the Crisis of Sugar in Puerto Rico, 1930–35" (PhD diss., State University of New York at Binghamton, 1989); César J. Ayala, *American Sugar Kingdom: The Plantation Economy of the Spanish Caribbean, 1898–1934* (Chapel Hill: University of North Carolina Press, 1999); Manuel R. Rodríguez, "Representing Development: New Perspectives about the New Deal in Puerto Rico, 1933–1936," *Centro Journal* 14, no. 2 (2002): 149–179; Teresita A. Levy, *Puerto Ricans in the Empire: Tobacco Growers and U.S. Colonialism* (New Brunswick, NJ: Rutgers University Press, 2014); César J. Ayala and Laird W. Bergad, *Agrarian Puerto Rico: Reconsidering Rural Economy and Society, 1899–1940* (Cambridge: Cambridge University Press, 2020). On the PRERA, see Manuel R. Rodríguez's landmark *A New Deal for the Tropics: Puerto Rico during the Depression Era, 1932–1935* (Princeton, NJ: Markus Wiener, 2010).

13 A mycologist by training, Carlos Chardón was chancellor of the University of Puerto Rico and one of the leading intellectuals of the Liberal Party. The Chardón Plan outlined the basic structure of the PRRA in 1934. Harold Ickes was a progressive Republican from Chicago chosen by Roosevelt to lead the Department of the Interior. He was a staunch proponent of publicly funded infrastructure and a longtime critic of unregulated monopolies. In addition to serving as secretary of the interior, he headed the PWA and was influential in the New Deal's environmental policy. As a former president of the Chicago NAACP, Ickes was (with Eleanor Roosevelt) one of the leading voices on race relations in Roosevelt's cabinet. Former editor of the *Nation*, Ernest Gruening was a diplomatic journalist who worked for the *Boston Herald*, *New York Tribune*, and *La Prensa*. He had an abiding interest in Latin American relations and was an unwavering advocate of the Good Neighbor Policy. Gruening was hired by Ickes to lead the Division of Territories and Island Possessions in 1934; he later served as governor of the Alaska Territory and, after it was granted statehood in 1959, as senator from Alaska.

14 Miles H. Fairbank was an administrator for the Maryland Farm Bureau who served as the head of the PRRA's Rural Rehabilitation Division before becoming its assistant administrator in 1937. Before serving as the regional and then assistant administrator of the PRRA, Guillermo Esteves Volkers was the commissioner of the insular Interior Department and one of the most respected civil engineers on the island.

15 While this book is centered on infrastructural and economic modernization led by the technocratic sector, there have been many other approaches to Puerto Rican modernization. For an excellent analysis of the cultural dimensions of modernization in education and school reform, see Solsiree del Moral, *Negotiating Empire: The Cultural Politics of Schools in Puerto Rico, 1898–1952* (Madison: University of Wisconsin Press, 2011). On how progressive science impacted race, gender, and reproduction, see Eileen J. Suárez Findlay, *Imposing Decency: The Politics of Sexuality and Race in Puerto Rico, 1870–1920* (Durham, NC: Duke University Press, 2000); Laura Briggs, *Reproducing Empire: Race, Sex, Science, and U.S. Imperialism in Puerto Rico* (Berkeley: University of California Press, 2002). For an analysis of radical and working-class visions of modernity, see Jorell Meléndez-Badillo, *The Lettered Barriada: Workers, Archival Power, and the Politics of Knowledge in Puerto Rico* (Durham, NC: Duke University Press, 2021).

16 On the end of the New Deal's reform impulse, see Alan Brinkley, *The End of Reform: New Deal Liberalism in Recession and War* (New York: Vintage, 1995). See also William E. Leuchtenburg, *Franklin D. Roosevelt and the New Deal: 1932–1940* (1963; repr., New York: Harper Collins, 2009); Michael Bernstein, *The Great Depression: Delayed Recovery and Economic Change in America, 1929–1939* (Cambridge: Cambridge University Press, 1987); Badger, *New Deal*; Steve Fraser and Gary Gerstle, *The Rise and Fall of the New Deal Order, 1930–1980* (Princeton, NJ: Princeton University Press, 1989); Jason Scott Smith, *Building New Deal Liberalism: The Political Economy of Public Works, 1933–1956* (Cambridge: Cambridge University Press, 2006); Robert D. Leighninger Jr., *Long-Range Public Investment: The Forgotten Legacy of the New Deal* (Charleston: University of South Carolina Press, 2007). On the New Deal in Puerto Rico, see Rexford G. Tugwell, *Changing the Colonial Climate* (1942; repr., New York: Arno Press, 1970); Thomas G. Mathews, *Puerto Rican Politics and the New Deal* (1960; repr., New York: Da Capo Press, 1974); Gordon K. Lewis, *Puerto Rico: Freedom and Power in the Caribbean* (New York: Monthly Review, 1963); Henry Wells, *The Modernization of Puerto Rico: A Political Study of Changing Values and Institutions* (Cambridge, MA: Harvard University Press, 1969); Gordon K. Lewis, *Notes on the Puerto Rican Revolution: An Essay on American Dominance and Caribbean Resistance* (New York: Monthly Review, 1974); James L. Dietz, *Economic History of Puerto Rico: Institutional Change and Capitalist Development* (Princeton, NJ: Princeton University Press, 1986); José Trias Monge, *Puerto Rico: The Trials of the Oldest Colony in the World* (New Haven, CT: Yale University Press, 1997); Rodríguez, "Representing Development"; Rodríguez, *New Deal for the Tropics*. On the more recent notion of a so-called Long New Deal lasting between 1933 and 1953, see Gary Gerstle, review of Ira Katznelson, *Fear Itself: The New Deal and the Origins of*

160 · Notes to Pages 12–13

Our Time (New York: Norton, 2013), *Journal of American History* 100, no. 4 (March 2014): 1171–1173.

17 Following George Rosen, this book uses the term "public health" to mean the "protection of the community against communicable diseases and sanitation of the environment." George Rosen, *A History of Public Health*, expanded ed. (Baltimore: Johns Hopkins University Press, 1993), 320. There is a rich historiography on Puerto Rican migration, including History Task Force of the Centro de Estudios Puertorriqueños, *Labor Migration under Capitalism: The Puerto Rican Experience* (New York: Monthly Review, 1979); Virginia E. Sánchez Korrol, *From Colonia to Community: The History of Puerto Ricans in New York City* (1983; repr., Berkeley: University of California Press, 1994); Jorge Duany, *The Puerto Rican Nation on the Move: Identities on the Island and in the United States* (Chapel Hill: University of North Carolina Press, 2002); Gina Pérez, *The Near Northwest Side Story: Migration, Displacement, and Puerto Rican Families* (Berkeley: University of California Press, 2004); Arlene Dávila, *Barrio Dreams: Puerto Ricans, Latinos, and the Neoliberal City* (Berkeley: University of California Press, 2004); Carmen Teresa Whalen and Víctor Vázquez-Hernández, *Puerto Rican Diaspora: Historical Perspectives* (Philadelphia: Temple University Press, 2005); Jorge Duany, *Blurred Borders: Transnational Migration between the Hispanic Caribbean and the United States* (Chapel Hill: University of North Carolina Press, 2011); Edgardo Meléndez, *Sponsored Migration: The State and Puerto Rican Postwar Migration to the United States* (Columbus: Ohio State University Press, 2017); Lorrin R. Thomas and Aldo A. Lauria Santiago, *Rethinking the Struggle for Puerto Rican Rights* (New York: Routledge, 2018); Ismael García-Colón, *Migrants at the Heart of Empire: Puerto Rican Workers on U.S. Farms* (Berkeley: University of California Press, February 2020). On urbanization, see Zaire Dinzey-Flores, "Temporary Housing, Permanent Communities: Public Housing Policy and Design in Puerto Rico," *Journal of Urban History* 33, no. 3 (2007): 467–492; Zaire Dinzey-Flores, *Locked In, Locked Out: Gated Communities in a Puerto Rican City* (Philadelphia: University of Pennsylvania Press, 2013); Carmelo Esterrich, *Concrete and Countryside: The Urban and the Rural in 1950s Puerto Rican Culture* (Pittsburgh: University of Pittsburgh Press, 2018).

18 Following Ellis Armstrong, this book uses the term "public works" to mean "the physical structures and facilities developed or acquired by public agencies to house government functions and provide water, waste disposal, power, transportation, and similar services to facilitate the achievement of common social and economic objectives." Ellis L. Armstrong, ed., *History of Public Works in the United States, 1776–1976* (Chicago: University of Chicago Press, 1976), 1. On the use of public authorities during the New Deal, see Robert Caro, *The Power Broker: Robert Moses and the Fall of New York* (New York: Vintage, 1975), 615–636; Gail Radford, *The Rise of the Public Authority: Statebuilding and Economic Development in Twentieth-Century America* (Chicago: University of Chicago Press, 2013), 14–15. Antonio Lucchetti, Puerto Rico's most prominent electrical engineer, led the insular Utilización de las Fuentes Fluviales (Water Resources Utility), the PRRA Rural Electrification

Notes to Pages 14–19 · 161

Division, and the Autoridad de las Fuentes Fluviales (Puerto Rico Water Resources Authority).

19 Rex Tugwell was the former assistant secretary of agriculture and head of the Resettlement Administration when he was named chancellor of the University of Puerto Rico and then appointed governor of Puerto Rico in 1941. An economist who favored central planning, Tugwell was one of the architects of the New Deal's agrarian policy and was influential to the creation of the AAA and Soil Conservation Service (both created in 1933), in addition to coauthoring the FDA's landmark Federal Food, Drug, and Cosmetic Act in 1938.

20 Michael Namorato, ed., *The Diary of Rexford G. Tugwell: The New Deal, 1932–1935* (New York: Greenwood, 1992), 312. See also Ismael García-Colón, *Land Reform in Puerto Rico: Modernizing the Colonial State, 1941–1969* (Gainesville: University Press of Florida, 2009).

21 On how mid-century economists and technocrats "gained a prominent space" in the intellectual world of Latin America, see Margarita Fajardo, *The World That Latin America Created: The United Nations Economic Commission for Latin America in the Development Age* (Cambridge, MA: Harvard University Press, 2022), 2.

22 The notion that we must read the public works of otherwise opaque bureaucrats and engineers draws from Adrián Gorelik, *The Grid and the Park: Public Space and Urban Culture in Buenos Aires, 1887–1936*, trans. Natalia Majluf (1998; repr., Latin America Research Commons, 2022), preface. The study of urbanization in Latin America is a burgeoning field. This book has benefited from the analysis of the technocratic vision of modernization in Healey, *Ruins of the New Argentina*; Tore C. Olsson, *Agrarian Crossings: Reformers and the Remaking of the U.S. and Mexican Countryside* (Princeton, NJ: Princeton University Press, 2017); Offner, *Sorting Out the Mixed Economy*; Idurre Alonso and Maristella Casciato, eds., *The Metropolis in Latin America, 1830–1930* (Los Angeles: Getty Research Institute, 2021).

23 For example, see Edwin Rosskam, photographer, "Examination of a child for hookworm in a P.R.R.A. (Puerto Rico Resettlement Administration) center, San Juan, Puerto Rico" and "Anti-malarial injection in a P.R.R.A. (Puerto Rico Resettlement Administration) health center," photographs, Farm Security Administration, Office of War Information Photograph Collection, Library of Congress. The photographer inadvertently mistook the name of the PRRA.

Chapter 1. San Felipe, San Ciprián, and the Election of 1932

1 Sidney W. Mintz, *Worker in the Cane: A Puerto Rican Life History* (1960; repr., New York: Norton, 1974), 111–114. On San Felipe, see Charles L. Mitchell, "The West Indian Hurricane of September 10–20, 1928," *Monthly Weather Review* 56, no. 9 (September 1928): 347–350; Oliver L. Fassig, "San Felipe—The Hurricane of September 13, 1928, at San Juan, P.R.," *Monthly Weather Review* 56, no. 9 (September 1928): 351; American National Red Cross, "The West Indies Hurricane Disaster, September, 1928: Official Report of Relief Work in Porto Rico, the Virgin Islands and Florida" (Washington, D.C.: American National Red Cross, 1929), 5; Thomas G. Mathews,

162 · Notes to Page 20

Puerto Rican Politics and the New Deal (1960; repr., New York: Da Capo Press, 1974), 1; Robert Mykle, *Killer 'Cane: The Deadly Hurricane of 1928* (Lanham, MD: Rowman & Littlefield, 2006), 113; Kerry Emmanuel, *Divine Wind: The History and Science of Hurricanes* (New York: Oxford University Press, 2005), 117–119; online appendix for Christopher W. Landsea, Steve Feuer, Andrew Hagen, David A. Glenn, Nicholas T. Anderson, Jamese Sims, Ramon Pérez, and Michael Chenoweth, "A Reanalysis of the 1921 to 1930 Atlantic Hurricane Database," *Journal of Climate* (February 2012).

2 San Felipe remained the most powerful storm to hit Puerto Rico for eighty-nine years until María struck as a Category 4 major hurricane on September 20, 2017, just two weeks after the powerful Irma made landfall on September 6. María had been classified as a Category 5 hurricane when it hit Dominica two days earlier. Prior to Katrina, which devastated New Orleans in 2005, San Felipe/Okeechobee was officially considered the deadliest natural disaster in U.S. history. A fictionalized version of the storm forms a harrowing section of Zora Neale Hurston's *Their Eyes Were Watching God* (1937; repr., New York: HarperPerennial, 1990). See also Emmanuel, *Divine Wind*, 121–123; Fassig, "San Felipe," 350–352; National Oceanic and Atmospheric Administration (NOAA), National Weather Service, Weather Forecast Office, Miami, Florida, "Memorial Web Page for the 1928 Okeechobee Hurricane," https://www.weather.gov/mfl/okeechobee; Mathews, *Puerto Rican Politics*, 2; Stuart B. Schwartz, *Sea of Storms: A History of Hurricanes in the Greater Caribbean from Columbus to Katrina* (Princeton, NJ: Princeton University Press, 2015), 233–234.

3 "Island Is Often Hit by Severe Storms: Puerto Rico Had Not Recovered Fully from Damage by the Big Hurricane of 1928," *New York Times*, September 28, 1932; Arturo Morales Carrión, *Puerto Rico: A Political and Cultural History* (New York: Norton, 1983), 212; Stuart B. Schwartz, "Hurricanes and the Shaping of Circum-Caribbean Societies," *Florida Historical Quarterly* 83, no. 4 (Spring 2005): 381–382, 404; Stuart B. Schwartz, "Differential Disasters: The 1928 Hurricane and the Shaping of the Circum-Caribbean Region," *ReVista: The Harvard Review of Latin America* (Winter 2007): 3; Schwartz, *Sea of Storms*, 233–234; Eric S. Blake and Christopher W. Landsea, "The Deadliest, Costliest, and Most Intense United States Tropical Cyclones from 1851 to 2010 (and Other Frequently Requested Hurricane Facts)," NOAA Technical Memorandum NWS NHC-6, National Hurricane Center, Miami, Florida, August 2011, 29, https://www.nhc.noaa.gov/pdf/nws-nhc-6.pdf. See also Horace Towner, *Twenty-Ninth Annual Report of the Governor of Puerto Rico* (Washington, D.C.: Government Printing Office, 1930), 1–4; Fassig, "San Felipe," 350–351; "Homeless Face Famine. Word by Crippled Wires Tells of Great Porto Rican Devastation," *New York Times*, September 16, 1928, 1; "Storm Crippled Porto Rican Trade," *New York Times*, September 25, 1928, 13. Ponce was flooded again in 1931. See "Porto Rico Storm and Flood Take Many Lives; Hurricane Moves Toward Southern Florida," *New York Times*, September 4, 1931, 1; Schwartz, "Differential Disasters," 5; Schwartz, *Sea of Storms*, 233.

4 Teresita A. Levy, *Puerto Ricans in the Empire: Tobacco Growers and U.S. Colonialism* (New Brunswick, NJ: Rutgers University Press, 2014), 31–32.

5 American National Red Cross, "West Indies Hurricane Disaster," 11–12; Levy, *Puerto Ricans in the Empire*, 32–36; James L. Dietz, *Economic History of Puerto Rico: Institutional Change and Capitalist Development* (Princeton, NJ: Princeton University Press, 1986), 100–101; Blake and Landsea, "Deadliest," 7; Miles H. Fairbank, "Statement of Miles H. Fairbank, Assistant Administrator, PRRA," *Hearings Before the Committee on Appropriations, United States Senate, May 16, 1938, on the Work Relief and Public Works Appropriation Act of 1938*, H. J. Res. 679, 75th Cong., 3rd sess. (Washington, D.C.: Government Printing Office, 1938), 50; Miles H. Fairbank, *The Chardon Plan and the Puerto Rico Reconstruction Administration, 1934–1954* (San Juan: Fairbank Corporation, 1978), 8–9; Towner, *Twenty-Ninth Annual Report*, 1–5.

6 James R. Beverley, *Thirty-Third Annual Report of the Governor of Puerto Rico* (San Juan: Bureau of Supplies, Printing, and Transportation, 1933), 1–2, 5.

7 Beverley, *Thirty-Third Annual Report*, 1–6, 157–159; Levy, *Puerto Ricans in the Empire*, 32; Dietz, *Economic History of Puerto Rico*, 137–139; Schwartz, *Sea of Storms*, 253–254; Department of Health of Porto Rico, "The Public Health Aspects of the Hurricane of San Ciprian," *Puerto Rico Journal of Public Health and Tropical Medicine* 8, no. 2 (1932); Miles H. Fairbank, "PRRA Organization, Financial Policies, and Functions Prepared Pursuant to the Requirements of Senate Resolution 150, 75th Congress, First Session," PRRA History Report folder, box 1, Records of the Finance Division, Record Group 323 (hereafter RG 323), National Archives and Records Administration–Northeast Division (New York City) (hereafter NARA-NYC).

8 César J. Ayala and Laird W. Bergad, *Agrarian Puerto Rico: Reconsidering Rural Economy and Society, 1899–1940* (Cambridge: Cambridge University Press, 2020), 20, 106–109. On the *agregado* class, see Sidney W. Mintz, "The Culture History of a Puerto Rican Sugar Cane Plantation: 1876–1949," *Hispanic American Historical Review* 33, no. 2 (May 1953). According to Ayala and Bergad, the "cultivation of food crops affected the life of the rural population in every region of the island," and their importance "cannot be overestimated as food expenditures were more than 50 percent of household expenses in all regions of Puerto Rico" (106). See also Laird W. Bergad, "Toward Puerto Rico's Grito de Lares: Coffee, Social Stratification, and Class Conflicts, 1828–1868," *Hispanic American Historical Review* 60, no. 4 (November 1980): 617–642; Laird W. Bergad, "Coffee and Rural Proletarianization in Puerto Rico, 1840–1898," *Journal of Latin American Studies* 15, no. 1 (May 1983): 83–100; César J. Ayala and Laird W. Bergad, "Rural Puerto Rico in the Early Twentieth Century Reconsidered: Land and Society, 1899–1915," *Latin American Research Review* 37, no. 2 (2002): 65–97.

9 Puerto Rico Emergency Relief Administration (PRERA), *Second Report of the Puerto Rican Emergency Relief Administration, from September 1, 1934, to September 30, 1935* and *Report of the Federal Emergency Relief Administration for Puerto Rico, from October 1, 1935 to June 30, 1936, in Liquidation to October 1937* (Washington, D.C.: Government Printing Office, 1939), 1–2; Oscar Costa Mandry and Pablo Morales Otero, "Report of Studies of the 1932 Epidemic of Influenza in Puerto Rico," *Puerto Rico Journal of Public Health and Tropical Medicine* 8, no. 2 (1932). San Nicolás resulted in only two official deaths. See Blake and Landsea, "Deadliest," 29.

164 · Notes to Pages 23–26

10 Progress Reports, box 3, Engineering Division Construction Projects, Swamp Land Filling and Draining for Malaria Control, Records Relating to Construction Projects Directed by the Engineering Division, RG 323, NARA-NYC; Progress Reports, General Records Relating to the Cement Plant Project, RG 323, NARA-NYC.

11 Marcos Ramírez Lavandero, ed., *Documents on the Constitutional Relationship of Puerto Rico and the United States* (Washington, D.C.: Puerto Rico Federal Affairs Administration, 1988), 24; Frank Mújica-Baker, Manuel A. Valverde Jr., and Awilda Lozano, *Huracanes y tormentas tropicales que han afectado a Puerto Rico* (San Juan: Estado Libre Asociado de Puerto Rico Agencia Estatal para el Manejo de Emergencias y Administracion de Desastres, n.d.); Stuart B. Schwartz, "The Hurricane of San Ciriaco: Disaster, Politics, and Society in Puerto Rico, 1899–1901," *Hispanic American Historical Review* 72, no. 3 (August 1992): 319; Schwartz, "Hurricanes and the Shaping of Circum-Caribbean Societies," 402. On Cuba, see Louis A. Pérez, *Winds of Change: Hurricanes and the Transformation of Nineteenth-Century* (Chapel Hill: University of North Carolina Press, 2001), 117–122.

12 On continuity between the Spanish and U.S. colonial systems, see Alfred W. McCoy, Francisco A. Scarano, and Courtney Johnson, "On the Tropic of Cancer: Transitions and Transformations in the U.S. Imperial State," in Alfred W. McCoy and Francisco A. Scarano, eds., *Colonial Crucible: Empire and the Making of the Modern American State* (Madison: University of Wisconsin Press, 2009), 11; Ann Zulawski, "Urban Development, Public Health, and the Environment," *Brown Journal of World Affairs* 22, no. 2 (Spring/Summer 2016): 197–214. On land concentration, see Laird W. Bergad, *Coffee and the Growth of Agrarian Capitalism in Nineteenth Century Puerto Rico* (Princeton, NJ: Princeton University Press, 1983); José O. Sola, "Colonialism, Planters, Sugarcane, and the Agrarian Economy of Caguas, Puerto Rico, between the 1890s and 1930," *Agricultural History* 85, no. 3 (Summer 2011): 349–372. On politics, see Schwartz, "Hurricane of San Ciriaco," 326–327; Schwartz, *Sea of Storms*, 199; Nicole Ferraiolo, "Charitable Imperialism and the Hurricane of San Ciriaco: Ideology, Humanitarian Partnerships and the Formation of American Relief Policy (Puerto Rico, 1899–1901)" (MA/MSc thesis, Columbia University / London School of Economics, 2011), 2–4.

13 George W. Davis, *Report of Brig. Gen. Geo. W. Davis, USV., on Civil Affairs of Puerto Rico, 1899* (Washington, D.C.: Government Printing Office, 1900), 67; Schwartz, "Hurricane of San Ciriaco," 304, 308, 324; Schwartz, *Sea of Storms*, 153.

14 Schwartz, "Hurricane of San Ciriaco," 316, 320, 326–328; Ferraiolo, "Charitable Imperialism," 19–22; Davis, *Report*, 293; *American Red Cross Bulletin* 10 (Washington: American National Red Cross, 1915), 283, 376; Schwartz, *Sea of Storms*, 197–198. On Davis's views, see Ferraiolo, "Charitable Imperialism," 16–19, and Davis, *Report*, 68–69.

15 Ferraiolo, "Charitable Imperialism," 3–4; Lizbeth Cohen, *Making a New Deal: Industrial Workers in Chicago, 1919–1939* (Cambridge: Cambridge University Press, 1990), 221–226.

16 John M. Barry, *Rising Tide: The Great Mississippi Flood of 1927 and How It Changed America* (New York: Simon & Schuster, 1998), 10–11, 170–171, 240, 262, 272; Matthew

T. Pearcy, "After the Flood: A History of the 1928 Flood Control Act," *Journal of the Illinois State Historical Society* 95, no. 2 (Summer 2002): 172–201.

17 Barry, *Rising Tide*, 365–369. The Federal Emergency Management Agency (FEMA), which coordinates disaster relief, emergency management, and civil defense today, was signed into law by Jimmy Carter in 1979.

18 William E. Leuchtenburg, *Herbert Hoover* (New York: Henry Holt, 2009), 70–71; Marian Moser Jones, *The American Red Cross from Clara Barton to the New Deal* (Baltimore: Johns Hopkins University Press, 2013), iix–ix. Interestingly, the Mississippi Flood also propelled Huey Long's successful campaign for governor in 1928. See Barry, *Rising Tide*, 351.

19 Towner, *Twenty-Ninth Annual Report*, 4–7; American National Red Cross, "West Indies Hurricane Disaster," 13.

20 Towner, *Twenty-Ninth Annual Report*, 3–5.

21 Schwartz, *Sea of Storms*, 237–238; Schwartz, "Hurricanes and the Shaping of Circum-Caribbean Societies," 404–406. The term "colono" can refer to both a "large farmer operating thousands of acres of land with wage labor and a small farmer working his cane land only with family labor." For more, see César J. Ayala, *American Sugar Kingdom: The Plantation Economy of the Spanish Caribbean, 1898–1934* (Chapel Hill: University of North Carolina Press, 1999), 124–125.

22 "Bingham Stresses Porto Rico's Needs: Senator Says There No Part of Nation Ever Suffered So Much as It Did in Hurricane," *New York Times*, November 22, 1928, 12; Puerto Rican Hurricane Relief Commission, December 21, 1928–June 18, 1935, RG 33, Records of the Extension Service, NARA-NYC; "History," Records of the Puerto Rican Hurricane Relief Commission, Records of the Office of Territories, RG 126, NARA-NYC; Edgar Kiess, testimony on "Relief of Porto Rico," *Congressional Record*–House, December 17, 1928, 773–775; Herbert Hoover, "Message to Congress Transmitting the Report of the Porto Rico Hurricane Relief Commission," January 14, 1930, *The American Presidency Project*, http://www.presidency.ucsb.edu/ws/?pid =22247. The work of the Hurricane Relief Commission and its successor, the Puerto Rican Hurricane Relief Loan Section, were later taken over by the PRRA.

23 Levy, *Puerto Ricans in the Empire*, 65, 82, 85, 72.

24 PRERA, *Second Report*, 2; Department of Health of Porto Rico, "Public Health Aspects"; Beverley, *Thirty-Third Annual Report*, 1–2. On the RFC, see Anthony J. Badger, *The New Deal: The Depression Years, 1933–1940* (Chicago: Ivan R. Dee, 1989), 48; Richard Polenberg, "Introduction: Franklin D. Roosevelt and American Liberalism," in Richard Polenberg, ed., *The Era of Franklin D. Roosevelt, 1933–1945* (Boston: Bedford/St. Martin's, 2000), 10. See also Cohen, *Making a New Deal*, 221–226, 261; Badger, *New Deal*, 35–37, 41–42; Joan Hoff Wilson, *Herbert Hoover: Forgotten Progressive* (Boston: Little, Brown, 1975), 137, 144–145; Ellis W. Hawley, *The Great War and the Search for a Modern World Order: A History of the American People and Their Institutions, 1917–1933*, 2nd ed. (New York: St. Martin's, 1992), 164, 174.

25 Beverley, *Thirty-Third Annual Report*, 4–5; Blake and Landsea, "Deadliest," 29; American National Red Cross, Puerto Rico Chapter, "Final Report of the Manager of Hurricane Relief, September 26, 1932," printed as appendix A in Beverley, *Thirty-*

166 · Notes to Pages 30–33

Third Annual Report, 38. For a scientific consideration of the long-term effects of hurricane damage, see Emery R. Boose, Mayra I. Serrano, and David R. Foster, "Landscape and Regional Impacts of Hurricanes in Puerto Rico," *Ecological Monographs* 74, no. 2 (May 2004): 335–352, https://www.jstor.org/stable/4539059.

26 American National Red Cross, Puerto Rico Chapter, "Final Report," 40–46.

27 Polling data are available at El Archivo de las Elecciones en Puerto Rico, https://electionspuertorico.org/archivo/1932.html. The election of 1932, which featured a turnout of more than 80 percent of registered voters, has been covered by several secondary sources. See Emilio Pantojas-García, *Development Strategies as Ideology: Puerto Rico's Export-led Industrialization Experience* (Boulder, CO: Lynne Rienner, 1990), chapters 1–2; Morales Carrión, *Puerto Rico*, chapters 11–12; César J. Ayala and Rafael Bernabe, *Puerto Rico in the American Century: A History since 1898* (Chapel Hill: University of North Carolina Press, 2007), chapters 4–7. Though Benigno Fernández García missed out on serving as the resident commissioner, he was later appointed the first regional administrator of the PRRA and the attorney general of Puerto Rico in 1935, positions he held simultaneously for at least one year. See also "Puerto Rico to Become 49th State, Two Island Senators Assert," *New York Times*, June 15, 1933.

28 Wilfredo Mattos Cintrón, "The Struggle for Independence: The Long March to the Twenty-First Century," in Edwin Meléndez and Edgardo Meléndez, eds., *Colonial Dilemma: Critical Perspectives on Contemporary Puerto Rico* (Boston: South End Press, 1993), 203; Ayala and Bernabe, *Puerto Rico in the American Century*, 108.

29 Mathews, *Puerto Rican Politics*, 31, 74, 219; Rexford G. Tugwell, *Changing the Colonial Climate* (1942; repr., New York: Arno Press, 1970), 10, 174; Edgardo Meléndez, *Puerto Rico's Statehood Movement* (New York: Greenwood, 1988), 33–55. While the Republican Party is often used as a kind of shorthand to mean the party of large sugar interests, by which is meant a collection of local, U.S., and international corporations, this shorthand is not fully correct as the party also featured coffee *hacendados* (estate owners) and other landed interests along with the electric and water-power corporations that supported sugar farming and milling and enjoyed virtual monopoly status on the island. It should be noted that the largest rivals of the Republican Party—the Union Party and (later) the Liberal Party—also had prominent members connected to big sugar. See Rafael Bernabe, "Prehistory of the Partido Popular Democrático: Muñoz Marin, the Partido Liberal and the Crisis of Sugar in Puerto Rico, 1930–35" (PhD diss., State University of New York at Binghamton, 1989), 56.

30 On the Socialist Party, see Blanca G. Silvestrini, *Los trabajadores puertorriqueqos y el Partido Socialista 1932–1940* (Río Piedras: University of Puerto Rico Press, 1979); A. G. Quintero-Rivera, "Socialist and Cigarmaker: Artisans' Proletarianization in the Making of the Puerto Rican Working Class," *Latin American Perspectives* 10, nos. 2/3 (Spring-Summer 1983); Gonzalo F. Córdova, *Resident Commissioner Santiago Iglesias and His Times* (Río Piedras: Editorial de la Universidad de Puerto Rico, 1993); Pedro Cabán, *Constructing a Colonial People: Puerto Rico and the United States, 1898–1932* (Boulder, CO: Westview, 1999), 235; Jorell Meléndez-Badillo, *The Lettered Barriada: Workers, Archival Power, and the Politics of Knowledge in Puerto*

Rico (Durham, NC: Duke University Press, 2021), 59–61, 111–113; Mathews, *Puerto Rican Politics*, 32. Although the FLT and Socialist Party were technically separate, they were largely run by the same leaders. See Ayala and Bernabe, *Puerto Rico in the American Century*, 63–64; Meléndez, *Puerto Rico's Statehood Movement*, 35; Quintero-Rivera, "Socialist and Cigarmaker," 35–36; Cabán, *Constructing a Colonial People*, 243–244. The FLT's connections to Samuel Gompers and the American Federation of Labor (AFL) were strong. In 1917, for example, Iglesias was chosen to serve as a member of the Pan-American Federation of Labor Conference Committee, which was designed to spread the AFL's reach into Latin America and the Caribbean. See Robert Jackson Alexander and Eldon M. Parker, *International Labor Organizations and Organized Labor in Latin America and the Caribbean: A History* (Santa Barbara, CA: Praeger/ABC-CLIO, 2009), 12–14. On Iglesias's view that Puerto Rican labor supported FDR but not Chardón, see "Puerto Rican Unions Urged to Enlarge: Iglesias Says New Deal Gives Impetus to Organized Labor—Back-to-Land Plans Told," *New York Times*, September 4, 1934.

31 Bernabe, "Prehistory," 192–194, 196–197; Gabriel Villaronga, "Constructing Muñocismo: Colonial Politics and the Rise of the PPD, 1934–1940," *Centro Journal* 12, no. 2 (2010): 177. For an analysis of the connection between women workers in the cigar industry (particularly leaf-strippers) and the Socialist Party, see Quintero-Rivera, "Socialist and Cigarmaker," 24–26. On Communist Party organizing, see "Huelgas," caja 674–678, Fondo Oficina del Gobernador, tarea 96–20, Archivo General de Puerto Rico; Ayala and Bernabe, *Puerto Rico in the American Century*, 136. Publicos were privately owned taxis that traversed regular routes in the absence of public transportation.

32 Gabriel Villaronga, *Toward a Discourse of Consent: Mass Mobilization and Colonial Politics in Puerto Rico, 1932–1948* (Westport, CT: Praeger, 2004), 14, 62–63. On the application of the Fair Labor Standards Act in Puerto Rico, Anne Macpherson has written that "two years of bitter struggle over the FLSA enforcement and amendment pitted employers in the sugar, needlework, and tobacco industries against a largely pro–New Deal mass-labor movement in Puerto Rico, and involved a variety of federal-cum-imperial actors." The struggle ended in a conservative amendment that lowered the minimum wage in Puerto Rico and the U.S. Virgin Islands, resulting in the birth of a colonial minimum wage untethered to the rate in the continental United States. The wage differential lasted from 1940 until 1983. Anne S. Macpherson, "Birth of the U.S. Colonial Minimum Wage: The Struggle over the Fair Labor Standards Act in Puerto Rico, 1938–1941," *Journal of American History* 104, no. 3 (December 2017): 656–680.

33 On Albizu Campos, see Gloria Tapia Ríos, *La Central Lafayette: Riqueza, Desarrollo, y Politica en el Sureste de Puerto Rico* (San Juan: Magna Cultura Ediciones, 2014), 228–229; Pantojas-García, *Development Strategies as Ideology*, 34; Luis Angel Ferrao, *Pedro Albizu Campos y el Nacionalismo Puertorriqueno* (San Juan: Editorial Cultural, 1990); Luis G. Collazo, *Pedro Albizu Campos: La espiritualidad de un revolucionario* (Río Piedras: Publicaciones Gaviota, 2015), 63–64. On the FLT and Socialist Party, see Bernabe, "Prehistory," 198–199, 202; Jorge Rodríguez Beruff, *Strategy as*

168 · Notes to Pages 34–38

Politics: Puerto Rico on the Eve of the Second World War (San Juan: La Editorial de la Universidad de Puerto Rico, 2007), 175, 180.

34 Bernabe, "Prehistory," 199–202; Radiogram, Miles Fairbank to Carlos Chardón, Carlos Chardón folder, box 1, Confidential Records of the Assistant Administrator, 1936–1952, RG 323, NARA-NYC; Progress Report, folder 1, box 1, Records of the Engineering Division, RG 323, NARA-NYC; "Federal Agencies Operating in Puerto Rico," in *Investigation of Political, Economic, and Social Conditions in Puerto Rico: Hearings before the Subcommittee of the House Committee of Insular Affairs, Part 19, Pursuant to HR 159*, 78th Cong., 2nd sess., 1944 (Washington, D.C.: Government Printing Office, 1944), 1763.

35 The 500-Acre Law was amended to the Foraker Act in 1900. It had been promoted by the U.S. beet sugar lobby, which sought to protect its interests against the expansion of the sugar trust and its cane holdings in the new American colonies. Congressman William Atkinson Jones (D-VA), whose career in Washington spanned from the Populist movement to the Progressive era, expressed his fear that "syndicates" in corporate agriculture were "being organized to buy up practically all the rich sugar, coffee, and tobacco lands." The amendment had many critics, including Charles Harcourt Forbes-Lindsay, who argued that the law "entirely nullified" the purpose of the Foraker Act—which was to "facilitate the introduction of American capital into Puerto Rico." See Matthew O. Edel, "Land Reform in Puerto Rico, 1940–1959: Part One," *Caribbean Studies* 2, no. 3 (1962), 28; Dietz, *Economic History of Puerto Rico*, 152–154; Ayala and Bergad, *Agrarian Puerto Rico*, 7–8; C. H. Forbes-Lindsay, *America's Insular Possessions*, vol. 1 (Philadelphia: J. C. Winston, 1906), 159–160.

36 Fairbank, *Chardon Plan*, 18–20, 21–24.

37 On the partisan control of the PRRA, see Harwood Hull to Stephen Early, July 20, 1935, folder 8: Puerto Rico, 1934–1935, box 255, Secretary of Interior File, Papers of Harold L. Ickes, Library of Congress. Stephen Early, who was the White House press secretary, forwarded Hull's letter to Harold Ickes. PRRA officials were somewhat bemused by the charges of favoritism toward the Liberal Party, noting internally that "Puerto Ricans are political to a fantastic degree" and that "there can be no question that politics is played fast and furiously by Puerto Ricans of every party." See Ernest Gruening to Harold Ickes, October 21, 1936, folder 9, Puerto Rico: 1936, box 255, Secretary of Interior File, Ickes Papers. On the "utter ideological sterility of the anti-Muñoz, anti-New Deal Coalition," see Robert W. Anderson, *Party Politics in Puerto Rico* (Stanford, CA: Stanford University Press, 1965), 35. See also "Puerto Rican Pleads for Reconstruction: Chancellor Chardon Urges Haste by Washington on Plan to Aid the Island," *New York Times*, September 21, 1934.

Chapter 2. From Relief to Reconstruction

1 A comparison between Puerto Rico and the U.S. Virgin Islands, which has been an unincorporated territory since they were sold to the U.S. by Denmark as part of the Treaty of the Danish West Indies in 1917, might be helpful. The population of Puerto Rico in 1935 was 1,723,534, which dwarfed the size of the population of the Virgin Islands—22,012 in 1930 and 24,889 in 1940. Unsurprisingly, New Deal activity in the

Virgin Islands was funded by a small fraction of the $1.7 billion budget in Puerto Rico. Relief work in 1934 amounted to just over $435,500 (about $9.8 million today). One of the major projects was the construction of Bluebeard's Castle Hotel, a tourist resort completed in 1938, which was funded by the PWA, WPA, and CCC for just over $271,800 (about $5.7 million today) and, upon its completion, leased to a private corporation. The most significant New Deal venture, however, was the incorporation of the Virgin Islands Company by Harold Ickes, Oscar L. Chapman (undersecretary of the interior), and Paul M. Pearson (governor of the Virgin Islands) for $1 million (about $22.6 million today) in 1934. The Virgin Islands Company was designed to purchase sugarcane lands and rum distilleries from the bankrupt West Indian Sugar Factory, Ltd., a Danish corporation that collapsed in 1930. By 1940, the Virgin Islands Company had spent over $3.4 million (about $73.3 million today) and recorded a net loss of almost $140,000 (about $3 million today). The company prospered during World War II, launched a rural electrification program in the late 1940s, and was seen by the Department of the Interior as the "backbone" of the local economy in 1955. Population statistics can be found at Puerto Rico Reconstruction Administration, Census of Puerto Rico: 1935, Population; U.S. Department of Commerce and Bureau of the Census, Fifteenth Census of the United States: 1930, Outlying Territories and Possessions: Virgin Islands; and U.S. Department of Commerce and Bureau of the Census, Fifteenth Census of the United States: 1940, Outlying Territories and Possessions: Virgin Islands. On the New Deal in the Virgin Islands, see Lawrence W. Cramer, *Annual Report of the Governor of the Virgin Islands to the Secretary of the Interior for the Fiscal Year Ended June 30, 1940* (Washington, D.C.: Government Printing Office, 1940); Living New Deal, "The Virgin Islands Company (1934)," https://livingnewdeal.org/glossary/virgin-islands-company-1934/ and "Bluebeard Castle Hotel–St. Thomas, VI," https://livingnewdeal.org/projects/bluebeard-castle-hotel-st-thomas-vi/. The "backbone" quotation is cited as *Annual Report of the Secretary of the Interior, Fiscal Year 1955*, p. 378.

2 FERA was in part modeled on the New York Temporary Emergency Relief Administration, which had been established while Roosevelt served as governor between 1929 and 1933. Between its creation in May 1933 to its liquidation at the end of 1937, FERA provided emergency relief to more than 20 million persons or about 16 percent of the total population of the United States. Territorial relief in Alaska, Hawaii, Puerto Rico, and the Virgin Islands under FERA fluctuated wildly from 4,000 cases of direct relief in August 1933 to 133,000 cases in July 1934 to less than 4,000 in June 1936 when general relief was discontinued. See Federal Works Agency, *Final Statistical Report of the Federal Emergency Relief Administration* (Washington, D.C.: U.S. Government Printing Office, 1942), 91–92, 98; Puerto Rico Emergency Relief Administration (PRERA), *Second Report of the Puerto Rican Emergency Relief Administration, from September 1, 1934, to September 30, 1935* and *Report of the Federal Emergency Relief Administration for Puerto Rico, from October 1, 1935 to June 30, 1936, in Liquidation to October 1937* (Washington, D.C.: Government Printing Office, 1939), 2; "Puerto Rico Seeks to Share in New Deal," *New York Times*, November 19, 1933.

170 · Notes to Pages 39–40

3 Manuel R. Rodríguez, "Representing Development: New Perspectives about the New Deal in Puerto Rico, 1933–1936," *Centro Journal* 14, no. 2 (2002): 157–158, 168. See also Manuel R. Rodríguez, *A New Deal for the Tropics: Puerto Rico during the Depression Era, 1932–1935* (Princeton, NJ: Markus Wiener, 2010), 38, 118–119; Dorothy Dulles Bourne and James Russell Bourne, *Thirty Years of Change in Puerto Rico: A Case Study of Ten Selected Rural Areas* (New York: Praeger, 1966), 131; PRERA, *Second Report*, 4–5; Miles H. Fairbank, *The Chardon Plan and the Puerto Rico Reconstruction Administration, 1934–1954* (San Juan: Fairbank Corporation, 1978), 10. On pre–New Deal federal interventions that impacted the daily lives of Puerto Ricans, see Eileen Findlay, *Imposing Decency: The Politics of Sexuality and Race in Puerto Rico, 1870–1920* (Durham, NC: Duke University Press, 2000); José Amador, *Medicine and Nation Building in the Americas, 1890–1940* (Nashville: Vanderbilt University Press, 2015).

4 Raymond Carr, *Puerto Rico: A Colonial Experiment* (New York: Vintage, 1984), 58–59.

5 For more on "Gore's Hell," see Thomas Mathews, *Puerto Rican Politics and the New Deal* (1960; repr., New York: Da Capo Press, 1974), 58–116; Arturo Morales Carrión, *Puerto Rico: A Political and Cultural History* (New York: Norton, 1983), 226–228; James L. Dietz, *Economic History of Puerto Rico: Institutional Change and Capitalist Development* (Princeton, NJ: Princeton University Press, 1986), 146–147; Maurine H. Beasley, *Ruby A. Black: Eleanor Roosevelt, Puerto Rico, and Political Journalism in Washington* (Lanham, MD: Lexington Books, 2017), 84–89; Harwood Hull, "Puerto Rico Hails Large Gore Family: With Nine Children, Governor Must Be 'Simpatico,' People Believe: Leaders Less Confident," *New York Times*, May 14, 1933. The article pejoratively asserts that Puerto Ricans saw Gore and his particularly large family as one of their own. See also "Patronage," *Newsweek*, May 6, 1933, quoted in Santiago Ortiz, *American Press Opinion with Reference to Politics and Government in Puerto Rico, 1932–1939* (Washington, D.C.: Office of Puerto Rico, 1946), 15. On the Coalition parade, see "San Juan Hails New Deal: Puerto Ricans, in Big Demonstration, Cheer Roosevelt and Gov. Gore," *New York Times*, October 16, 1933.

6 Jorge Rodríguez Beruff, *Strategy as Politics: Puerto Rico on the Eve of the Second World War* (San Juan: La Editorial de la Universidad de Puerto Rico, 2007), 175–176.

7 Within a year, however, it was clear that rather than representing the reform impulse of the New Deal, the Coalition represented "markedly conservative interests in power" on the island. See Mathews, *Puerto Rican Politics*, 20; Beasley, *Ruby A. Black*, 84–89. On the removal of Gore and appointment of Winship, see "Liberals May Seek to Oust Governor Gore; Barceló Party in Puerto Rico Would Avoid Embarrassing President, However," *New York Times*, September 17, 1933; "Nature of Choice of Winship Hailed; Puerto Rico Credits Roosevelt Alone for It, While Gore Was Held a Farley Man," *New York Times*, January 28, 1934; "Winship Assumes Puerto Rican Post; New Governor Announces Plan to Extend the AAA and NRA Fully to the Island," *New York Times*, February 6, 1934; "Puerto Rico Unity Urged on Parties; Democrats Ask the Governor to Extend 'New Deal' as Far as Local Condi-

tions Permit," *New York Times*, February 16, 1934. The article incorrectly (but tellingly) refers to members of the Liberal Party as Democrats.

8   Telegram, Muñoz Marín to Ickes, July 31, 1935, and Ickes to Muñoz Marín, August 2, 1935, folder 8: Puerto Rico, 1934–1935, box 255, Secretary of Interior File, Papers of Harold L. Ickes, Library of Congress (hereafter Ickes Papers). See also Antonio Ayuso Valdirresa, "¡Fuera Winship!" *El Imparcial*, July 23, 1935, 1; "Reily, Gore, and Winship," *El Imparcial*, 1935; Cesar Borgia, "¿Se Va Winship?," *La Correspondencia de Puerto Rico*, July 23, 1935, 1; Cesar Borgia, "Los planes de reconstrucción económica en peligro de fracasar," *La Correspondencia*, n.d.; Cesar Borgia, "La Huella Imborrable," *La Correspondencia*, July 9, 1935; "Es unánime el clamor público: ¡Fuera Winship!," *El Imparcial*, July 24, 1935; "La danza de los expertos . . . y del despilfarro," *El Mundo*, July 18, 1935, 6; "¿Insistirá el Gobernador en crear un 'supergobierno' deprimente para el país?" *El Mundo*, June 30, 1935. Clippings, folder 8: Puerto Rico, 1934–1935, box 255, Secretary of Interior File, Ickes Papers. Antonio Ayuso was the editor of *El Imparcial* and a former leader of the Nationalist Party. See "Antonio Ayuso, Publisher, Dies," *New York Times*, April 27, 1970.

9   Though the PRERA initially had five divisions, this book uses the explanation of its bureaucracy provided by Manuel Rodríguez, who expertly distilled its structure into three categories. See Rodríguez, *New Deal for the Tropics*, 55–56; PRERA, *Second Report*, 6–7. On Dorothy and James Bourne, see Bourne and Bourne, *Thirty Years of Change*, 3 (and the erratum to page 3). Dorothy Dulles Bourne was the cousin of John Foster and Allen Dulles, the Republican secretary of state under Dwight Eisenhower and director of the CIA, respectively. After her time with the PRERA, Dorothy Bourne served as the executive director of the Civil Defense Volunteers and was a professor and dean at Bard College, among other ventures. In 1962, she was awarded $100,000 by the anthropology department of Cornell University to return to Puerto Rico to study the same rural areas she had surveyed before and during the New Deal. The result was the book, cowritten with her husband. See also "Mrs. Dorothy Dulles Bourne, Educator in Puerto Rico, Dies," *New York Times*, April 19, 1969; Francisco Vizcarrondo, *Education in Puerto Rico: The Second-Unit Rural Schools of Porto Rico, Pre-Vocational Schools for Pupils of Intermediate Grades* (San Juan: Bureau of Supplies, Printing, and Transportation, 1930). On the PRERA birth control program, which was run through the Bureau of Social Services, see Laura Briggs, *Reproducing Empire: Race, Sex, Science, and U.S. Imperialism in Puerto Rico* (Berkeley: University of California Press, 2002), 96–98.

10   PRERA, *Second Report*, 2, 7; Fairbank, *Chardon Plan*, 10.

11   Rodríguez, *New Deal for the Tropics*, 55–57; Rodríguez, "Representing Development," 172.

12   PRERA, *Second Report*, 5, 7; Mathews, *Puerto Rican Politics*, 130–131; Dietz, *Economic History of Puerto Rico*, 147; "Puerto Rico to Aid 200,000 Families," *New York Times*, February 25, 1934; "Puerto Rico Gets Relief; Direct Aid Supplemented by a Wide Program of Civil Works," *New York Times*, April 8, 1934.

13   Rodríguez, *New Deal for the Tropics*, 127–128; "Relief Chief Posts Bond in Puerto Rico; Denies Charge of Slandering Legislature by Saying It Includes Criminals," *New*

172 · Notes to Pages 43–45

York Times, April 7, 1935; "Relief Aide's Home Afire; Puerto Rican Police Find Oil Poured on Bourne's Residence," *New York Times*, July 15, 1935. Following his time with the PRERA, James Bourne joined Harry Hopkins at the WPA before retiring from public service in 1937.

14 Mathews, *Puerto Rican Politics*, 56–57, 129–130; Rodríguez, *New Deal for the Tropics*, 53–55, 125, 128–130; Beasley, *Ruby A. Black*, 84–85.

15 Dietz, *Economic History of Puerto Rico*, 147; Rodríguez, "Representing Development," 171–172; Fernando Picó, *History of Puerto Rico: A Panorama of Its People* (Princeton, NJ: Markus Weiner, 2006), 265–266; Rodríguez Beruff, *Strategy as Politics*, 175–176. See also "Two Tons of Quinine Curb Malaria in Puerto Rico," *New York Times*, February 19, 1934; "Puerto Rico to Aid 200,000 Families," *New York Times*, February 25, 1934; "Puerto Rico Gets Relief; Direct Aid Supplemented by a Wide Program of Civil Works," *New York Times*, April 8, 1934; "Puerto Rico Relief Funds Pay for New Lifeguards," *New York Times*, June 19, 1934.

16 Chardón was a younger cousin of Antonio Lucchetti, the island's most prominent electrical engineer, who also graduated from Cornell. Carlos E. Chardón, personal communication to author, May 2018. For more on the island's "reformist elite" class of mostly white, male intellectuals and politicians who were educated at elite U.S. universities, see Gabriel Villaronga, *Toward a Discourse of Consent: Mass Mobilization and Colonial Politics in Puerto Rico, 1932–1948* (Westport, CT: Praeger, 2004), 17, 25; Ismael García-Colon, *Land Reform in Puerto Rico: Modernizing the Colonial State, 1941–1969* (Gainesville: University Press of Florida, 2009), 41. This book's understanding of the Chardón Plan is indebted to Juan Giusti, who provided insight through personal conversations with the author in July 2022.

17 Eleanor Roosevelt's tour has been discussed in several sources, including Blanche Wiesen Cook, *Eleanor Roosevelt: 1932–1938*, vol. 2 (New York: Viking, 1999) and Beasley, *Ruby A. Black*, 93–99. Tugwell was in Puerto Rico to help establish the CCC on the island. See Rexford G. Tugwell, *Changing the Colonial Climate* (1942; repr., New York: Arno Press, 1970), 9. See also PRRA, *Album de Oro de Puerto Rico: Obra divulgacíon cultural en pro de la fraternidad americana*, ed. Antonio M. Monteagudo and Antonio Escámez (Havana: Artes Graficas, 1939), n.p.; Dietz, *Economic History of Puerto Rico*, 150–151; Fairbank, *Chardon Plan*, 5, 10–11; "First Lady Hailed on Tour in Island: Puerto Rican Villagers Press around Her Car with Bouquets and Pleas," *New York Times*, March 10, 1934; "2,000 at Reception to Mrs. Roosevelt: She Shakes Hands with All at Puerto Rican Fete after 300-Mile Drive," *New York Times*, March 14, 1934. After touring the island in 1936, Ickes wrote that the island contained the "worst slums that I have ever seen. The dwellings looked as if a breath would blow them over. . . . Open sewage runs through the streets and around the buildings and there are no sanitation facilities at all. The children play in this sewage, which in many cases is covered with a thick, green scum. The houses appear to be dirty and unkempt. The cooking is done on little charcoal stoves, and the furniture is of the simplest and scantiest. . . . Such slums are a reflection not only upon the [Puerto Rican] Government but upon that of the United States. It is unbelievable that human beings can be permitted to live in such noisome cesspools." See Harold L. Ickes, *The*

Secret Diary of Harold L. Ickes, vol. 1: *The First Thousand Days* (New York: Simon & Schuster, 1953), 504.

18 Franklin D. Roosevelt, "Remarks in San Juan, Puerto Rico," July 7, 1934, *The American Presidency Project*, https://www.presidency.ucsb.edu/documents/remarks-san -juan-puerto-rico. See also "New Deal Delays Vex Puerto Ricans," *New York Times*, August 26, 1934.

19 Juan Giusti Cordero, "El profesor de la UPR y el plan que transformó al país," *80 Grados*, September 20, 2019, https://www.80grados.net/el-profesor-de-la-upr-y-el -plan-que-trasnsformo-al-pais/.

20 Carlos Chardón to Tugwell, March 29, 1934, quoted in Mathews, *Puerto Rican Politics*, 161; Giusti, "El profesor de la UPR"; "Puerto Rico Plan Asks Estate Cuts; Policy Committee Recommends Large Tracts Be Broken Up–Sets 500-Acre Limit," *New York Times*, July 28, 1934; Harwood Hull, "Puerto Rico Wants Teeth in Its Land Law; Pending Bills Would Extend Present 500-Acre Limitations to Individuals," *New York Times*, March 10, 1935.

21 Fairbank, *Chardon Plan*, 18–20, 21–24; "Puerto Rico Relief Board Urges Garlic Cultivation," *New York Times*, March 20, 1935.

22 "Puerto Rico Votes Legislative Strike; Session Adjourned in Protest against 'Dictatorship' from Washington," *New York Times*, April 15, 1935. Albizu Campos and Iglesias Santíago had been against the Chardón Plan for some time. See "Puerto Rico Upset by Chardon Plan," *New York Times*, August 12, 1934.

23 "Puerto Rico Spurs Statehood Drive; Coalitionists Plan Permanent Commission in Washington to Further Aims," *New York Times*, April 16, 1935.

24 Mathews, *Puerto Rican Politics*, 237–238; "Puerto Rico Group Fights Tugwell Plan," *New York Times*, May 6, 1934; "Various Problems Upset Puerto Rico; Uncertainty as to Action of Our Government Vexes Sugar Industry," *New York Times*, July 29, 1934; "Puerto Rico Upset by Chardon Plan."

25 "Executive Order 7057 Establishing the Puerto Rico Reconstruction Administration," May 28, 1935, *The American Presidency Project*, https://www.presidency .ucsb.edu/documents/executive-order-7057-establishing-the-puerto-rico -reconstruction-administration.

26 W. I. Myers to Ickes, August 29, 1934, and Ickes to Myers, September 1, 1934, folder 8: Puerto Rico, 1934–1935, box 255, Secretary of Interior File, Ickes Papers; Harwood Hull, "Relief Suggested for Puerto Ricans," *New York Times*, November 18, 1934. Years later, some insiders tried to downplay the political jockeying that took place. For example, Leona Bachrach Gerard, who ran the Liaison Office of the PRRA in Washington, added several corrections to Fairbank's manuscript on the Chardón Plan and the PRRA. Where Fairbank wrote that Puerto Rican political, professional, and civic leaders all "maneuvered rapidly to gain a position" in the New Deal, Gerard suggested that this line be changed to "pressed forward early to join the wide-spread efforts at many levels to rescue a whole Island people." Fairbank kept "maneuvered" in the final version. See Miles H. Fairbank, "The Chardon Plan and the Puerto Rico Reconstruction Administration, 1934–1954," 8, draft copy, edited by

174 · Notes to Pages 49–53

Leona Bachrach Gerard, folder 1, Miles H. Fairbank Papers, 1975–1978, Franklin D. Roosevelt Presidential Library.

27 *Annual Report of the Secretary of the Interior for the Fiscal Year Ending June 30, 1937* (Washington, D.C.: Government Printing Office, 1937), 318–319.

28 Franklin D. Roosevelt, August 1, 1935, Information and Research Section, PRRA, "Facts about the Puerto Rico Reconstruction Administration," Franklin and Eleanor Roosevelt Institute (FERI) New Deal Network, located on the Internet Archive Wayback Machine, https://web.archive.org/web/20120205043811/http://newdeal.feri.org:80/pr/pr10.htm; Miles H. Fairbanks (*sic*), "Puerto Rico Reconstruction Administration," *Annual Report of the Secretary of the Interior for the Fiscal Year Ending June 30, 1939* (Washington, D.C.: Government Printing Office, 1939), 353. See also "Urges Roosevelt to Act: Puerto Rican Liberal Says President Could End Delays," *New York Times*, December 9, 1934; "Puerto Ricans Ask for Independence," *New York Times*, December 9, 1934; "President Insures Aid to Puerto Rico," *New York Times*, December 23, 1934.

29 Memo, Chardón to Gruening, "Administrative Coordination in the PRRA" folder, General Records Relating to the Cement Plant Project, RG 323, NARA-NYC. See also "New Set-Up Ordered in Puerto Rico Relief: Roosevelt Ends Controversy by Appointment of Administration Headed by Gruening," *New York Times*, May 30, 1935.

30 "A.D. Personnel-Employment Record" folder, box 2, General Records Relating to Administration, RG 323, NARA-NYC; *Annual Report of the Secretary of the Interior for the Fiscal Year Ending June 30, 1937*, 319–320; "Para el 16 diciembre 23,258 trabajaban en la Administración de reconstrucción de Puerto Rico," *El Pais*, December 23, 1939.

31 "Federal Agencies Operating in Puerto Rico," in *Investigation of Political, Economic, and Social Conditions in Puerto Rico: Hearings before the Subcommittee of the House Committee of Insular Affairs, Part 19, Pursuant to HR 159*, 78th Cong., 2nd sess., 1944 (Washington, D.C.: Government Printing Office, 1944), 1756, 1760; *Annual Report of the Secretary of the Interior for the Fiscal Year Ending June 30, 1937*, 320; "Bars Hiring of Non–Puerto Ricans," *New York Times*, October 24, 1935.

32 Fairbank, *Chardon Plan*, 53.

33 Fairbank, *Chardon Plan*, 53; see also PRRA, *Puerto Rico: A Guide to the Island and Boriquén: Compiled and Written by the Puerto Rico Reconstruction Administration in Co-Operation with the Writers' Program of the Works Progress Administration* (1940; repr., New York: Gordon Press, 1979), 28.

34 *El Dia: El Periodico de Ponce*, October 4, 1935, folder 1, Slum Clearance Division, RG 323, NARA-NYC.

35 Memo, Gruening to Ickes, August 6, 1935, folder 8: Puerto Rico, 1934–1935, box 255, Secretary of Interior File, Ickes Papers.

36 Robert David Johnson, *Ernest Gruening and the American Dissenting Tradition* (Cambridge, MA: Harvard University Press, 1998), 111, 116, 123. See also Anne O'Hare McCormick, "The New Deal Looks Overseas," *New York Times*, January 20, 1935.

Notes to Pages 53–55 · 175

37 Johnson, *Ernest Gruening*, 121.

38 A. W. Maldonado, *Luis Muñoz Marín: Puerto Rico's Democratic Revolution* (San Juan: La Editorial, Universidad de Puerto Rico, 2006), 137.

39 César J. Ayala and Rafael Bernabe, *Puerto Rico in the American Century: A History since 1898* (Chapel Hill: University of North Carolina Press, 2007), 110; Arturo Morales Carrión, *Puerto Rico: A Political and Cultural History* (New York: Norton, 1983), 234; Maldonado, *Luis Muñoz Marín*, 139–141. Like Winship, Riggs was retired from the military; he had served in World War I and various diplomatic roles during the Wilson administration. In Washington, where he was born, he was a neighbor and friend of Millard Tydings, the influential Democratic senator from Maryland.

40 "El Coronel de la Policía muerto a balazos: Dos nacionalistas, uno de ellos el matador, fueron luego Muertos por la Uniformada en el Cuartel: En Utuado fue herido gravemente el Jefe de Policía y levemente un guardia—Otra nacionalistas result allí muerto," *El Mundo*, February 24, 1936, 1; "2 in Puerto Rico Kill Police Head and Are Shot Dead," *New York Times*, February 24, 1936, 1.

41 Maldonado, *Luis Muñoz Marín*, 120, 138.

42 Quoted in Federico Ribes Tovar, *Albizu Campos: Puerto Rican Revolutionary* (New York: Plus Ultra, 1971), 58–59.

43 Maldonado, *Luis Muñoz Marín*, 137–138; "2 in Puerto Rico Kill Police Head"; Mathews, *Puerto Rican Politics*, 249–250.

44 Ribes Tovar, *Albizu Campos*, 58–59.

45 Maldonado, *Luis Muñoz Marín*, 137–138; "2 in Puerto Rico Kill Police Head."

46 "7 in Puerto Rico Arrested in Plot: Albizu Campos and Six of His Nationalist Aides Later Are Freed on $10,000 Bonds Each," *New York Times*, March 6, 1936, 1; "Washington informa los tramites que se siguieron: en conexion con el proceso contra los lideres nacionalistas de Puerto Rico," *El Mundo*, March 7, 1936, 1; "Albizu Campos Gets Bond: Puerto Rican Nationalist Is Freed, but Companions Are Held," *New York Times*, April 8, 1936, 17.

47 "Puerto Rican Assails 'Yankee Despotism': Albizu Campos, Nationalist Chief, Says Followers Are Ready to Die for Independence," *New York Times*, April 17, 1936, 1.

48 Mathews, *Puerto Rican Politics*, 251; Morales Carrión, *Puerto Rico*, 235–236; Ayala and Bernabe, *Puerto Rico in the American Century*, 110–112; Ribes Tovar, *Albizu Campos*, 63–66. In addition to the Albizu Campos trials, Cooper was involved in several other prominent cases during the 1930s, including siding against the PRRA in a suit by the Porto Rico Railway, Light, and Power Company in 1938, and in favor of the PPD-led government's case for defending its land reform law (Law 26), which enforced the 500-Acre Law, in 1941. Born in South Carolina, Cooper received a law degree from the Polytechnic Institute in San Germán, where he first visited as a Presbyterian missionary. While serving his second term as governor of South Carolina, Cooper accepted an appointment to the Federal Farm Loan Board and was later asked by Roosevelt to help organize the Commodity Credit Corporation, for which he briefly served as general counsel. Following this, Roosevelt appointed him to serve on the U.S. District Court for Puerto Rico from 1934 to 1947. See "Robert Archer Cooper," National Governors Association, https://www.nga.org/governor/

176 · Notes to Pages 55–57

robert-archer-cooper/; "Polytechnic Institute, San Germán," Presbyterian Historical Society, https://digital.history.pcusa.org/islandora/object/islandora:142269.

49 "Los líderes politicos y el Proyecto Tydings," *El Mundo*, April 25, 1936. See also Frank Otto Gatell, "Independence Rejected: Puerto Rico and the Tydings Bill of 1936," *Hispanic American Historical Review* 38, no. 1 (February 1958): 25–44.

50 For example, see Gatell, "Independence Rejected"; Mathews, *Puerto Rican Politics and the New Deal*, 254–55; Fairbank, *Chardon Plan*, 38–39; Roberta Ann Johnson, *Puerto Rico: Commonwealth or Colony?* (New York: Praeger, 1980), 134–135; Morales Carrión, *Puerto Rico*, 234; Carr, *Puerto Rico*, 62–63; Nancy Morris, *Puerto Rico: Culture, Politics, and Identity* (Westport, CT: Praeger, 1995), 39–40; Maldonado, *Luis Muñoz Marín*, 142–145. An exact quote from Tydings appears in numerous places, including Gatell (33), Carr (62), Morris (39), and Johnson (135). See also "Territories: Unwanted Freedom," *Time*, May 4, 1936; Murray Paddack, "Puerto Rico's Plight," *Current History* 44, no. 3 (June 1936): 91–96. In response to the Tydings Bill, New York congressman Vito Marcantonio proposed a rival bill that would have offered Puerto Rican independence on its own terms without any changes to U.S. tariff or emigration policy. See Gatell, "Independence Rejected," 36. Gruening preferred an approach to independence similar to the Philippine bill. See Gruening to Ickes, March 13, 1936, folder 9, Puerto Rico: 1936, box 255, Secretary of Interior File, Ickes Papers.

51 Ickes, *Secret Diary*, 1: 399; Harold L. Ickes, *The Secret Diary of Harold L. Ickes*, vol. 2: *The Inside Struggle* (New York: Simon & Schuster, 1954), 95.

52 Ickes, *Secret Diary*, 1: 393.

53 Jo Ann E. Argersinger, *Toward a New Deal in Baltimore: People and Government in the Great Depression* (Chapel Hill: University of North Carolina Press, 1988), 196–197; James T. Patterson, *Congressional Conservatism and the New Deal: The Growth of the Conservative Coalition in Congress, 1933–1939* (Lexington: University Press of Kentucky, 1967), 348–349. For more on the influence and opposition of conservative and largely southern congressional Democrats of the era, see Patterson, 24–25; Ira Katznelson, *Fear Itself: The New Deal and the Origins of Our Time* (New York: Norton, 2013), 259. At the same time, the focus on Tydings's conservatism and anti–New Deal posturing does not paint the entire picture of him. Born in Havre de Grace, Maryland, in 1890, Millard Evelyn Tydings graduated from the University of Maryland's law school and served in World War I before being elected to the Maryland House of Delegates, the House of Representatives, and eventually the Senate, where he served from 1927 to 1950. In 1934, he wrote a resolution condemning Nazism and antisemitism and after World War II called for nuclear disarmament and led investigations against Joseph McCarthy, the Republican senator from Wisconsin whose destructive anticommunism crusade defined the cultural Cold War. By all measures, McCarthy's unfounded counterattacks in the press cost Tydings his senatorial reelection in 1950 and ended his political career. See "Millard Evelyn Tydings (1890–1961)," Biographical Directory of the United States Congress, https://bioguide.congress.gov/search/bio/T000446.

54 By this time, James Bourne had also become a critic of the PRRA. See "Relief Head

Scores Puerto Rican Work: J. R. Bourne Says Gruening Projects Fail to Give Aid to Many People," *New York Times*, June 22, 1936.

55 Ickes, *Secret Diary*, 2: 5; "Gruening Agency Shifted; Puerto Rican Reconstruction Aid Is Put Under Ickes," *New York Times*, November 18, 1936. See also "Executive Order 7493—Placing the Administrative Acts of the Puerto Rico Reconstruction Administration under the Control and Supervision of the Secretary of the Interior until Further Order," November 14, 1936, *The American Presidency Project*, https://www.presidency.ucsb.edu/documents/executive-order-7493-placing-the -administrative-acts-the-puerto-rico-reconstruction.

56 "Chardón dice que Gruening ha desprestigiado su cargo," *El Mundo*, November 13, 1936. See also "Gruening afirma que no quiere aceptarle la renuncia a Chardón," *El Mundo*, November 7, 1936; "Chardón cree 'muy posible' una solución satisfactoria," *El Mundo*, November 8, 1936. On Chardón's influence in other parts of Latin America, see Timothy W. Lorek, "The Puerto Rican Connection: Recovering the 'Cultural Triangle' in Global Histories of Agricultural Development," *Agricultural History* 94, no. 1 (Winter 2020): 108–140.

57 "7 Die in Puerto Rico Riot, 50 Injured as Police Fire on Fighting Nationalists," *New York Times*, March 22, 1937; "Aumentan a quince los muertos de Ponce," *El Mundo*, March 23, 1937; "Se Mantiene un refuerzo de 200 policias en Ponce," *El Mundo*, March 24, 1937.

58 Ickes, *Secret Diary*, 2: 5–6, 47, 150, 160, 329; "Chardón rechazo el cargo: De decano de Colegio de Agricultural," *El Mundo*, November 12, 1936; "Chardón to Study Wild Potato," *New York Times*, November 17, 1936.

59 "El Partido Liberal pide 'una investigación minuciosa que depure toda la verdad de lo occurido' el domingo en Ponce," *El Mundo*, March 24, 1937. See also Maldonado, *Luis Muñoz Marín*, 151–153; Mathews, *Puerto Rican Politics*, 312; Ayala and Bernabe, *Puerto Rico in the American Century*, 116; Ronald Fernández, *The Disenchanted Island: Puerto Rico and the United States in the Twentieth Century* (Westport, CT: Praeger, 1996), 131–132; Jorge Rodríguez Beruff, "From Winship to Leahy: Crisis, War, and Transition in Puerto Rico," in Alfred W. McCoy and Francisco A. Scarano, eds., *Colonial Crucible: Empire and the Making of the Modern American State* (Madison: University of Wisconsin Press, 2009), 433; José Paralitici, "Imprisonment and Colonial Domination, 1898–1958," in Ramón Bosque Pérez and José Javier Colón Morera, eds., *Puerto Rico under Colonial Rule: Political Persecution and the Quest for Human Rights* (Albany: SUNY Press, 2006), 74–75.

60 "Barceló declara que una asemblea debe eliminar todos los radicalismos que had pertubado la marcha de nuestra partido," *El Mundo*, March 24, 1937. See also Maldonado, *Luis Muñoz Marín*, 155–157.

61 Pedro A. Cabán, "Puerto Rico: State Formation in a Colonial Context," *Caribbean Studies* 30, no. 2 (July-December 2002), 184; Rodríguez Beruff, *Strategy as Politics*, 185–187; Maldonado, *Luis Muñoz Marín*, 155–157.

62 Letter regarding organizational set up of the PRRA, October 22, 1936, folder 9, Puerto Rico: 1936, box 255, Secretary of Interior File, Ickes Papers.

63 Muñoz Marín to Ruby Black, October 26, 1936 (forwarded to Ickes by Black on

178 · Notes to Pages 59–60

November 5), folder 9, Puerto Rico: 1936, box 255, Secretary of Interior File, Ickes Papers.

64 As Jason Scott Smith has argued, the large-scale public works of the PWA and WPA were "the New Deal's central enterprise" and have proven to be "extraordinarily successful method[s] of state-sponsored economic development." Jason Scott Smith, *Building New Deal Liberalism: The Political Economy of Public Works, 1933–1956* (Cambridge: Cambridge University Press, 2006), 19, 84, 88, 118. See also Robert D. Leighninger Jr., *Long-Range Public Investment: The Forgotten Legacy of the New Deal* (Charleston: University of South Carolina Press, 2007).

65 According to Leona Bachrach Gerard, Roosevelt replaced Gruening with Ickes to capitalize on his reputation as "Honest Harold," who had instilled several anticorruption measures within the PWA. One of his closest executive assistants, Gerard wrote that the Ickes promotion came with the "clear understanding that management of the . . . program would emanate from the Assistant Administrator in San Juan." See Leona Bachrach Gerard, "Mission to Puerto Rico—1937," 7–8, n.d. (probably written 1978), folder 2, Miles H. Fairbank Papers, 1975–1978, Franklin D. Roosevelt Presidential Library. See also "Ickes Named to New Post: Becomes Head of Reconstruction Administration in Puerto Rico," *New York Times*, August 18, 1937.

66 Fairbank, "Chardon Plan," draft copy; Harold Ickes to E. K. Burlew, November 15, 1937, folder 2: 1937, box 256, Secretary of Interior File, Ickes Papers.

67 Fairbank's agricultural roots in the Baltimore area were strong. Along with owning a sixty-acre farm in Howard County, Fairbank was the secretary-treasurer (along with several other positions) of the Maryland Farm Bureau. See "Miles H. Fairbank Gets Job in Puerto Rico: Appointed to Organize Productive Credit Associations on Island," *Baltimore Sun*, January 31, 1934; "Fairbank Inspects Thin Suits Looking to Puerto Rico Post," *Baltimore Sun*, February 6, 1934; "Change in San Juan Post: Miles H. Fairbank, of Maryland, Replaces Dr. Chardón," *Baltimore Sun*, November 10, 1936; "Gets Puerto Rican Post: Miles H. Fairbank Heads $42,000,000 Reconstruction Program," *New York Times*, November 10, 1936; "Fairbank hablo ayer por telefono con Gruening: Dice que la orden del Presidente no affecta la estructura de la PRRA," *El Mundo*, November 19, 1936; Harwood Hull, "Priming the Puerto Rican Pump: A Marylander Is Directing the Island's Recovery Program," *Baltimore Sun*, January 31, 1937; "Fairbank Appointment Is Confirmed by Senate: Catonsville Man Will Be Regional Administrator for Puerto Rico Agency," *Baltimore Sun*, January 17, 1937; "Puerto Rico Office Given Up by Gruening: Miles H. Fairbank Gets Post as Head of Reconstruction Administration of Island," *New York Times*, July 14, 1937; "Ickes Named to New Post: Becomes Head of Reconstruction Administration in Puerto Rico," *New York Times*, August 18, 1937. See also Teresita A. Levy, *Puerto Ricans in the Empire: Tobacco Growers and U.S. Colonialism* (New Brunswick, NJ: Rutgers University Press, 2014), 102–103.

68 "El Gobernador Winship deseoso de renunciar: en Washington consideren a Fairbank para el caso de que actual Ejecutivo persista en sus propósitos," *El Mundo*, April 13, 1937.

Notes to Pages 60–64 · 179

69 "Martínez Nadal dice Fairbank es non grato para Governador: Acusa le jefe de 'PRRA' de estar construyendo una maquinaria política en Puerto Rico," *El Mundo*, November 14, 1938. The story was picked up and expanded by the Associated Press.

70 "CCC Camps in Puerto Rico Torn Down, Unused, Is Charge: Island Senate President Calls Construction Unnecessary Because People Rebel at Regimentation," *Baltimore Sun*, September 15, 1938. The CCC operated in Puerto Rico from 1933 to its permanent closure in 1942. On the CCC in Puerto Rico, see Manuel Valdés Pizzini, Michael González Cruz, and José Eduardo Martínez, *La transformación del paisaje puertorriqueño y la disciplina del Cuerpo Civil de Conservación, 1933–1942* (Río Piedras: Centro de Investigaciones Sociales, Universidad de Puerto Rico, 2011), 262–263.

71 "Fairbank sucesor de Chardón," *El Mundo*, November 10, 1936. Fairbank himself only commented that he was sorry to see Chardón leave under such circumstances. See also "Fairbank espera que el nuevo plan cafetero de la PRRA," *El Mundo*, October 29, 1936; "Ickes tendra ahora la jefatura suprema de la 'PRRA,'" *El Mundo*, November 16, 1936; "Munoz Marín declara que Roosevelt no podia 'permanencer indiferente ante la situación en la 'PRRA,'" *El Mundo*, November 16, 1936.

72 Ickes to Coll y Cuchí, July 19, 1937, folder 1: 1937, box 256, Secretary of Interior File, Ickes Papers.

73 Tufts College, *Announcement of the Engineering School* (Boston: Tufts College, 1916), 105; John W. Leonard, *Who's Who in Engineering: A Biographical Dictionary of Contemporaries* (Brooklyn: John W. Leonard Corporation, 1922), 1311; Fairbank, *Chardon Plan*, 31–32, 36. His brother, Major General Luis Raúl Esteves, was the first leader of the Puerto Rican National Guard and the first head of the PRRA Personnel Division before resigning in 1936. "Se hara un reajuste del personal de la PRRA," *El Mundo*, November 11, 1936; "Luis R. Esteves (1893–1958)," in Alexander M. Bielakowski, ed., *Ethnic and Racial Minorities in the U.S. Military: An Encyclopedia* (Santa Barbara, CA: ABC-CLIO, 2013).

74 Fairbanks (*sic*), "Puerto Rico Reconstruction Administration," 354.

75 Fairbank, *Chardon Plan*, 49–51.

Chapter 3. *Para Permanencia*

1 "La fábrica de cemento que construye la PRRA en Cataño," *El Mundo*, January 23, 1938. The term "Portland" comes from Victorian England, where this type of cement was first manufactured and thought to resemble a kind of building stone from the Isle of Portland.

2 The largest recorded period of mangrove decline took place during the long era of agricultural expansion between 1800 and 1940. Sebastián Martinuzzi, William A. Gould, Ariel E. Lugo, and Ernesto Medina, "Conversion and Recovery of Puerto Rican Mangroves: 200 Years of Change," *Forest Ecology and Management* 257 (2009): 75–84, https://data.fs.usda.gov/research/pubs/iitf/ja_iitf_2009_martinuzzi001.pdf. For more on the environmental importance of mangroves in Puerto Rico and present-day efforts to restore them, see Aaron M. Ellison and Elizabeth J. Farn-

sworth, "Anthropogenic Disturbance of Caribbean Mangrove Ecosystems: Past Impacts, Present Trends, and Future Predictions," *Biotropica* 28, no. 4, part A (December 1996): 549–565; Benjamin L. Branoff and Sebastián Martinuzzi, "The Structure and Composition of Puerto Rico's Urban Mangroves," *Forests* 11, no. 10 (2020), https://www.mdpi.com/1999-4907/11/10/1119; Benjamin Lee Branoff, "Quantifying the Influence of Urbanization on Puerto Rico's Mangrove Ecosystems" (PhD diss., University of Puerto Rico, Río Piedras, 2018); Adriana Colón Adorno, "Analyzing Changes in Puerto Rican Mangroves and Local Conditions to Identify Restoration Opportunities," *Tropical Resources* 39 (2020), https://tri.yale.edu/tropical-resources/tropical-resources-vol-39/analyzing-changes-puerto-rican-mangroves-and-local; Ann Grauvogl, "Restoring Mangroves in Puerto Rico Supports Human Health and Well-Being," Global Health Institute, July 15, 2021, https://ghi.wisc.edu/restoring-mangroves-in-puerto-rico-supports-human-health-and-well-being/; David Thill, "Setting Down Roots: Mangroves Interlock with Communities on Puerto Rico's North Coast," WWF Environment and Disaster Management, June 2, 2022, https://envirodm.org/resource/setting-down-roots-mangroves-interlock-with-communities-on-puerto-ricos-north-coast/.

3 On Operation Bootstrap's place in the literature, see Emilio Pantojas-García, "End-of-the-Century Studies of Puerto Rico's Economy, Politics, and Culture: What Lies Ahead?," *Latin American Research Review* 35, no. 3 (2000): 227–240.

4 Congress allocated $850,000 from the Emergency Relief Appropriation Act of 1935 for the Cataño plant and additional allotments totaling $616,500 in 1936, 1937, and 1938. In 1978, Fairbank wrote that the total construction cost of the cement plant was $1,444,831.14 (just below the $1,466,500 allocated). Manuel Font to Arturo Cordova Infante, March 18, 1938, Puerto Rico Cement Corporation folder (PRCC), General Records Relating to the Cement Plant Project, RG 323, NARA-NYC (hereafter Cement Plant Records); "Outline of the History of the Cement Plant Project," box 2, Accounting and Cost folder, Cement Plant Records; Miles H. Fairbank, Testimony, *Hearings before the Subcommittee of the Committee on Appropriations: Making Appropriations for Work Relief and Relief, Fiscal Year 1941*, U.S. Congress, House of Representatives, 76th Cong., 3rd sess. (Washington, D.C.: Government Printing Office, 1940), 149–151; Miles H. Fairbank, *The Chardon Plan and the Puerto Rico Reconstruction Administration, 1934–1954* (San Juan: Fairbank Corporation, 1978), 8–9. The military base was renamed Fort Buchanan in 1940.

5 "Memorandum on the Cement Plant," January 16, 1939, Accounting and Cost folder, box 2, Cement Plant Records.

6 Beatriz Del Cueto, "The Development of Hydraulic Mortars, Cement, and Concrete in Puerto Rico," *Journal of Preservation Technology* 42, no. 1 (2011): 45.

7 Del Cueto, "Development of Hydraulic Mortars," 45–46; Beatriz Del Cueto, "Portland Cements in the Spanish Caribbean as Agents of Change: Hydraulic Mosaics and Concrete Blocks," paper presented at the Fifth International Congress on Construction History, Chicago, June 3–7, 2015, 3–5.

8 Del Cueto, "Development of Hydraulic Mortars," 5–7; Del Cueto, "Portland Cements," 47.

Notes to Pages 65–69 · 181

9 Del Cueto, "Portland Cements," 48, 52n18.

10 Manuel Font to Arturo Cordova Infante, March 18, 1938, PRCC folder, box 1, Cement Plant Records. See American Society of Engineers, *Year Book* (1933), 62; House of Representatives History Office, "Pagán, Bolívar," https://history.house.gov/People/Listing/P/PAGÁN,-Bolívar-(P000013)/.

11 "La fábrica de cemento que construye la PRRA en Cataño," *El Mundo*, January 23, 1938, 11; "Puerto Rico to Build Factory for Cement," *New York Times*, April 23, 1936, 10.

12 "La fábrica de cemento." Larrínaga was born in Trujillo Alto in 1847 and educated at the Rensselaer Polytechnic Institute in upstate New York just after the Civil War—a time when it was unusual for Puerto Ricans to attend college in the United States. Larrínaga designed and built the first railroad line in Puerto Rico extending from San Juan to Río Piedras and helped found the Partido Federalista de Puerto Rico (precursor to the Partido de Unión) with Luis Muñoz Rivera in 1900. After joining the Union Party, Larrínaga served as the second resident commissioner from 1905 to 1911. See House of Representatives History Office, "Larrínaga, Tulio (1847–1917)," https://history.house.gov/People/Detail/16721; E. Fernandez Garcia, Francis W. Hoadley, and Eugenio Astol, eds., *El Libro de Puerto Rico* (San Juan: El Libro Azul, 1923), 311. Antonio Romero is also noteworthy as the husband of Josefina Barceló Bird and thus the son-in-law of Liberal Party leader Antonio Barceló.

13 "Memorandum on the Cement Plant," January 16, 1939; Harwood Hull, "Puerto Rico Hopes for Speedy Action: Winship's Washington Stay Strengthens Belief in Rehabilitation Plan," *New York Times*, November 4, 1934, 81. On the longer history of imported salted fish in Puerto Rico during the Spanish colonial era, including cod, haddock, and herring, see David Griffith, Carlos Garcia-Quijano, and Manuel Valdés Pizzini, "A Fresh Defense: A Cultural Biography of Quality in Puerto Rican Fishing," *American Anthropologist* 115, no. 1 (2013): 21–22.

14 Albert W. Buel, "The Industrial Development of the Island of Porto Rico, Suggestions and Warnings from a Recent Investigation," *Engineering Magazine*, August 1900, 683–696.

15 Del Cueto, "Portland Cements," 48–49.

16 "Memorandum on the Cement Plant," January 16, 1939; "PRCC Accounting Report," July 1944, box 2, Accounting and Cost folder, Cement Plant Records; General Records Relating to the Cement Plant Project, RG 323, NARA-NYC; "Puerto Rico Gets Plant: $1,000,000 Cement Factory to Be Run by Government," *New York Times*, March 19, 1938, 5.

17 "PRCC Accounting Report," July 1944, box 2, Accounting and Cost folder, Cement Plant Records; "Statement of Under Secretary of Puerto Rico Cement Corporation," June 16, 1943, General Accounting Office, *Reference Manual of Government Corporations* (Washington, D.C.: General Printing Office, 1945), 460.

18 "La fábrica de cemento pasó ya al gobierno insular: Ayer se hizo el primer despacho del producto a una firma privada en virtud de una negociación efectuado el sábado," *El Mundo*, January 17, 1939.

19 For example, see James L. Dietz, *Economic History of Puerto Rico: Institutional*

182 · Notes to Pages 69–71

Change and Capitalist Development (Princeton, NJ: Princeton University Press, 1986), 156; Emilio Pantojas-García, *Development Strategies as Ideology: Puerto Rico's Export-led Industrialization Experience* (Boulder, CO: Lynne Rienner, 1990), 44.

20 Michael Grey, *New Deal Medicine: The Rural Health Programs of the Farm Security Administration* (Baltimore: Johns Hopkins University Press, 1999), 99.

21 Grey, *New Deal Medicine*, 186n18, 208–209n70; William E. Leuchtenburg, *Franklin D. Roosevelt and the New Deal: 1932–1940* (1963; repr., New York: Harper Collins, 2009), 133; Jason Scott Smith, *Building New Deal Liberalism: The Political Economy of Public Works, 1933–1956* (Cambridge: Cambridge University Press, 2006), 94, 113, 156; Fairbank, *Chardon Plan*, 41–42; Miles H. Fairbank to Governor Blanton Winship, March 20, 1937, folder 1, Toro Negro Hydroelectric Project, Records of the Rural Electrification Division, RG 323, NARA-NYC; Antonio S. Lucchetti, *Second General Report on the Utilization of the Water Resources of Puerto Rico, 1935–45 / Segunda memoria general sobre la utilización de las fuentes fluviales de Puerto Rico, 1935–45* (San Juan: Government of Puerto Rico Printing Office, 1945), 8; *Creating the Puerto Rico Water Resources Authority: Hearings before the Committee of Insular Affairs on HR 8239*, House of Representatives, 76th Cong., 3rd sess., March 19–22, 25–29, and April 15–16, 18–19, 1940 (Washington, D.C.: Government Printing Office, 1940).

22 Miles Fairbank, "Puerto Rico Reconstruction Administration," in Harold L. Ickes, *Annual Report of the Secretary of the Interior for the Fiscal Year Ended June 30, 1938* (Washington, D.C.: Government Printing Office, 1938), 285.

23 Outline of the History of the Cement Plant Project, box 2, Accounting and Cost folder, Cement Plant Records; Fairbank, "Puerto Rico Reconstruction Administration," 290.

24 See "Increase in Prices of Construction Materials," Carlos Chardón to Ernest Gruening, February 21, 1936, box 1, Carlos Chardón folder, Confidential Records of the Assistant Administrator, 1936–1952, RG 323, NARA-NYC; Miles Fairbank, radiogram to Guillermo Esteves, January 20, 1938; Esteves, radiogram to E. E. Glover, Department of the Interior, January 20, 1938; Fairbank to B. S. Sloeau, Procurement Division of the Treasury Department, January 26, 1938, all box 1, Cement folder, Confidential Records of the Assistant Administrator, 1936–1952, RG 323, NARA-NYC.

25 On organized labor and the New Deal in Puerto Rico, see Blanca G. Silvestrini, *Los trabajadores puertorriqueqos y el Partido Socialista 1932–1940* (Río Piedras: University of Puerto Rico Press, 1979); Miles Galvin, *The Organized Labor Movement in Puerto Rico* (London: Associated University Presses, 1979); Antonio Lauria-Perricelli, "Puerto Rico in the 1930s," in Constance R. Sutton, ed., *Revisiting Caribbean Labour* (Kingston, Jamaica: Ian Randle, 2005), 3–5; Héctor Reyes, "Puerto Rico: The Last Colony," *International Socialist Review* 3 (Winter 1997); Anne S. Macpherson, "Birth of the U.S. Colonial Minimum Wage: The Struggle over the Fair Labor Standards Act in Puerto Rico, 1938–1941," *Journal of American History* 104, no. 3 (December 2017): 656–680.

26 See Robert W. Lesley, "Cement—A Review," *Concrete: A Monthly Magazine Dedi-*

cated to Concrete Construction and Cement Manufacture 13, no. 6 (December 1918): 59; Teo A. Babún Jr., "Cuba's Cement Industry," *Annual Proceedings of the Association for the Study of the Cuban Economy*, vol. 7 (1997); Ana Lense-Larrauri, "Cement Transforms Mariel—and My Family," *Miami Herald*, August 29, 2010. Cement production in the Caribbean region has expanded since World War II and remains an essential factor in combating disease and insulating infrastructure from hurricanes. Today, local cement is produced in Barbados, Cuba, the Dominican Republic, El Salvador, Guatemala, Haiti, Honduras, Jamaica, Nicaragua, Panama, Puerto Rico, and Trinidad and Tobago. Most of these plants were financed by foreign capital and run by foreign corporations, with Scandinavian investments in Caribbean cement particularly high. The 7.0 earthquake that struck Haiti in 2010 killed over 200,000 people and caused massive damage to the country's cement-based architecture. On cement production in the Caribbean, see Peter Edwards, "Central America and the Caribbean—Regional Cement Focus,"*Global Cement Magazine*, August 22, 2012. The PRCC was later privatized, purchased by the private Ponce Cement Corporation in 1950 and sold to CEMEX of Mexico in 2002. "Puerto Rican Cement to Be Sold to CEMEX, Mexican Cement Producer to Pay $160 Million," *Puerto Rico Herald*, September 28, 2000; "Cemex to Buy Puerto Rican Cement," *Wall Street Journal*, June 13, 2002.

27 "Correspondencia de la Puerto Rico Cement Corporation," caja 356, "Puerto Rico Cement Corporation," Fondo Oficina de Gobierno, tarea 96–20, parte 1, Archivo General de Puerto Rico; Miles Fairbank, letter to Manuel Font, January 25, 1939, Accounting and Cost folder, box 2, Cement Plant Records.

28 Rupert Emerson to Rexford G. Tugwell, January 17, 1945, and Harold Ickes to Leo T. Crowley, June 6, 1945, in "Correspondencia de la Puerto Rico Cement Corporation." On the history of the Dominican cement industry, see Del Cueto, "Development of Hydraulic Mortars," 3. It has also been reported that the Dominican Republic did not have its own functioning cement plant until 1973, over ten years after Trujillo's assassination. See Edwards, "Central America and the Caribbean."

29 "Texto del convenio collectivo firmando entre la C.G.T. y la Puerto Rico Cement Corporation: Este es el primero en su clase que se firma en Puerto Rico," *El Mundo*, December 16, 1943, 10; "PRCC Accounting Report," box 2, Accounting and Cost folder, Cement Plant Records.

30 For example, see Assistant Administrator's Office folder, box 1, General Records relating to Administration, RG 323, NARA-NYC; Records of the Engineering Division, RG 323, NARA-NYC.

31 Manuel Font to PRCC Board of Directors, box 2, Accounting and Cost folder, Cement Plant Records; Miles Fairbank to E. K. Burlew, assistant secretary of the interior, May 1, 1941, box 1, Cement Plant folder, Confidential Records of the Assistant Administrator, 1936–1952, RG 323, NARA-NYC; "Federal Agencies Operating in Puerto Rico," in *Investigation of Political, Economic, and Social Conditions in Puerto Rico: Hearings before the Subcommittee of the House Committee of Insular Affairs, Part 19, Pursuant to HR 159*, 78th Cong., 2nd sess., 1944 (Washington, D.C.: Government Printing Office, 1944), 1758.

32 Guillermo Esteves to Ernest Gruening, May 3, 1937, box 2, Construction Projects—General Memoranda, Reports on Activities, etc., folder, Records Relating to Construction Projects Directed by the Engineering Division, RG 323, NARA-NYC. See also Harwood Hull, "Priming the Puerto Rican Pump: A Marylander Is Directing the Island's Recovery Program," *Baltimore Sun*, January 31, 1937.

33 José Ferré to PRCC, Letters, June 1939–January 1941, box 2, Accounting and Cost folder, Cement Plant Records. José Ferré's father, Antonio Ferré Bacallao, founded the Puerto Rico Iron Works in 1918.

34 Governor Winship to Ponce Cement Corporation, Letters, June 1939–January 1941, box 2, Accounting and Cost folder, Cement Plant Records.

35 The privatization of these public resources has been discussed in A. W. Maldonado, *Boom and Bust in Puerto Rico: How Politics Destroyed an Economic Miracle* (Notre Dame, IN: University of Notre Dame Press, 2021), 45–46; Maldonado, *Teodoro Moscoso and Puerto Rico's Operation Bootstrap* (Gainesville: University Press of Florida, 1997), 63–68, 170.

36 Fomento is still in operation today. Born in Barcelona in 1910, Moscoso attended elementary school in New York before graduating from Ponce High School. He attended the Philadelphia School of Pharmacy and graduated from the University of Michigan in 1932. After returning to Ponce and working in his family's pharmacy for several years, Moscoso was recruited to work for the local branch of the Puerto Rico Housing Authority and led several "slum clearance" programs before joining Luis Muñoz Marín in the PPD and, later, the Kennedy administration. See Maldonado, *Teodoro Moscoso*, 7–9.

37 Enteritis is the inflammation of the small intestine, most commonly associated with contaminated water or food. Progress Reports, box 3, Engineering Division Construction Projects, "Swamp Land Filling and Draining for Malaria Control" folder, Records Relating to Construction Projects Directed by the Engineering Division, RG 323, NARA-NYC; Progress Reports, General Records Relating to the Cement Plant Project, RG 323, NARA-NYC; Elisa M. González, "Food for Every Mouth: Nutrition, Agriculture, and Public Health in Puerto Rico, 1920s–1960s" (PhD diss., Columbia University, 2016); Eduardo Garrido Morales, *Annual Report of the Commissioner of Health of Porto Rico, 1937–1938* (San Juan, 1938).

38 "PRRA Organization, Financial Policies, and Functions Prepared Pursuant to the Requirements of Senate Resolution 150, 75th Congress, First Session," PRRA History Report folder, box 1, Records of the Finance Division, RG 323, NARA-NYC. See also Puerto Rico Emergency Relief Administration (PRERA), *Second Report of the Puerto Rican Emergency Relief Administration, from September 1, 1934, to September 30, 1935* and *Report of the Federal Emergency Relief Administration for Puerto Rico, from October 1, 1935 to June 30, 1936, in Liquidation to October 1937* (Washington, D.C.: Government Printing Office, 1939), 2.

39 Miles Fairbank to Governor Blanton Winship, June 30, 1939, box 3, Construction Projects, "Swamp Land Filling and Draining for Malaria Control" folder, Records Relating to Construction Projects Directed by the Engineering Division, RG 323, NARA-NYC; "Federal Agencies Operating in Puerto Rico," 1757.

40 Miles Fairbank to Blanton Winship, November 14, 1938, box 1, Carlos Chardón folder, Confidential Records of the Assistant Administrator, 1936–1952, RG 323, NARA-NYC. In 1942, Benitez Rexach built the Normandie Hotel in San Juan.

41 Jorell Meléndez-Badillo, *The Lettered Barriada: Workers, Archival Power, and the Politics of Knowledge in Puerto Rico* (Durham, NC: Duke University Press, 2021), 20–21. On Egozcue, see Thomas Mathews, *Puerto Rican Politics and the New Deal* (1960; repr., New York: Da Capo Press, 1974), 238–239.

42 César J. Ayala and Laird W. Bergad, *Agrarian Puerto Rico: Reconsidering Rural Economy and Society, 1899–1940* (Cambridge: Cambridge University Press, 2020), 126.

43 Luz Marie Rodríguez, "[Re]visions on Social Housing in San Juan: Notes on Workers' Housing (1930s–1950s)," in Jorge Lizardi and Martin Schwegmann, eds., *Ambivalent Spaces: Memory and Oblivion in Modern Social Architecture* (San Juan: Ciu(a) d y Callejón, 2012), 2; Luz Marie Rodríguez, "New Deal Communities for Puerto Rico: The Urban Housing Projects of the Puerto Rico Reconstruction Administration" (MS thesis, Mississippi State University, 1994), 31–32; Insular Department of Health, Annual Reports for 1934 and 1935, Progress Report folder, Cement Plant Records.

44 James Bourne to Joseph Hyde Pratt, February 13, 1935, box 2, Records of the Engineering Division, RG 323, NARA-NYC.

45 Progress Report, General Records Relating to the Cement Plant Project, RG 323, NARA-NYC; Harold Ickes, *The Secret Diary of Harold L. Ickes*, vol. 1: *The First Thousand Days* (New York: Simon & Schuster, 1953), 504.

46 *Problems in Connection with Slum Clearance in Puerto Rico: With Special Reference to the San Juan Area*, 2–3, 1939, box 1, Slums folder, Records of the Engineering Division, and folder 1, Records of the Engineering Division, Slum Clearance Division, RG 323, NARA-NYC. Agustín M. de Andino later served as the head of the insular Office of Housing Administration. See "Statement of Under Secretary of Puerto Rico Cement Corporation," 460.

47 *Problems in Connection with Slum Clearance*, 1.

48 *Problems in Connection with Slum Clearance*, 2–3.

49 Adolfo Noñes, "Slums and Settlements," February 24, 1936, box 2, Ponce Slum Clearance Division, Records of the Engineering Division, RG 323, NARA-NYC. On Mayagüez, see "Housing of the Poor, Mayagüez," box 2, Slum Clearance Division, Records of the Engineering Division, RG 323, NARA-NYC.

50 *Problems in Connection with Slum Clearance*, 6–7. On the Fajardo Sugar Company's construction of relief houses, see Harwood Hull, "Views from Fajardo, Puerto Rico," Prints and Photographs Division, Library of Congress.

51 *Problems in Connection with Slum Clearance*, 1–3, 6–7; Bourne to Pratt, February 13, 1935. See also Jack Delano, photographer, "Ponce, Puerto Rico. House for sale in the slums [1941]," photograph, Farm Security Administration—Office of War Information Photograph Collection, Library of Congress, https://www.loc.gov/resource/fsa .8c07849/.

52 Progress Reports, 1938, Cement Plant Records; *Problems in Connection with Slum Clearance*, 5. For Miranda and Ponce data, see appendix A (pp. 23–29). See also

186 · Notes to Pages 81–93

Zaire Dinzey-Flores, "Temporary Housing, Permanent Communities: Public Housing Policy and Design in Puerto Rico," *Journal of Urban History* 33, no. 3 (2007): 471.

53 *Problems in Connection with Slum Clearance*, 4–5.

54 *Problems in Connection with Slum Clearance*, 11.

55 *Problems in Connection with Slum Clearance*, 20–22.

Chapter 4. The Road to Modernization

1 Manuel Zeno Gandía, *The Pond*, trans. Kal Wagenheim (1894; repr., Princeton, NJ: Markus Wiener, 1999), 54. The original text reads: "Para llegar a ella era neccesario descender una vertiene, vadear, saltando de pedra el río y subir después el empinado cerro. El camino era estrecho, y con frequencia interrumpido por escalones formados por el pie de los caminantes en el terreno barroso del monte. Espesos bosques cubrían las veredas y casi podia afirmarse que el sol no bañaba nunca con rayos directos aquellos lugares." Manuel Zeno Gandía, *La Charca* (1894; repr., Buenos Aires: Stock Cero, 2005), 19.

2 Pablo Morales Otero and Manuel A. Pérez, "Health Work in the Rural Areas of Puerto Rico," *Puerto Rico Journal of Public Health and Tropical Medicine* 15, no. 1 (1939).

3 "Federal Agencies Operating in Puerto Rico," in *Investigation of Political, Economic, and Social Conditions in Puerto Rico: Hearings before the Subcommittee of the House Committee of Insular Affairs, Part 19, Pursuant to HR 159*, 78th Cong., 2nd sess., 1944 (Washington, D.C.: Government Printing Office, 1944), 1763.

4 Progress Reports, box 3, Engineering Division Construction Projects, "Swamp Land Filling and Draining for Malaria Control" folder, Records Relating to Construction Projects Directed by the Engineering Division, RG 323, NARA-NYC (hereafter Engineering Division Construction Projects Records); Progress Reports, 1938, PRCC folder, General Records Relating to the Cement Plant Project, RG 323, NARA-NYC.

5 Walter C. Earle, Luis D. Palacios, and Antonio Arbona, "Methods Used to Control Malaria in Puerto Rico," *Puerto Rico Journal of Public Health and Tropical Medicine* 11, no. 3 (1936).

6 Garrido Morales to Harold Ickes, December 2, 1937, and Blanton Winship to Franklin D. Roosevelt, July 21, 1937, box 3, Engineering Division Construction Projects, "Swamp Land Filling and Draining for Malaria Control" folder, Engineering Division Construction Projects Records.

7 Progress Reports, 1938, General Records Relating to the Cement Plant Project, RG 323, NARA-NYC. See also Progress Reports, box 3, Engineering Division Construction Projects, "Swamp Land Filling and Draining for Malaria Control" folder, Engineering Division Construction Projects Records. See also Nicole Elise Trujillo-Pagan, "Worms as a Hook for Colonising Puerto Rico," *Social History of Medicine* 26, no. 4 (2013); Jose Amador, *Medicine and Nation Building in the Americas, 1890–1940* (Nashville: Vanderbilt University Press, 2015).

8 Pablo Morales Otero to Miles Fairbank, January 10, 1938, Carlos Chardón folder, box 1, Confidential Records of the Assistant Administrator, 1936–1952, RG 323, NARA-NYC; José Rodríguez Pastor, Pablo Morales Otero, George C. Payne, R. Ramírez

Santos, and Euripides Silva, "Tuberculosis Surveys in Puerto Rico: II. A Study of Two Urban Communities. Preliminary Report," *Puerto Rico Journal of Public Health and Tropical Medicine* 10, no. 4 (1935): 514–515.

9 Pablo Morales Otero, Assistant Professor Bacteriology and Hygiene, to Miles Fairbank, box 1, Carlos Chardón folder, Confidential Records of the Assistant Administrator, 1936–1952, RG 323, NARA-NYC; Eduardo Garrido Morales, *Annual Report of the Commissioner of Health of Porto Rico, 1937–1938* (San Juan, 1938), 37–42.

10 Eduardo Garrido Morales, "Developing a Comprehensive Health Service in Puerto Rico: An Address at the Inaugural Meeting of the Puerto Rico Public Health Association, San Juan, September 23, 1941," *American Journal of Public Health and the Nation's Health* 32, no. 1 (January 1942): 59–62; Garrido Morales, "Discurso pronunciado por el Honorable Comisionado de Sanidad en la Primera Asamblea de la Asociación de Salud Pública de Puerto Rico," *Puerto Rico Journal of Public Health and Tropical Medicine* 17, no. 3 (1942). On his political views, see Miles Fairbank to Harold Ickes, March 10, 1938, Assistant Administrator's Office folder, box 1, General Records Relating to Administration 1935–1954, RG 323, NARA-NYC; Miles Fairbank, letter to Lorena Graham, Carlos Chardón folder, box 1, Confidential Records of the Assistant Administrator, 1936–1952, RG 323, NARA-NYC; Francisco A. López Domínguez to M. S. Huberman, n.d., folder 1, box 2, Records of the Rural Electrification Division, PRRA Land Options, RG 323, NARA-NYC.

11 George W. Bachman, *Report of the Director of the School of Tropical Medicine for the Fiscal Year Ending June 1941* (San Juan: University of Puerto Rico, 1941).

12 Section 3, "Luis Muñoz Marín: El Politico 1920–1940," Fundación Luis Muñoz Marín; General Memoranda, box 1, Records of the Engineering Division, RG 323, NARA-NYC; box 4, Construction Projects, UPR Projects, School of Tropical Medicine, Engineering Division Construction Projects Records. A planned three-hundred-bed hospital at the University of Puerto Rico's School of Tropical Medicine was not built.

13 Pablo Morales Otero to Miles Fairbank, November 10, 1938, Carlos Chardón folder, box 1, Confidential Records of the Assistant Administrator, 1936–1952, RG 323, NARA-NYC; Progress Reports, folder 1, box 1, Records of the Engineering Division, RG 323, NARA-NYC; "Federal Agencies Operating in Puerto Rico," 1763.

14 Miles Fairbank, "Puerto Rico Reconstruction Administration," in Harold L. Ickes, *Annual Report of the Secretary of the Interior for the Fiscal Year Ended June 30, 1938* (Washington, D.C.: Government Printing Office, 1938), 285; folder 1, box 1, Records of the Engineering Division, RG 323, NARA-NYC.

15 Otero and Pérez, "Health Work in the Rural Areas of Puerto Rico."

16 Fairbank, "Puerto Rico Reconstruction Administration," 285; PRRA, *Album de Oro de Puerto Rico: Obra divulgacíon cultural en pro de la fraternidad americana*, ed. Antonio M. Monteagudo and Antonio Escámez (Havana: Artes Graficas, 1939), n.p.

17 J. C. Hitchman to Miles Fairbank, August 19, 1938, Farmers Houses—General Memoranda folder, Engineering Division Construction Projects Records.

18 *Problems in Connection with Slum Clearance in Puerto Rico*, 8–10, 1939, box 1, "Slums" folder, Records of the Engineering Division, RG 323, NARA-NYC.

188 · Notes to Pages 96–98

19 Rafael A. González to Carlos Chardón, July 18, 1936, box 1, Experimental Prefabricated Houses, Engineering Division Construction Projects Records, as cited by Luz Marie Rodríguez, PRRA Architecture, Facebook, June 22, 2018, https://www.facebook.com/prraarchitecture.

20 *Greenbelt Towns: A Demonstration in Urban Planning* (Washington, D.C.: Resettlement Administration, 1936), n.p. See also Paul K. Conkin, *Tomorrow a New World: The New Deal Community Program* (1959, repr., Ithaca, NY: Cornell University Press, 2019); Robert D. Leighninger Jr., *Long-Range Public Investment: The Forgotten Legacy of the New Deal* (Columbia: University of South Carolina Press, 2007); Julie D. Turner, *Best-Laid Plans: The Promises and Pitfalls of the New Deal's Greenbelt Towns* (Cincinnati: University of Cincinnati Press, 2022).

21 Telesforo Carrero, *Housing in Puerto Rico: Technical Paper No. 5* (Santurce: Puerto Rico Planning Board, 1950), 26–27.

22 Carrero, *Housing in Puerto Rico*, 20; *Problems in Connection with Slum Clearance in Puerto Rico, 7–10*, 1939, box 1, "Slums" folder, Records of the Engineering Division, RG 323, NARA-NYC. Jorge Ramírez de Arellano attended Syracuse University along with fellow architects Pedro Méndez and Rafael Hernández Romero, who also worked for PRRA. "Los arquitectos de la PRRA: Jorge Ramírez de Arellano (1903–1978)," PRRA Architecture, Facebook, January 31, 2019.

23 Dinzey-Flores, "Temporary Housing," 472–473; Marygrace Tyrrell, "Colonizing Citizens: Housing Puerto Ricans, 1917–1952," (PhD diss., Northwestern University, 2009), 190–194, 199.

24 "Dos millones y medio de dólares ha gastado ya la PRRA: En la construcción de viviendas que dan acomodo a cinco mil personas," *El Mundo,* August 22, 1938. After its completion, PRRA headquarters were moved from Old San Juan to the Eleanor Roosevelt development in Hato Rey. Miles H. Fairbank, *The Chardon Plan and the Puerto Rico Reconstruction Administration, 1934–1954* (San Juan: Fairbank Corporation, 1978), 55.

25 Tyrell, 190; Luz Marie Rodríguez, "New Deal Communities," 169.

26 Adolfo Noñes, "Slums and Settlements," February 24, 1936, box 2, Ponce Slum Clearance Division, Records of the Engineering Division, RG 323, NARA-NYC.

27 Zaire Dinzey-Flores, "Temporary Housing, Permanent Communities: Public Housing Policy and Design in Puerto Rico," *Journal of Urban History* 33, no. 3 (2007): 470–473, 482–485, 489n24, 491n62; Luz Marie Rodríguez, "[Re]visions on Social Housing in San Juan: Notes on Workers' Housing (1930s–1950s)," in Jorge Lizardi and Martin Schwegmann, eds., *Ambivalent Spaces: Memory and Oblivion in Modern Social Architecture* (San Juan: Ciu(a)d y Callejón, 2012), 12.

28 Guillermo Esteves, "Activities of the Puerto Rico Reconstruction Administration in Connection with the Agrarian Reforms in Puerto Rico," in *Caribbean Research Council, Caribbean Land Tenure Symposium of the Caribbean Committee on Agriculture, Nutrition, Fisheries, and Forestry of the Caribbean Research Council* (Washington, D.C., 1946), 163–164.

29 Manuel Font to Miles Fairbank and Guillermo Esteves, January 19, 1937, box 2,

Notes to Pages 98–102 · 189

Farmers Houses—General Memoranda folder, Engineering Division Construction Projects Records.

30 Manuel Font to Guillermo Esteves, February 1, 1937, box 2, Farmers Houses—General Memoranda folder, Engineering Division Construction Projects Records.

31 Fairbank to J. C. Hitchman, Principal Construction Engineer, Work Relief Division, January 29, 1938, box 2, Farmers Houses—General Memoranda folder, Engineering Division Construction Projects Records.

32 J. C. Hitchman to Guillermo Esteves, January 5, 1937, box 1, General Memoranda, Records of the Engineering Division, RG 323, NARA-NYC; Blanton Winship, *Thirty-Ninth Annual Report of the Governor of Puerto Rico* (San Juan: Bureau of Supplies, Printing, and Transportation, 1939), 83.

33 Fairbank, "Puerto Rico Reconstruction Administration," 283.

34 Esteves, "Activities," 164, 165.

35 Contrato de Usufructo Condicional, October 1, 1940, Records Relating to the Rural Rehabilitation Division, RG 323, NARA-NYC; Memo, box 3, Construction Projects—Patillas Bridge folder, Engineering Division Construction Projects Records; Weekly Progress Report, August 26, 1936, Work Relief Division, box 1, General Memoranda, Records of the Engineering Division, RG 323, NARA-NYC.

36 Box 2, La Granja Development Housing Management General Memoranda, Records of the Office of Housing Management, Assistant Administrator, RG 323, NARA-NYC, as cited by PRRA Architecture, "Booklet published for the first anniversary of La Granja Housing Development in Caguas (December 18, 1938)," Facebook, June 21, 2018. On tobacco, see Teresita A. Levy, *Puerto Ricans in the Empire: Tobacco Growers and U.S. Colonialism* (New Brunswick, NJ: Rutgers University Press, 2014). On the growth of sugarcane in Caguas, see José O. Sola, "Colonialism, Planters, Sugarcane, and the Agrarian Economy of Caguas, Puerto Rico, between the 1890s and 1930," *Agricultural History* 85, no. 3 (Summer 2011): 349–372. For population numbers, see PRRA, *Census of Puerto Rico: 1935, Population, Bulletin No. 1: Number and Distribution of Inhabitants*.

37 Avery S. Hoyt, Acting Chief of Bureau of Etymology and Plant Quarantine, USDA, to Ernest Gruening, March 25, 1936, Assistant Administrator's Office folder, box 1, General Records Relating to Administration, RG 323, NARA-NYC; César J. Ayala and Laird W. Bergad, *Agrarian Puerto Rico: Reconsidering Rural Economy and Society, 1899–1940* (Cambridge: Cambridge University Press, 2020), 232–234.

38 Fairbank, "Puerto Rico Reconstruction Administration," 284; Fairbank, *Chardon Plan*, 22, 45; "Federal Agencies Operating in Puerto Rico," 1763; Angela M. Pelzel, "Cattle Fever Tick Surveillance in Texas," *USDA National Animal Health Surveillance System Outlook* (August 2005), 1–2.

39 Fairbank, *Chardon Plan*, 45–46.

40 PRRA, *Puerto Rico: A Guide to the Island and Boriquén: Compiled and Written by the Puerto Rico Reconstruction Administration in Co-Operation with the Writers' Program of the Works Progress Administration* (1940; repr., New York: Gordon Press, 1979), 291; *Maricao Fish Hatchery* (brochure), Puerto Rico Department of Natural and Environmental Resources; "Micropterus salmoides," National Estuarine and

190 · Notes to Pages 102–104

Marine Exotic Species Information System, Smithsonian Institution Environmental Research Center, https://invasions.si.edu/nemesis/species_summary/168160.

41 Fairbank, "Puerto Rico Reconstruction Administration," 293; U.S. Department of Agriculture, *Caribbean National Forest of Puerto Rico* (Washington, D.C.: Government Printing Office, 1936), 19–20; "Federal Agencies Operating in Puerto Rico," 1763; Manuel Valdés Pizzini, Michael González Cruz, and José Eduardo Martínez, *La transformación del paisaje puertorriqueño y la disciplina del Cuerpo Civil de Conservación, 1933–1942* (Río Piedras: Centro de Investigaciones Sociales, Universidad de Puerto Rico, 2011).

42 Esteves, "Activities," 163–164.

43 Miles H. Fairbank, *The Economic Outlook for Puerto Rico: An Address Delivered before the Faculty and Student Body of the University of Puerto Rico* (San Juan: Bureau of Supplies, Printing, and Transportation, 1935), 13–14; "Federal Agencies Operating in Puerto Rico," 1763. See also Blanton Winship, *Thirty-Ninth Annual Report of the Governor of Puerto Rico* (San Juan: Bureau of Supplies, Printing, and Transportation, 1939), 83.

44 Miles H. Fairbank to William D. Leahy, March 20, 1940, Re: Political Affiliations of the Board of Directors of Cooperatives Financed by the Puerto Rico Reconstruction Administration, box 4, Lafayette Central Complaint Folder, Investigations, RG 323, NARA-NYC.

45 Esteves, "Activities," 166–167.

46 Esteves, "Activities," 168; "Living in Peace in a Time of War: The Civilian Public Service Story," https://civilianpublicservice.org/.

47 Luis Muñoz Marín, Amendments to Land Law, Cartapacio 330, Tierras, series 10, Legislatura, 1948–40, subsection 22, Leyes, section 4, Luis Muñoz Marín, Presidente del Senado, 1941–1948, Fundación Luis Muñoz Marín.

48 Gloria Tapia Ríos, *La Central Lafayette: Riqueza, Desarrollo, y Politica en el Sureste de Puerto Rico* (San Juan: Magna Cultura Ediciones, 2014), 241–242; Esteves, "Activities," 168. The Fantauzzi family (originally from Corsica) had many landholdings in southeastern Puerto Rico dating back to 1815, when the Spanish Crown first allowed immigration to Puerto Rico from areas outside of Spain. The family owned many combined businesses in commerce, credit, finance, agriculture, and sugar refining and founded the Central Lafayette on the grounds of the former Central Cuatro Calles in 1905. It was named for the family's business offices on Rue La Fayette in the 9th and 10th arrondissements of Paris, a street named for the French hero of the American Revolution. See Tapia Ríos, *La Central Lafayette*, 52–53, 69–70, 99–101, 126–127; César J. Ayala, *American Sugar Kingdom: The Plantation Economy of the Spanish Caribbean, 1898–1934* (Chapel Hill: University of North Carolina Press, 1999), 144, 226. Arroyo and the southeastern sugar region, which had one of the island's largest rates of landlessness, was noted for its large population of Black Puerto Ricans, who made up over half of the area's population from 1855 to 1935. One trait of the Fantauzzi brothers' businesses, however, seems to have been the ability to adapt, as the family business—which owned hundreds of enslaved persons—

Notes to Pages 105–106 · 191

withstood the abolition of slavery in 1873 and the recession of the 1880s. See César J. Ayala and Laird W. Bergad, "Rural Puerto Rico in the Early Twentieth Century Reconsidered: Land and Society, 1899–1915," *Latin American Research Review* 37, no. 2 (2002): 78; Gloria Tapia Ríos, "Central Lafayette de Arroyo: Eje económico y de cambio social en el sureste puertorriqueño," in Félix R. Huertas González and Juan E. Roque Rivera, eds., *Los pueblos de la región centro oriental y su historia*, vols. 19 and 20 (Gurabo, PR: Universidad del Turabo, Sistema Universitario Ana G. Méndez, 2013), 109; Pablo Morales Otero et al., "Health and Socio-Economic Conditions on a Sugar Cane Plantation," *Puerto Rico Journal of Public Health and Tropical Medicine* 12, no. 4 (1937): 413. In addition to the Central Lafayette, the Fantauzzi family operated the Central Columbia in Maunabo and the Central Providencia in Patillas. The combined holdings were profitable, as Central Columbia alone was once the fifth largest sugar producer in Puerto Rico. Following San Felipe, which caused extensive damage to the mill and the cane fields, the Fantauzzi brothers bought out the other investors of the Columbia and transferred its machinery to enlarge the Central Lafayette. After San Ciprián, the family rebuilt several parts of Lafayette and repaired its service roads and railway lines. In 1932, the family contracted the Puerto Rico Iron Works, owned by Ferré Enterprises of Ponce, to build a single-span steel-truss railroad bridge over the Maunabo River and replace a wooden deck bridge. The railroad bridge would be used to bring cane from the isolated Maunabo valley, where it was transported by truck and reloaded on the railroad to Lafayette. See "Batey Columbia Railroad Bridge," *Historical American Engineering Record* PR-33, National Park Service, Southeast Region, Department of the Interior, 2–5, available at http://lcweb2.loc.gov/master/pnp/habshaer/pr/pr1400/pr1461/data/pr1461data .pdf (accessed October 23, 2023).

49 Tapia Ríos, *La Central Lafayette*, 242, 228–229.

50 Weekly Progress Report, October 28, 1937, box 1, folder 1, General Memoranda, Records of the Engineering Division, RG 323, NARA-NYC.

51 "El president de la Cámara comenta la compra," *El Mundo*, April 15, 1936. See also Tapia Ríos, *La Central Lafayette*, 257.

52 Confidential letter, Miles Fairbank to Governor Leahy, March 20, 1940, box 4, Lafayette Central, Complaint Folder, Investigations, RG 323, NARA-NYC. A five-star admiral in the U.S. Navy, Leahy served as governor from September 1939 to November 1940. For more on his time in office, see Jorge Rodríguez Beruff, ed., *Las memorias de Leahy* (Río Piedras: Fundación Luis Muñoz Marín, 2002).

53 "Claiborne se propone presentar una demanda contra la Central Lafayette," *El Mundo*, October 31, 1939; "Demanda sobre salarios contra la Cooperativa Lafayette," *El Mundo*, November 8, 1939; Anne S. Macpherson, "Birth of the U.S. Colonial Minimum Wage: The Struggle over the Fair Labor Standards Act in Puerto Rico, 1938–1941," *Journal of American History* 104, no. 3 (December 2017): 665. For biographical information on Claiborne, see "Guide to the Papers of Robert Watson Claiborne, 1934–1966," Special Collections, University of Virginia Library. Ernesto Ramos Antonini later joined the Popular Democratic Party and served as Speaker of the

192 · Notes to Pages 106–110

House between 1945 and 1953. Victor Gutierrez Franqui was the attorney general and secretary of justice between 1951 and 1952 and served as the acting governor of Puerto Rico in 1952.

54 Tapia Ríos, *La Central Lafayette*, 265–268; "Co-operative Land Venture Fails," *New York Times*, August 13, 1940.

55 Weekly Reports, box 2, Reports on Activities folder, General Memoranda, Engineering Division Construction Projects Records.

56 "La Central Lafayette ha inaugurado su hospital," *El Mundo*, April 30, 1939. See also "Se hace un estudio de la dieta de los trajabadores agricolas de P.R.," *El Mundo*, April 28, 1937, in Efemérides de la P.R.R.A., *La PRRA según la prensa puertorriqueña, Tomo 4* (1937).

57 Morales Otero et al., "Health and Socio-Economic Conditions," 407–409. See also Pablo Morales Otero et al., "Health and Socio-Economic Conditions in the Tobacco, Coffee and Fruits Regions," *Puerto Rico Journal of Public Health and Tropical Medicine* 14, no. 3 (1939).

58 Morales Otero et al., "Health and Socio-Economic Conditions," 409–413.

59 Weekly Reports, box 2, Reports on Activities folder, General Memoranda, Engineering Division Construction Projects Records.

60 Emilio Serra, Rural Engineering Section, Weekly Construction Progress Report on School Construction, March 7, 1938, box 3, Construction Projects—School Building Program, Engineering Division Construction Projects Records.

61 Jose Gallardo to Harold Ickes, December 9, 1938, box 3, Construction Projects—School Building Program, Engineering Division Construction Projects Records; Evangelista Rosario to Miles Fairbank, November 1939, box 3, Construction Projects—School Building Program, Engineering Division Construction Projects Records. Barceloneta had recently gained notoriety as the home of bantamweight Sixto Escobar, Puerto Rico's first world-champion boxer.

62 Santos Vega to PRRA, September 19, 1937, box 3, Construction Projects—School Building Program, Engineering Division Construction Projects Records; Fairbank to Rufino Gómez, February 13, 1940, box 3, Construction Projects—School Building Program, Engineering Division Construction Projects Records; Memo, Fairbank to Hitchman, *April 23, 1937,* box 1, General Memoranda, Engineering Division Construction Projects Records.

63 Memo, R. B. Pérez Mercado, October 18, 1937, General Folder, box 3, Construction Projects—School Building Program, Engineering Division Construction Projects Records.

64 School Construction Progress Report, August 29, 1937, General Folder, box 3, Construction Projects—School Building Program, Engineering Division Construction Projects Records.

65 School Construction Progress Report, August 29, 1937.

66 Henry A. Hirshberg to Governor William Leahy, May 15, 1940, box 6, William Leahy folder, Confidential Records of the Assistant Administrator, 1936–1952, RG 323, NARA-NYC. See also R. N. Elliott, *Decisions of the Acting Comptroller General of the*

Notes to Pages 110–115 · 193

United States, vol. 17, *July 1, 1937 to June 30, 1938* (Washington, D.C.: Government Printing Office, 1938), 1005.

67 Memo, Jackson C. Hitchman, box 1, General Memoranda, Records of the Engineering Division, RG 323, NARA-NYC; Fairbank to Winship, April 13, 1937, box 1, Investigations, RG 323, NARA-NYC.

68 Miles Fairbank to Guillermo Esteves, July 23, 1937, box 4, University Projects folder, Engineering Division Construction Projects Records; Winship, *Thirty-Ninth Annual Report*, 84.

69 In the 1960s and 1970s, the University of Puerto Rico system was expanded to include campuses in Aguadilla, Arecibo, Bayamón, Carolina, Cayey, Humacao, Ponce, and Utuado.

70 Progress Reports, box 3, Construction Projects, Patillas Bridge folder, Engineering Division Construction Projects Records; *Weekly Report, Work Relief Division, Engineering Section, Auguest 26, 1936,* box 1, folder 1, Records of the Engineering Division, RG 323, NARA-NYC; Progress Reports, box 3, Construction Projects—Patillas Bridge folder, Engineering Division Construction Projects Records; "Federal Agencies Operating in Puerto Rico," 1763.

71 Manuel Marín to Miles Fairbank, February 1, 1937, and Miles Fairbank to Manuel Marín, February 5, 1937, both box 2, folder 1, Slum Clearance Division, Records of the Engineering Division, RG 323, NARA-NYC.

72 Eugenio Orsini to Miles Fairbank, May 21, 1937; Germanico Belaval to PRRA Engineering Division, December 1937, both box 1, folder 1, Records of the Engineering Division, RG 323, NARA-NYC; Agricultures y comerciantes del Bo. Río Prieto de la municipalidad de Yauco to Governor William Leahy, February 16, 1940, box 3, Construction Projects, Río Prieto Highway folder, Engineering Division Construction Projects Records.

73 Levy, *Puerto Ricans in the Empire*, 16; Efrén Rivera Ramos, *American Colonialism in Puerto Rico: The Judicial and Social Legacy* (Princeton, NJ: Markus Weiner, 2007), 228.

74 Juan E. Cortes to PRRA, n.d., box 3, Construction Projects, Sewerage Systems folder, Engineering Division Construction Projects Records; Weekly Progress Reports, *November 22, 1937, through April 30, 1938,* box 1, folder 1, Records of the Engineering Division, Public Utilities and Misc. Section, Records of the Engineering Division, RG 323, NARA-NYC; *Jackson C. Hitchman to Guillermo Esteves, July 5, 1938,* box 1, General Memoranda, Records of the Engineering Division.

75 Fairbank, "Puerto Rico Reconstruction Administration," 291; Winship, *Thirty-Ninth Annual Report*, 83.

Chapter 5. Rural Electrification

1 On rural electrification in the continental United States, see Alvin E. Heutchy, "The Rural Electrification Administration and Its Work in Pennsylvania" (MA thesis, Pennsylvania State College, 1938); William E. Leuchtenburg, *Flood Control Politics: The Connecticut River Valley Problem, 1927–1950* (Cambridge, MA: Har-

194 · Notes to Pages 115–116

vard University Press, 1953); Arthur Morgan, *The Making of the TVA* (Buffalo, NY: Prometheus, 1974); D. Clayton Brown, *Electricity for Rural America: The Fight for the REA* (Westport, CT: Greenwood, 1980); Paul Conkin, *TVA: Fifty Years of Grass Roots Bureaucracy* (Urbana: University of Illinois Press, 1983); Jason Scott Smith, *Building New Deal Liberalism: The Political Economy of Public Works, 1933–1956* (Cambridge: Cambridge University Press, 2006); David Billington and Donald Jackson, *Big Dams of the New Deal Era: A Confluence of Engineering and Politics* (Norman: University of Oklahoma Press, 2006).

2 William Leuchtenburg has shown that electricity did not arrive in rural parts of Connecticut until the 1950s, about ten years after Puerto Rico. See Leuchtenburg, *Flood Control Politics.*

3 Rural Puerto Ricans made up about 70 percent of the population of Puerto Rico throughout the 1930s. They were 72 percent of the population in 1930, 70.3 percent in 1935, and 69.7 percent in 1940. The total population of Puerto Rico was 1,543,913 in 1930, 1,723,534 in 1935, and 1,869,255 in 1940. See Census of the United States, 1940, "Población: Boletín Núm. 1: Número de los Habitantes, Puerto Rico/Population: First Series: Number of Inhabitants, Puerto Rico," 1. Whereas 90 percent of urban residents in the United States had electricity during the 1930s, only 10 percent of rural residents had access to electric power. Although there were more urban than rural residents in the United States beginning with the 1920 census, during the Depression there were over 54 million rural residents and rural majorities or near-majorities in 31 of the 48 states. In all, about 44 percent of the population lived in rural areas. Of these, roughly 32.7 million people lived on farms (26.5 percent of the total population), the vast majority of whom lived without electric light or indoor plumbing just as they did in the nineteenth century. While Appalachia and the South are obvious examples, rural areas also included large swaths of the Midwest, Southwest, Northeast, and Pacific Northwest. See U.S. Census Bureau, *Table 1, Urban and Rural Population: 1900 to 1990* (October 1995), https://www2.census.gov/programs-surveys/decennial/tables/1990/1990-urban-pop/urpop0090.txt.

4 Victor S. Clark, *Porto Rico and Its Problems* (1930; repr., New York: Arno Press, 1975), 15–17; Sidney W. Mintz, *Worker in the Cane: A Puerto Rican Life History* (1960; repr., New York: Norton, 1974), 51; Fernando Picó (introduction), *Puerto Rico Remembered/Recuerdos de Puerto Rico: Photographs from the Collection of Tom Lehman* (San Diego: Thunder Bay Press, 2010), 82–85; Brown, *Electricity for Rural America*, xiii–xiv.

5 Odette Keun, *A Foreigner Looks at TVA* (New York: Longmans, Green, 1937), 30–31; Grey, 21–22, 27–28.

6 Public Health Data, Progress Report folder, General Records Relating to the Cement Plant Project, RG 323, NARA-NYC.

7 While rarely fatal, hookworm stunted growth, caused lethargy and anemia, and contributed to regional socioeconomic stagnation. By 1910, the so-called Vampire of the South had infected 40 percent of all school-aged children in the U.S. South and was one of the leading reasons for comparatively low school attendance numbers in the region, affecting its long-term development. See Hoyt Bleakley, "Disease

and Development: Evidence from Hookworm Eradication in the American South," *Quarterly Journal of Economics* 122, no. 1 (2007): 74–75, 77. More broadly, the FSA estimated that sickness and disease were the cause of 50 percent of all farm mortgage defaults in the United States during the Great Depression. See Farm Security Administration, *Medical Care for Farm Security Administration Borrowers* (Washington, D.C.: Government Printing Office, 1939), 2. For more on the history of outhouses, including the New Deal construction of sanitary outhouses, see Holly Bollinger, *Outhouses* (Saint Paul, MN: MBI Publishing, 2005), 20–21; Sue Wunder, "A Depression-Era Outhouse Gets a Makeover: Old 'WPA 830' Stands Tall and Strong Once Again," *Christian Science Monitor*, August 20, 2007.

8 "Swamp Land Filling and Draining for Malaria Control," box 3, Engineering Division Construction Projects, Records Relating to Construction Projects Directed by the Engineering Division, RG 323, NARA-NYC; Public Health Data, Progress Report folder, General Records Relating to the Cement Plant Project, RG 323, NARA-NYC; Joint Report by the School of Tropical Medicine and PRRA, March 1939, quoted in Edward J. Bash, Food Distribution Administration, "A Statement on Operations in Puerto Rico and the Virgin Islands by Division of Territories and Island Possessions," in U.S. Congress, House Committee on Insular Affairs, Division of Territories and Island Possessions, Department of the Interior, *Investigation of Political, Economic, and Social Conditions in Puerto Rico: Hearings before the Subcommittee of the House Committee of Insular Affairs, Pursuant to HR 159*, 78th Cong., 2nd sess., 1944, 410.

9 Antonio S. Lucchetti, *Second General Report on the Utilization of the Water Resources of Puerto Rico, 1935–45 / Segunda memoria general sobre la utilización de las fuentes fluviales de Puerto Rico, 1935–45* (San Juan: Government of Puerto Rico Printing Office, 1945), 3; Oliver L. Fassig, "On the Average Monthly and Annual Rainfall of Porto Rico," *Porto Rico Journal of Public Health and Tropical Medicine* 5, no. 3 (1930); PRRA, *Puerto Rico: A Guide to the Island and Boriquén: Compiled and Written by the Puerto Rico Reconstruction Administration in Co-Operation with the Writers' Program of the Works Progress Administration* (1940; repr., New York: Gordon Press, 1979), 29–30, 31; "Puerto Rico Surface-Water Resources," in *U.S. Geology Survey Water-Supply Paper 2299* (Washington, D.C.: Government Printing Office, 1987), 399; U.S. Energy Information Administration, "Puerto Rico Territory Energy Profile," https://www.eia.gov/state/print.php?sid=RQ; Rexford G. Tugwell, *Changing the Colonial Climate* (1942; repr., New York: Arno, 1970), 71.

10 Luis Fortuño, testimony regarding the Caribbean National Rainforest Act of 2005, House of Representatives, 109th Congress, 1st Sess., September 13, 2005, *Congressional Record*, House, vol. 151, pt. 15 (Washington, D.C.: Government Printing Office, 2005).

11 U.S. Bureau of the Census, *Electrical Industries of Porto Rico: 1907* (Washington, D.C.: Government Printing Office, 1909), 22–27; A. G. Quintero-Rivera, "Socialist and Cigarmaker: Artisans' Proletarianization in the Making of the Puerto Rican Working Class," *Latin American Perspectives* 10, nos. 2/3 (Spring-Summer 1983), 23.

12 U.S. Bureau of the Census, *Electrical Industries of Porto Rico*, 24–27.

196 · Notes to Pages 117–120

13 Antonio Lucchetti, "Rural Electricity in Puerto Rico: An Insular Government Undertaking," *Third World Power Conference—1936* (Washington, D.C.: Government Printing Office, 1936), 7.

14 César J. Ayala, *American Sugar Kingdom: The Plantation Economy of the Spanish Caribbean, 1898–1934* (Chapel Hill: University of North Carolina Press, 1999), 74–75; Alfred D. Chandler, *The Visible Hand: The Managerial Revolution in American Business* (Cambridge, MA: Harvard University Press, 1977); Martin J. Sklar, *The Corporate Reconstruction of American Capitalism, 1890–1916: The Market, the Law, and Politics* (Cambridge: Cambridge University Press, 1988); Kim Phillips-Fein, *Invisible Hands: The Businessmen's Crusade against the New Deal* (New York: W. W. Norton, 2010).

15 *Electrical Industries of Porto Rico: 1907*, 9–10. See also Gricel M. Surillo Luna, "Moving Forward: Railways in Puerto Rico," PhD Diss., The Graduate Center, City University of New York (2017), 63–64.

16 U.S. Bureau of the Census, *Electrical Industries of Porto Rico*, 29; PRRA, *Puerto Rico*, 30–31.

17 Lucchetti, *Second General Report*, 10; U.S. Bureau of the Census, *Electrical Industries of Porto Rico*, 29.

18 Antonio S. Lucchetti, "Concerning the Construction and Operation of the Hydro-Electric and Irrigation Systems of the South Coast and of the Hydro-Electric System of Utilization of the Water Resources of the Government of Puerto Rico," *Bulletin of the Department of the Interior* (San Juan: Government of Puerto Rico, 1936), 26–28; Lucchetti, *Second General Report*, 10.

19 Lucchetti, *Second General Report*, 9; Lucchetti, "Rural Electricity in Puerto Rico," 7, 16.

20 Taller de Formación Política, *La cuestión nacional* (Río Piedras: Ediciones Huracán, 1982), 109, quoted in Serafín Méndez Méndez and Gail A. Cuesto, eds., *Notable Caribbeans and Caribbean Americans: A Biographical Dictionary* (Westport, CT: Greenwood, 2003), 5; César J. Ayala and Rafael Bernabe, *Puerto Rico in the American Century: A History since 1898* (Chapel Hill: University of North Carolina Press, 2007), 41–42, 105.

21 Unión Protectora de Desempleados, quoted in Gabriel Villaronga, *Toward a Discourse of Consent: Mass Mobilization and Colonial Politics in Puerto Rico, 1932–1948* (Westport, CT: Praeger, 2004), 51–52, 55–56; Ayala and Bernabe, *Puerto Rico in the American Century*, 140–141; Gerald Meyer, "Vito Marcantonio: Congressman for Puerto Rico, 1934–1936, 1938–1950," http://vitomarcantonio.com/gerald-meyer-articles/vito-marcantonio-congressman-for-puerto-rico/.

22 J. Fred Rippy, "Electrical Utilities in Puerto Rico," *Journal of Business of the University of Chicago* 19, no. 4 (October 1946): 223. On Cuba, see Thomas F. O'Brien, "The Revolutionary Mission: American Enterprise in Cuba," *American Historical Review* 98, no. 3 (June 1993): 765; Louis A. Pérez Jr., *Cuba: Between Reform and Revolution*, 3rd ed. (New York: Oxford University Press, 2006), 205.

23 Lucchetti, Second General Report, 8; U.S. Congress, House Committee on Insular Affairs, Creating the Puerto Rico Water Resources Authority: Hearings before

the Committee of Insular Affairs on HR 8239, 76th Cong., 3rd sess., March 19–22, March 25–29, April 15–16, April 18–19, 1940 (Washington, D.C.: Government Printing Office, 1940).

24 Miles Fairbank to Leona Graham, August 6, 1938, box 2, General Memoranda, Records of the Rural Electrification Division, RG 323, NARA-NYC.

25 Alanson A. Van Fleet, *The Tennessee Valley Authority* (New York: Chelsea House, 1987), 33. TVA chairman David Lilienthal, for example, was raised in Indiana.

26 "Efemérides de la PRRA," Personal Directivo de la PRRA, Epoca 1935–1936, Fundación Luis Muñoz Marín.

27 Lucchetti, "Rural Electricity in Puerto Rico," 14.

28 Miles H. Fairbank, *The Chardon Plan and the Puerto Rico Reconstruction Administration, 1934–1954* (San Juan: Fairbank Corporation, 1978), 41–42; Miles Fairbank to Blanton Winship, March 20, 1937, folder 1, Toro Negro Hydroelectric Project, Records of the Rural Electrification Division, RG 323, NARA-NYC; Memo, November 12, 1936, box 1, Las Garzas Hydroelectric Project folder, Records of the Rural Electrification Division, RG 323, NARA-NYC (hereafter Las Garzas folder).

29 Fairbank to Winship, March 20, 1937, folder 1, Toro Negro Hydroelectric Project, Records of the Rural Electrification Division, RG 323, NARA-NYC.

30 Antonio Lucchetti to Carlos Chardón, September 6, 1935, box 3, folder 1, Toro Negro Hydroelectric Project, Records of the Rural Electrification Division, RG 323, NARA-NYC; Lands Necessary for Construction of Toro Negro Hydroelectric Plant, Toro Negro Hydroelectric Project, Records of the Rural Electrification Division, RG 323, NARA-NYC; Progress Report, General Memoranda, box 1, folder 2, Records of the Engineering Division, RG 323, NARA-NYC; Lucchetti, *Second General Report*, 19.

31 Antonio Lucchetti to Miles Fairbank, March 24, 1938, box 1, Las Garzas folder. See also Blanton Winship, *Thirty-Ninth Annual Report of the Governor of Puerto Rico* (San Juan: Bureau of Supplies, Printing, and Transportation, 1939), 84–85.

32 Lucchetti, *Second General Report*, 22. The peak of Monte Guilarte is 3,934 feet above sea level, making it the fifth highest peak in the Cordillera Central.

33 Miles Fairbank, "Puerto Rico Reconstruction Administration," in Harold L. Ickes, *Annual Report of the Secretary of the Interior for the Fiscal Year Ended June 30, 1938* (Washington, D.C.: Government Printing Office, 1938), 288; "Puerto Rico Opens Garza Dam," *New York Times*, November 10, 1941, 3.

34 Fairbank, "Puerto Rico Reconstruction Administration," 289; Lucchetti, *Second General Report*, 1935–45, 23; J. Wesley Neal et al., "The Mystery of Dos Bocas Reservoir, Puerto Rico: Explaining Extreme Spatial Heterogeneity in Largemouth Bass Distribution," *Caribbean Journal of Science* 41, no. 4 (2005): 805. The Río Caonillas is known for its Taino petroglyphs. See Monica Flaherty Frassetto, "A Preliminary Report on Petroglyphs in Puerto Rico," *American Antiquity* 25, no. 3 (1960), https://www.latinamericanstudies.org/taino/pr-petroglyphs.pdf. As of 2005, sedimentation has reduced the reservoir's storage capacity to 17.26 million cubic meters—a storage loss of about 54 percent. See Luis R. Soler-López, "Sedimentation History of Lago

198 · Notes to Pages 124–129

Dos Bocas, Puerto Rico, 1942–2005" (2005), USGS Publications Warehouse, https://www.science.gov/topicpages/l/lago+dos+bocas.

35 Manuel Font to Stanley McCaskey, Assistant General Counsel of the PRRA, November 18, 1938; Miles Fairbank to Manuel Font, November 25, 1938; Antonio Lucchetti to Miles Fairbank, November 25, 1938, all in box 4, Cement Plant: Transportation Charges for the Cement Shipments Folder, Records of the Assistant Administrator, RG 323, NARA-NYC. Rail service in Puerto Rico had been almost entirely used for agricultural purposes, mostly in sugar. The American Railroad Company had been in operation since 1902, when it was formed to take control of all existing rail lines from the Spanish era.

36 Fairbank, *Chardon Plan*, 41–42.

37 "Governor's Message at Dos Bocas Dam, November 19, 1942," in Tugwell, *Changing the Colonial Climate*, 265.

38 Lucchetti, *Second General Report*, 24–25; U.S. Congress, *Creating the Puerto Rico Water Resources Authority*, 12.

39 For a thorough debunking of the "Myth of the Disappeared Legion of Proprietors," see César J. Ayala and Laird W. Bergad, *Agrarian Puerto Rico: Reconsidering Rural Economy and Society, 1899–1940* (Cambridge: Cambridge University Press, 2020), 15–40.

40 "Statement of Miles H. Fairbank, Assistant Administrator, PRRA," *Hearings Before the Committee on Appropriations*, United States Senate, May 16, 1938, on the Work Relief and Public Works Appropriation Act of 1938, H. J. Res. 679, 75th Cong., 3rd sess. (Washington, D.C.: Government Printing Office, 1938), 50.

41 Antonio Lucchetti to Carlos Chardón, September 6, 1935, box 3, folder 1, Records of the Rural Electrification Division, RG 323, NARA-NYC.

42 Land Appraisal Memos, box 3, folder 1, Records of the Rural Electrification Division, RG 323, NARA-NYC.

43 Antonio Lucchetti to Miles Fairbank, n.d., box 3, folder 1, Records of the Rural Electrification Division, RG 323, NARA-NYC.

44 See boxes 1–8, alphabetical by last name, Records of the Land and Title Section of the Legal Division, Title Opinions on Lands Intended For Rural Electrification Projects, 1936–1938, RG 323, NARA-NYC; boxes 1–19, alphabetical by last name, Records of the Land and Title Section of the Legal Division, Land Acquisition Case Files for Rural Electrification Projects, 1937–1941, RG 323, NARA-NYC (hereafter Land Acquisition Case Files).

45 Land Acquisition Case Files.

46 Land Acquisition Case Files; "Puerto Rican Hurricane Relief Loan Section," in U.S. Congress, *Investigation of Political, Economic, and Social Conditions in Puerto Rico*, 1753–1754.

47 Land Acquisition Case Files.

48 Land Acquisition Case Files; "Puerto Rican Hurricane Relief Loan Section," 1753–1754.

49 Title Opinions on Lands Intended for Rural Electrification Projects, 1936–1938, Records of the Land and Title Section of the Legal Division, RG 323, NARA-NYC.

Notes to Pages 130–134 · 199

50 Gerónimo Fontánes to Miles Fairbank, n.d.; Manuel V. Torres to Miles Fairbank, June 2, 1937; Lucchetti to Miles Fairbank and Tomás Bernardini Palés, June 1937, all in box 1, Las Garzas folder.

51 Neighbors and taxpayers of Peñuelas to Miles Fairbank, August 10, 1936; Memorandum de Esta Administración Municipal de Peñuelas to Miles Fairbank [translation by author], September 8, 1937, both in box 1, Las Garzas folder.

52 U.S. Congress, *Creating the Puerto Rico Water Resources Authority*, 23, 31, 55, 66.

53 U.S. Congress, *Creating the Puerto Rico Water Resources Authority*, 42–45, 23, 31, 55, 66.

54 Crawford later served as the director of the Michigan National Bank and the Refiners Transport and Petroleum Corporation of Detroit. See "Crawford, Fred Lewis, 1888–1957," Biographical Directory of the United States Congress, http://bioguide .congress.gov/scripts/biodisplay.pl?index=C000889.

55 "Lucchetti contesta las declaraciones de Martinez Nadal—Dice que el president del Senado está mal asesorado y peor impresionado," *El Mundo*, August 23, 1938, 9; "Puerto Rican 'Little TVA' Barred by a Pocket Veto," *New York Times*, September 16, 1938.

56 John Bauer and Nathaniel Gold, *The Electric Power Industry: Development, Organization, and Public Policies* (New York: Harper & Brothers, 1939), 216. Puerto Rico is about 100 miles wide; the Tennessee valley is over 880 miles long.

57 "Puerto Rico Electric Power Authority Act," Act No. 83 of May 12, 1941, Estado Libre Asociado de Puerto Rico. Guy Swope served as acting governor between February and August 1941. He was appointed to replace José Miguel Gallardo, the former insular commissioner of education who twice served as acting governor.

58 U.S. Congress, *Creating the Puerto Rico Water Resources Authority*, 36.

59 "Puerto Rican 'TVA' Gets Hearing Today—House Committee Expects Row," *New York Times*, March 19, 1940.

60 U.S. Congress, *Creating the Puerto Rico Water Resources Authority*, 24, 351, 391, 396. See also House of Representatives, 76th Cong., 3rd Sess., Hearings, June 20, 1940, *Congressional Record* (Bound Edition), vol. 86, part 8 (June 13, 1940 to July 8, 1940), 8741.

61 "Celebramos el acuerdo de la Asociación de Agricultores," *El Mundo*, October 17, 1939. See also "Puerto Rico Plans 'TVA'' Corporation," *New York Times*, April 28, 1938.

62 See Rafael Alberto Bernabe, "Prehistory of the Partido Popular Democrático: Muñoz Marin, the Partido Liberal and the Crisis of Sugar in Puerto Rico, 1930–35" (PhD diss., State University of New York at Binghamton, 1989), 199–201; Eugenio Latimer Torres, "Historia de la Autoridad de Energía Eléctrica," *ENCICLOPEDI-APR: Una Proyecto de la Fundación Puertorriqueña de las Humanidades*, March 23, 2021, https://enciclopediapr.org/content/historia-de-la-autoridad-de-energia -electrica/.

63 "There Is No Excuse for Not Passing the Bill to Create the Water Resources Authority of Puerto Rico," *El Imparcial*, February 20, 1940, translated and quoted in U.S.

200 · Notes to Pages 134–136

Congress, *Creating the Puerto Rico Water Resources Authority*, 433. Edited by Antonio Valdivieso, *El Imparcial* was the island's second leading newspaper and supported independence.

64 José Enrique Colom, "Tarifas de Fuentes Fluviales más bajas que las privadas," *El Mundo*, August 23, 1938. A civil engineer with a degree from the University of Pennsylvania, Colom briefly served as acting governor in 1939.

65 E. Colon Baerga, "The Joke Will End This Year," *La Correspondencia*, March 19, 1940, translated by Antonio Lucchetti, quoted in U.S. Congress, *Creating the Puerto Rico Water Resources Authority*, 435. *La Correspondencia* (1890–1940) generally supported autonomy and self-determination.

66 "Editorial: Why Does Not the Governor Intercede?," *La Correspondencia*, March 13, 1940; E. Colon Baerga, "And Now Shall They Persist in Their Error?," *La Correspondencia*, April 6, 1940; "Topic of the Day—the Veto of the Water Resources Bill," *La Correspondencia*, July 5, 1940, all translated by Antonio Lucchetti and quoted in U.S. Congress, *Creating the Puerto Rico Water Resources Authority*, 435–440.

67 Bauer and Gold, *Electric Power Industry*, 326–327. The legacy of this model of public financing will be discussed in the conclusion.

68 U.S. Congress, *Creating the Puerto Rico Water Resources Authority*, 19, 21.

69 U.S. Congress, *Creating the Puerto Rico Water Resources Authority*, 122–123.

70 "Litigation–Puerto Rico Railway, Light and Power Company" folder, Claims, RG 323, NARA-NYC; "Utility Sues to Halt Puerto Rico Project," *New York Times*, March 16, 1936. On June 16, 1938, Judge Robert Cooper of the U.S. District Court for Puerto Rico sided with the Railway, Light, and Power Company, which was contesting the rural electrification program of the PRRA. However, the Supreme Court overturned his decision and dismissed the case, citing the rejection of two other recent attacks on New Deal rural electrification programs in *Alabama Power Company v. Ickes* and *Tennessee Electric Power Company v. TVA*.

71 Puerto Rico Water Resources Authority, *Power and Irrigation in Puerto Rico, 1945–1955: A Third General Report on the Utilization of the Water Resources of Puerto Rico* (San Juan: Commonwealth of Puerto Rico, 1958), 9–10. See also "Island Utility in Court—Acts to Bar Federal Purchase of Puerto Rican Properties," *New York Times*, July 7, 1942; "Utility Seizure Is Upset," *New York Times*, November 28, 1942; "Utility Is Taken Over: Government Expropriates Property of Porto Rico Light and Power," *New York Times*, December 29, 1942; "Puerto Rico Utilities Sold to Government: Power Companies Submit after Court Upholds Seizure," *New York Times*, December 10, 1943; "Lastra dice que es constitucional—Su proyecto para comprar la 'P.R. Light,'" *El Mundo*, August 23, 1938; Tugwell, *Changing the Colonial Climate*, 141.

72 Luis Muñoz Marin, "Mensaje del gobernador Luis Muñoz Marín, en la inauguración de la planta termoeléctrica de Palo Seco, en Cataño, 17 de febrero de 1951" (Message of Governor Luis Muñoz Marin, at the inauguration of the Palo Seco thermoelectric plant in Cataño, February 17, 1951), Fundación Luis Muñoz Marín.

73 Puerto Rico Water Resources Authority, *Power and Irrigation in Puerto Rico*, 14, 18; Henry Wells, *The Modernization of Puerto Rico: A Political Study of Changing Values and Institutions* (Cambridge, MA: Harvard University Press, 1969), 172–173.

74 Lucchetti, *Second General Report*, 28–29; "Widens Puerto Rico 'TVA': Court Turns Over Operation of San Juan's Water Supply," *New York Times*, April 22, 1944.

75 Puerto Rico Water Resources Authority, *Power and Irrigation in Puerto Rico*, 7; Villaronga, *Toward a Discourse of Consent*, 17.

76 "Puerto Rico Aqueduct and Sewer Authority Act," Act No. 40, May 1, 1945, Estado Libre Asociado de Puerto Rico; Wells, *Modernization of Puerto Rico*, 173.

77 See James L. Dietz, *Economic History of Puerto Rico: Institutional Change and Capitalist Development* (Princeton, NJ: Princeton University Press, 1986), 186–194; Ayala and Bernabe, *Puerto Rico in the American Century*, 188–189; A. W. Maldonado, *Teodoro Moscoso and Puerto Rico's Operation Bootstrap* (Gainesville: University Press of Florida, 1997), 25–45.

Conclusion

1 On the population, see America Counts, "Puerto Rico Population Declined 11.8% from 2010 to 2020," August 25, 2021, https://www.census.gov/library/stories/state-by-state/puerto-rico-population-change-between-census-decade.html. On the makeup of the Financial Oversight and Management Board, see "About Us," Financial Oversight and Management Board for Puerto Rico, https://oversightboard.pr.gov/about-us/.

2 For example, see: Hilda Lloréns, "Imaging Disaster: Puerto Rico through the Eye of Hurricane María," *Transforming Anthropology* 26, no. 2 (2018); Yarimar Bonilla and Marisol LeBrón, eds., *Aftershocks of Disaster: Puerto Rico Before and After the Storm* (Chicago: Haymarket, 2019); Yarimar Bonilla, "The Coloniality of Disaster: Race, Empire, and the Temporal Logics of Emergency in Puerto Rico, USA," *Political Geography* 78 (April 2020); Pedro Cabán, "Puerto Rico in Crisis and the Shifting Dictates of Empire," *Centro Journal* 33, no. 1 (Spring 2021); César J. Ayala, "Puerto Rico: Hurricanes and Neoliberal Ravages," *Against the Current* 221 (November/December 2022); Ivis García and Nicolas Hernandez, "'They're Just Trying to Survive': The Relationship between Social Vulnerability, Informal Housing, and Environmental Risks in Loíza, Puerto Rico, USA," *World Development Sustainability* 2 (June 2023), https://doi.org/10.1016/j.wds.2023.100062. For an audio excursion on these topics, listen to the widely available podcast *La Brega*, cocreated by Alana Casanova-Burgess for WNYC. For a corporate examination of post-María conditions in Puerto Rico, see Public-Private Analytic Exchange Program, "Threats to Pharmaceutical Supply Chains: The Public-Private Analytic Exchange Program Research Findings" (July 2018), https://mil.wa.gov/asset/5cefeb671410c. For a broader reading list on the aftermath of María, see "What the Storm Revealed," Puerto Rico Syllabus Project, https://puertoricosyllabus.com/syllabus/hurricane-maria/what-the-storm-revealed/.

3 César J. Ayala and Rafael Bernabe, *Puerto Rico in the American Century: A History since 1898* (Chapel Hill: University of North Carolina Press, 2007), 337–342.

4 Gail Radford, *The Rise of the Public Authority: Statebuilding and Economic Development in Twentieth-Century America* (Chicago: University of Chicago Press, 2013), 3–6.

202 · Notes to Pages 140–142

5 Radford, *Rise of the Public Authority*, 6–7. Radford succinctly describes the New Deal's emphasis on revenue bonds as both a "strategy . . . for enlarging state and local borrowing capacity" and as a "methodology to by which to achieve desired outcomes, first and foremost the evasion of legal constraints on borrowing" (128–129).

6 "Pinceladas de Nuestra Historia," Autoridad de Energía Eléctrica, https://aeepr .com/es-pr/Quienes-Somos.

7 Puerto Rico Water Resources Authority, *Power and Irrigation in Puerto Rico, 1945–1955: A Third General Report on the Utilization of the Water Resources of Puerto Rico* (San Juan: Commonwealth of Puerto Rico, 1958), 44. The Atomic Energy Commission, which was created by the Atomic Energy Act of 1946, controlled all aspects of nuclear power in the United States.

8 In November 1968, Rincón hosted the World Surfing Championships at the so-called Domes Beach, which is adjacent to the still-standing reactor and continues to be one of the most popular surfing spots in the Caribbean. See "History," Rincón Surf Fest, https://rinconsurffest.com/history/. On nuclear development, see "Pinceladas de Nuestra Historia"; U.S. Department of Energy Legacy Management, "Hoja de Datos: BONUS, Puerto Rico, Planta del Reactor Clausurado," June 2020, https:// www.energy.gov/sites/default/files/2020/06/f76/BONUS%2C%20Puerto%20Rico %2C%20Planta%20del%20Reactor%20Clausurado%20Hoja%20de%20Datos_0 .pdf; Ray O. Haroldsen, *The Story of the Borax Nuclear Reactor and the EBR-I Meltdown* (Idaho Falls, ID: Arco, 2008).

9 "Pinceladas de Nuestra Historia." According to the U.S. Energy Information Administration, as of 2020 about 50 percent of the electricity in Puerto Rico is generated by petroleum, 29 percent by natural gas, 19 percent by coal, and 2.5 percent by renewable energy sources included hydropower. Signed in 2019, the Puerto Rico Energy Public Policy Act required PREPA to generate 40 percent of its electricity from renewable resources by 2025, 60 percent by 2040, and 100 percent by 2050. PREPA is also mandated to phase out coal-fired generation by 2028. Results from this law remain to be seen.

10 For an investigative video on the health and environmental dangers of this plant and lack of accountability from the insular government, see "El Peso de las Cenizas/Burning Ashes," February 20, 2023, season 5, episode 4, *Puerto Rican Voices*, CENTRO, directed by Ismael Cubero and produced by Juan C. Dávila, Yarimar Bonilla, and Ángel Antonio Ruíz, video blog, https://centropr.hunter.cuny.edu/ media/burning-ashes/. The AES-PR coal plant continues to produce an average of 800 tons of coal ash per day, much of it stored in a five-story open pile. For more on the plant's environmental and health effects on other areas, including the Dominican Republic (where coal ash was also sold as filler), Florida, and Georgia, see Valerie Volcovici, "US EPA Chief Views Pollution in Puerto Rico, Vows to Fight for Change," Reuters, July 28, 2022, https://www.reuters.com/business/environment/ us-epa-chief-views-pollution-puerto-rico-vows-fight-change-2022-07-28/; Peter Winslow, "How Puerto Rico's Banned Coal Ash Winds Up in Rural Georgia," *Ener-*

gy News, September 20, 2022, https://energynews.us/2022/09/20/how-puerto-ricos
-banned-coal-ash-winds-up-in-rural-georgia/; "Toxic Coal Ash in Puerto Rico: The
Hazardous Legacy of the AES-PR Coal Plant," *Earth Justice*, May 4, 2023, https://
earthjustice.org/feature/coal-ash-states/puerto-rico.

11 The repeal of the corporate tax exemptions was influenced by the Clinton administration's agreement to balance the federal budget following two Republican-led
government shutdowns between November 1995 and January 1996.

12 There are a variety of sources on the repeal of Section 936, including Sherrie L.
Baver, "The Rise and Fall of Section 936: The Historical Context and Possible Con-
sequences for Migration," *Centro Journal* 11, no. 2 (Spring 2000); Susan M. Col-
lins, Barry P. Bosworth, and Miguel A. Soto-Class, *The Economy of Puerto Rico:
Restoring Growth* (Washington, D.C.: Brookings Institution Press and Center for the
New Economy, 2006); Scott Greenberg and Gavin Ekins, "Tax Policy Helped Create
Puerto Rico's Fiscal Crisis," Tax Foundation, June 30, 2015, https://taxfoundation
.org/tax-policy-helped-create-puerto-rico-fiscal-crisis/; Emma Scully, "Puerto
Rico: The Financial Implications of Dependency," Council on Hemispheric Affairs,
August 21, 2015, https://www.coha.org/puerto-rico-the-financial-implications-of
-dependency/; John W. Schoen, "Here's How an Obscure Tax Change Sank Puerto
Rico's Economy," *CNBC*, September 26, 2017, https://www.cnbc.com/2017/09/26/
heres-how-an-obscure-tax-change-sank-puerto-ricos-economy.html; Félix Cór-
dova Iturregui, *La Eliminación de la Sección 936: La historia que se intenta suprimir*
(San Juan: Publicaciones Gaviota, 2020); U.S. Energy Information Administration,
"Puerto Rico Territory Energy Profile," https://www.eia.gov/state/print.php?sid
=RQ; Mario Cancel, "Reflexiones: ¿Qué hacer después de la muerte de las 936?,"
Claridad, February 9, 2021, https://www.claridadpuertorico.com/reflexiones-que
-hacer-despues-de-la-muerte-de-las-936/; Frances Robles, "Months after Puerto
Rico Earthquakes, Thousands Are Still Living Outside," *New York Times*, April 8,
2021. See also Manuel Suarez, "Puerto Rico Sees Harm in Tax Plan," *New York Times*,
August 25, 1985, 35; "Puerto Rico Fighting to Keep Its Tax Breaks for Businesses,"
New York Times, May 10, 1993, 1, 55; Clifford Krauss, "Threat of Statehood in Puerto
Rico Leads to a Restored Tax Break," *New York Times*, July 24, 1993; Sandra Lilley,
"Former Puerto Rico Gov. Carlos Romero Barceló Dies at 88," *NBC News*, May 4,
2021, https://www.nbcnews.com/news/latino/carlos-romero-barcel-former-puerto
-rico-governor-dead-88-rcna816; "Puerto Rico Energy Public Policy Act," Act. No.
17, April 11, 2019, https://bvirtualogp.pr.gov/ogp/Bvirtual/leyesreferencia/PDF/2
-ingles/17-2019.pdf. For an account of the long history of opposition to 936 by the
statehood movement, see A. W. Maldonado, *Boom and Bust in Puerto Rico: How
Politics Destroyed an Economic Miracle* (Notre Dame, IN: University of Notre Dame
Press, 2021).

13 Dánica Coto, "Puerto Rico Selects Company to Privatize Power Generation," *Associated Press*, January 25, 2023, https://apnews.com/article/united
-states-government-caribbean-puerto-rico-climate-and-environment-business
-12587fe080ed71f545dddle520db50e4; Nicole Acevedo, "Puerto Rico Officially

Privatizes Power Generation amid Protests, Doubts," *NBC News*, January 25, 2023, https://www.nbcnews.com/news/latino/puerto-rico-officially-privatizes-power-generation-genera-pr-rcna67284; Autoridad de Asesoría Financiera y Agencia Fiscal de Puerto Rico, "Genera PR Tapped to Run Puerto Rico's Energy Generation," n.d., https://www.aafaf.pr.gov/press-room-articles/genera-pr-tapped-to-run-puerto-ricos-energy-generation/; "Pase de batón en la generación de energía eléctrica en Puerto Rico," *El Vocero de Puerto Rico*, June 30, 2023, https://www.elvocero.com/gobierno/agencias/pase-de-bat-n-en-la-generaci-n-de-energ-a/article_c945f21a-1688-11ee-a5ad-1759969017fc.html; "Se materializa la transición a Genera PR como operador de la flota generatriz de la AEE," *El Nuevo Dia*, June 30, 2023, https://www.elnuevodia.com/noticias/noticias/notas/se-materializa-la-transicion-a-genera-pr-como-operador-de-la-flota-generatriz-de-la-aee/.

14 "Puerto Rican Cement to Be Sold to CEMEX, Mexican Cement Producer to Pay $160 Million," *Puerto Rico Herald*, September 28, 2000; "Cemex to Buy Puerto Rican Cement," *Wall Street Journal*, June 13, 2002. See also A. W. Maldonado, *Teodoro Moscoso and Puerto Rico's Operation Bootstrap* (Gainesville: University Press of Florida, 1997), 63–68, 170. Recent reports indicate that CEMEX may close the Ponce plant due to declining revenues since 2006. See "Cemex Puerto Rico Switches Ponce Cement Plant to Grinding," *Global Cement*, January 11, 2018. Luis A. Ferré also founded the Ponce Art Museum.

15 José L. Bolívar, *The Caribbean Front in World War II: The Untold Story of U-Boats, Spies, and Economic Warfare* (Princeton, NJ: Markus Weiner, 2021), 33; César J. Ayala and José L. Bolívar, *Battleship Vieques: Puerto Rico from World War II to the Korean War* (Princeton, NJ: Markus Weiner, 2011), 167; José L. Bolívar, *Guerra (banca) y desarrollo: El Banco de Fomento y la industrialización de Puerto Rico* (San Juan: Fundación Luis Muñoz Marín / Instituto de Cultura Puertorriqueña, 2011), 26, 31–35, 39.

16 Relief and Construction Appropriations and Expenditures of the WEP for the Fiscal Years 1942–43 to 1945–46, Cartapacia 76, series 1—Gobierno Federal, Correspondencia, subseries 34, War Emergency Program 1945–43, subsection 1: Datos y Estadísticas, section 4, Luis Muñoz Marín, Presidente del Senado, 1941–1948, Fundación Luis Muñoz Marín; Gerardo M. Piñero Cádiz, "La Base Aeronaval Roosevelt Roads: El Pearl Harbor del Caribe" and Carlos M. González Morales, "Borinquen Field y Aguadilla: Un Municipio en la Guerra," both in *Puerto Rico en la Segunda Guerra Mundial: Baluarte del Caribe*, ed. Jorge Rodríguez Beruff and José L. Bolívar Fresneda (San Juan: Ediciones Callejón, 2012), 293, 261; Bolívar, *Caribbean Front*, 123–136; Ayala and Bolívar, *Battleship Vieques*, 23–24.

17 Bolívar, *Caribbean Front*, 123–126; Ayala and Bolívar, *Battleship Vieques*, 23–24. As Jason Scott Smith has written, wartime development "was constructed on the deep and vital foundations that had been laid down by the New Deal and the public works programs created state capacities essential to the preparedness effort." See Smith, *Building New Deal Liberalism: The Political Economy of Public Works, 1933–1956* (Cambridge: Cambridge University Press, 2006),192–193.

18 Buenaventura J. Jane, Chief Administrative Assistant, War Department, U.S. Engineer's Office, Puerto Rico District, San Juan, Monthly Civilian Personnel Report, November 1, 1943, folder 1, Strength Reports—District Engineer, 1940–1943, Records of the Office of the Chief of Engineers, Puerto Rico District, box 5, Correspondence Relating to Civil and Military Construction Projects, 1941–1950, RG 77, NARA-NYC (hereafter Strength Reports); "Report upon the Improvement of Rivers and Harbors in the Panama District," Civil Works—Miscellaneous Administrative Matters, Strength Reports.

19 Ayala and Bolívar calculated that wartime spending in Puerto Rico equated to nearly 4.6 times the amount per capita spent by the United States on Western Europe during the Marshall Plan. Ayala and Bolívar, *Battleship Vieques*, 25. In 1941, Tugwell wrote that wartime construction equaled the total income of the entire sugar industry. Tugwell, *Changing the Colonial Climate* (1942; repr., New York: Arno, 1970), 32n1. On the construction of naval, air, and military bases throughout Latin America and the Caribbean, see Rebecca Herman, *Cooperating with the Colossus: A Social and Political History of US Military Bases in World War II Latin America* (New York: Oxford University Press, 2022).

20 There are many excellent sources on Puerto Rico and the Caribbean during the war. This book has relied on Gaylord T. M. Kelshall, *The U-Boat War in the Caribbean* (1988; repr., Annapolis, MD: Naval Institute Press, 1994); Fitzroy André Baptiste, *War, Cooperation and Conflict: The European Possessions in the Caribbean, 1939–1945* (New York: Greenwood, 1988); Jorge Rodríguez Beruff, *Strategy as Politics: Puerto Rico on the Eve of the Second World War* (San Juan: La Editorial de la Universidad de Puerto Rico, 2007); Ayala and Bolívar, *Battleship Vieques*; Bolívar, *Guerra (banca) y desarrollo*; Rodríguez Beruff and Bolívar Fresneda, *Puerto Rico en la Segunda Guerra Mundial*, particularly Piñero Cádiz, "La Base Aeronaval Roosevelt Roads" and González Morales, "Borinquen Field y Aguadilla"; Karen E. Eccles and Debbie McCollin, eds., *World War II and the Caribbean* (Kingston, Jamaica: University of the West Indies Press, 2017); Bolívar, *Caribbean Front*.

21 "Victims of U-Boat Trailed as Lure—Raider Followed Lifeboat Five Days but Men Refused to Hail Passing Ships," *New York Times*, April 4, 1942. A sampling of newspaper accounts conveys the direct, menacing impact of the submarine war on Puerto Rico, the Dominican Republic, Aruba, Curaçao, Uruguay, Chile, and Brazil. See "Submarines Off Our Coast," *New York Times*, September 23, 1939; "Dominican Cutter Seen a War Victim," *New York Times*, October 3, 1939; "Nazi Fueling Bases for U-Boats and Raiders Set Up in Caribbean," *New York Times*, August 21, 1940; "Nazi Threat to Puerto Rico Recalled by Raid on Aruba," *New York Times*, February 17, 1942; "U-Boat Lair Hunted in Caribbean Area," *New York Times*, February 18, 1942; "39 Die on Tanker Fired Off Curaçao," *New York Times*, February 22, 1942; "U-Boat Raids Used for Axis Propaganda," *New York Times*, February 22, 1942; "Puerto Rican Isle Is Shelled by Enemy," *New York Times*, March 4, 1942; "Escapes 4 U-Boats, Is Sunk by a 5th," *New York Times*, April 6, 1942; "Sinking Hints Italy Has U-Boats: Brazilian Freighter Is Sent to Bottom Off Virginia," *New York Times*, May 30, 1942;

"Axis Mines off Atlantic Coast New Menace to Our Shipping," *New York Times*, June 21, 1942; "2 More Ships Sunk by U-Boat Raiders," *New York Times*, June 27, 1942; "Submarines Plague Caribbean Coast," *New York Times*, July 12, 1942; "Uruguayan Taken Captive by U-Boat," *New York Times*, August 8, 1942.

22 Bolívar, *Caribbean Front*, 83–84. Food shortages plagued the circum-Caribbean region, including in Puerto Rico, the Dominican Republic, Haiti, Cuba, Trinidad and Tobago, Guatemala, Honduras, Nicaragua, Costa Rica, and Panama. All looked to the United States for assistance. On the insular government's attempts to get sugar producers to grow more food crops during the war, including Governor Tugwell's effort to secure $15 million (about $285 million today) from Roosevelt for this purpose, see Tugwell, *Changing the Colonial Climate*, 195, 207. According to Tugwell, the effort was thwarted by resident commissioner Bolivar Pagán, who convinced Congress that the funds were unnecessary. On food insecurity and public health in the broader region, see Rita Pemberton, "War, Food, and Security: Feeding Trinidad and Tobago in Wartime, 1939–1945" and Debbie McCollin, "Ravages and Rejuvenation: World War II and Public Health in the British Caribbean," both in Karen E. Eccles and Debbie McCollin, eds., *World War II and the Caribbean* (Kingston, Jamaica: University of the West Indies Press, 2017).

23 José Bolívar estimates that 60 percent of the WPA's 14,500 employees in Puerto Rico were working on military projects. See Bolívar, "Las Inversiones y los Programmeas Militares: Construyendo la Infrastructura y los Recursos Humanos de la Posguerra," in Rodríguez Beruff and Bolívar Fresneda, *Puerto Rico en la Segunda Guerra Mundial*, 151. Rodríguez Beruff contends that over 32,000 New Deal employees were directly working on defense projects and many more indirectly. See Rodríguez Beruff, *Strategy as Politics*, ix.

24 Jane, Monthly Civilian Personnel Reports, November 1 and 30, 1943.

25 Jane, Monthly Civilian Personnel Report, November 1, 1943; Major Gus A. Draper, Corps of Engineers, to Chief of Engineers, U.S. Army, March 31, 1943, Civil Works—Miscellaneous Administrative Matters, Strength Reports; W. D. Tomlin, Chief Administrative Assistant, to Post Utilities Officer, U.S. Engineer's Office, Ponce, Puerto Rico, March 10, 1942, Civil Works—Miscellaneous Administrative Matters, folder 2, Strength Reports.

26 Draper to Chief of Engineers, March 31, 1943; Tomlin to Post Utilities Officer, March 10, 1942.

27 Kelshall, *U-Boat War*, xiii, 8, 16; Baptiste, *War, Cooperation and Conflict*, 79–81, 129–130, 160. On life in the Vichy-controlled and Axis-aligned French Caribbean colonies of Guadeloupe and Martinque, see Eric T. Jennings, "The French Caribbean in World War II: Upheavals, Repression, and Resistance," in Eccles and McCollin, *World War II and the Caribbean.*

28 The emergence of populism in Latin America and the Caribbean during the 1930s and 1940s was varied and uneven. While historical scholarship has been dominated by discussion of Juan Perón in Argentina, Getulio Vargas in Brazil, and the consolidation of the Institutional Revolutionary Party (PRI) under Lázaro Cárdenas in

Mexico, others have called for a more nuanced understanding of populist expressions in the Caribbean. Using the example of Puerto Rico, Antonio Gaztambide-Géigel argues that proximity to the United States and broader North Atlantic economy has had a greater influence on the internal political developments of Caribbean societies than has been widely acknowledged. Similarly, Jorge Duany and Emilio Pantojas-Garcia noted that the island's relationship with the United States and its colonial form of democracy separate it from other places of the Caribbean. Writing that "paradoxically, Puerto Rico is one of the most democratic countries in the Caribbean region, as measured by massive electoral participation, a competitive party system, and legal protection of individual rights and freedoms," Duany and Pantojas-Garcia remind us that Puerto Rico is also "one of the most undemocratic" countries in the area due to its colonial status and limited nature of citizenship for residents on the island. Another undemocratic area of the region, the Dominican Republic under Trujillo, constructed a broad array of infrastructural projects that were directly modeled on the PRRA's hurricane-proof public works built in Puerto Rico. In Cuba, by contrast, the constitution of 1940 under Batista codified many of the populist social and economic reforms of the New Deal years into law, becoming (for a time) the most democratic framework of government in the Americas. See Antonio Gaztambide-Géigel, *Tan lejos de Dios . . . Ensayos sobre las relaciones del Caribe con Estados Unidos* (San Juan: Ediciones Callejon, 2006), 135–136; Jorge Duany and Emilio Pantojas-Garica, "Fifty Years of Commonwealth: The Contradictions of Free Associated Statehood in Puerto Rico," in Lammert de Jong and Dirk Krujit, eds., *Extended Statehood in the Caribbean: Paradoxes of Quasi-colonialism, Local Autonomy, and Extended Statehood in the USA, French, Dutch, and British Caribbean* (Amsterdam: Rozenberg, 2005), 45. On the Dominican Republic under Trujillo, see Eric Roorda, *The Dictator Next Door: The Good Neighbor Policy and the Trujillo Regime in the Dominican Republic, 1930–1945* (Durham, NC: Duke University Press, 1998); Richard Lee Turits, *Foundations of Despotism: Peasants, the Trujillo Regime, and Modernity in Dominican History* (Stanford, CA: Stanford University Press, 2003); Lauren Derby, *The Dictator's Seduction: Politics and the Popular Imagination in the Era of Trujillo* (Durham, NC: Duke University Press, 2009); Lorgia García-Peña, *The Borders of Dominicanidad: Race, Nation, and Archives of Contradiction* (Durham, NC: Duke University Press, 2016). On Batista and the Cuban constitution of 1940, see Marifeli Pérez-Stable, *The Cuban Revolution: Origins, Course, and Legacy*, 2nd ed. (New York: Oxford University Press, 1999); Robert Whitney, *State and Revolution in Cuba: Mass Mobilization and Political Change, 1920–1940* (Chapel Hill: University of North Carolina Press, 2001); Robert Whitney, "The Architect of the Cuban State: Fulgencio Batista and Populism in Cuba, 1937–1940," *Journal of Latin American Studies* 32, no. 2 (May 2000); George Reid Andrews, *Afro-Latin America: 1800–2000* (New York: Oxford University Press, 2004); Louis A. Pérez, Jr., *Cuba: Between Reform and Revolution Third Edition* (New York: Oxford University Press, 2006); Frank Argote-Freyre, *Fulgencio Batista: From Revolutionary to Strongman* (New Brunswick, NJ: Rutgers University Press, 2007); Kaitlyn Henderson,

208 · Notes to Pages 147–148

"Race, Discrimination, and the Cuban Constitution of 1940," *Hispanic American Historical Review* 100, no. 2 (May 2020).

29 Memo, Miles Fairbank to Leona Graham, June 1, 1939, Fairbank to Graham folder, Confidential Records of the Assistant Administrator, 1936–1952, RG 323, NARA-NYC.

30 Antonio Cruz y Nieves to Miles Fairbank, August 18, 1937, and June 23, 1939, Information and Research Section, General Memoranda folder, box 2, General Records Relating to Administration, RG 323, NARA-NYC; "Lista de Publicaciones Hispano-americanas Sobre Agricultura," Information and Research Section—General Memoranda folder, box 2, General Records Relating to Administration, RG 323, NARA-NYC; PRRA, *Puerto Rico: A Guide to the Island and Boriquén: Compiled and Written by the Puerto Rico Reconstruction Administration in Co-Operation with the Writers' Program of the Works Progress Administration* (1940; repr., New York: Gordon Press, 1979); Tugwell, *Changing the Colonial Climate*, 97.

31 Rodríguez Beruff, *Strategy as Politics*, 185–188, 305–306; Pedro A. Cabán, "Puerto Rico: State Formation in a Colonial Context," *Caribbean Studies* 30, no. 2 (2002): 185. The rise of the PPD has been extensively covered, including in Emilio González Díaz, "Class Struggle and Politics in Puerto Rico during the Decade of the 1940s: The Rise of the P.D.P.," *Two Thirds* 2, no. 1 (1979); Juan José Baldrich, "Class and the State: The Origins of Populism in Puerto Rico, 1934–1952" (PhD diss., Yale University, 1981); Juan R. Torruella, *The Supreme Court and Puerto Rico: The Doctrine of Separate and Unequal* (Río Piedras: Editorial de la Universidad de Puerto Rico, 1985); Rafael Alberto Bernabe, "Prehistory of the Partido Popular Democrático: Muñoz Marin, the Partido Liberal and the Crisis of Sugar in Puerto Rico, 1930–35" (PhD diss., State University of New York at Binghamton, 1989); Emilio Pantojas-García, *Development Strategies as Ideology: Puerto Rico's Export-led Industrialization Experience* (Boulder, CO: Lynne Rienner, 1990); Juan A. Giusti Cordero, "Labour, Ecology, and History in a Puerto Rican Plantation Region: 'Classic' Rural Proletarians Revisited," *International Review of Social History* 41 (1996); Nathaniel I. Córdova, "In His Image and Likeness: The Puerto Rican Jíbaro as Political Icon," *Centro Journal* 17, no. 2 (Fall 2005); Ayala and Bernabe, *Puerto Rico in the American Century*, 109, 138; Gabriel Villaronga, *Toward a Discourse of Consent: Mass Mobilization and Colonial Politics in Puerto Rico, 1932–1948* (Westport, CT: Praeger, 2004); "Puerto Rican Populism Revisited: The PPD during the 1940s," *Latin American Studies* 21, no. 3 (1989); A. W. Maldonado, *Luis Muñoz Marín: Puerto Rico's Democratic Revolution* (San Juan: La Editorial, Universidad de Puerto Rico, 2006), 187–188; Nathaniel I. Córdova, "Luis Muñoz Marín's Stump Speech in the Partido Popular Democrático Campaign of 1938–1940," *Advances in the History of Rhetoric* 10 (2007); Gabriel Villaronga, "Constructing Muñocismo: Colonial Politics and the Rise of the PPD, 1934–1940," *Centro Journal* 22, no. 2 (2010).

32 As Villaronga has argued, Muñoz viewed the PRERA and PRRA as failures and by 1940 "saw the New Deal crumble along with his vision of transforming Puerto Rico into a modern society." But Muñoz also understood that taking control of PRRA re-

Notes to Pages 148–150 · 209

construction projects, patronage networks, and land reform platforms was key and hoped that a revived New Deal would offer him a "platform to enhance the appeal of economic development." See Villaronga, *Toward a Discourse of Consent*, 162–163.

33 Julio A. Pérez to Guillermo Alicea, September 26, 1942, Cartapacio 68, subseries 29, PRRA 1944–1942, series 1—Gobierno Federal, Correspondencia, section 4, Luis Muñoz Marín, Presidente del Senado, 1941–1948, Fundación Luis Muñoz Marín; Relief and Construction Appropriations and Expenditures of the WEP for the Fiscal Years 1942–43 to 1945–46, Cartapacia 76, series 1—Gobierno Federal, Correspondencia, subseries 34, War Emergency Program 1945–43, subsection 1: Datos y Estadisticas, section 4, Luis Muñoz Marín, Presidente del Senado, 1941–1948, Fundación Luis Muñoz Marín; Guillermo Esteves to Luis Muñoz Marín, November 3, 1943, Cartapacio 67, subseries 29, PRRA 1944–1942, series 1—Gobierno Federal, Correspondencia, section 4, Luis Muñoz Marín, Presidente del Senado, 1941–1948, Fundación Luis Muñoz Marín.

34 Memo, Fairbank to Ickes, February 2, 1938, folder 3: 1937, box 256, Secretary of Interior File, Papers of Harold L. Ickes, Library of Congress. See also "Distinguidas personalidades del país celebran. El plan de industrialización presentado por el señor Miles H. Fairbank," *El Mundo*, February 19, 1938, 1; "New Credit Sought to Aid Puerto Rico," *New York Times*, November 21, 1938, 1, 3; "Puerto Ricans Split on New Credit Plan," *New York Times*, February 15, 1939; "Plan de 100,000,000 para Puerto Rico," *El Mundo*, February 16, 1939; "President Favors an Insular 'RFC,'" *New York Times*, January 31, 1940; "Creation of Insular Reconstruction Authority Favored by President Roosevelt, According to Governor Leahy of Puerto Rico," *Commercial and Financial Chronicle* 150, no. 3893 (February 3, 1940), 774. On the proposed Insular Reconstruction Authority offices, see Records Relating to Construction Projects, Assistant Administrator General Records, Records of the Puerto Rico Reconstruction Administration, RG 323, NARA-NYC, as cited by PRRA Architecture, Facebook, July 5, 2019.

35 Villaronga, *Toward a Discourse of Consent*, 103; Ayala and Bernabe, *Puerto Rico in the American Century*, 145–146; Rodríguez Beruff, *Strategy as Politics*, 190.

36 Rexford G. Tugwell, *Puerto Rican Public Papers of R. G. Tugwell, Governor* (1945; repr., New York: Arno Press, 1975), 340.

37 Luis Muñoz Marín, Amendments to Land Law, Cartapacio 330, Tierras, series 10, Legislatura, 1948–40, subsection 22, Leyes, section 4, Luis Muñoz Marín, Presidente del Senado, 1941–1948, Fundación Luis Muñoz Marín; Pantojas-Garcia, "Puerto Rican Populism Revisited," 535.

38 Tugwell, *Puerto Rican Public Papers*, 45, 346–347; "Land Law of Puerto Rico, Act No. 26 of April 22, 1941," Puerto Rico Budget Office; César J. Ayala and Laird W. Bergad, *Agrarian Puerto Rico: Reconsidering Rural Economy and Society, 1899–1940* (Cambridge: Cambridge University Press, 2020), 279.

39 Tugwell, *Changing the Colonial Climate*, 147.

40 Ismael García-Colón, "Buscando ambiente: Hegemony and Subaltern Tactics of Survival in Puerto Rico's Land Distribution Program," *Latin American Perspectives*

210 · Notes to Pages 150–152

33, no. 1 (January 2006), 2–3. See also Ismael García-Colón, *Land Reform in Puerto Rico: Modernizing the Colonial State, 1941–1969* (Gainesville: University Press of Florida, 2009).

41 Ismael García-Colón, "Playing and Eating Democracy: The Case of Puerto Rico's Land Distribution Program, 1940s–1960s," *CENTRO Journal* 18, no. 2 (Fall 2006): 185. Muñoz Marín, who had cultivated the ability to speak to audiences of Washington officials and the Puerto Rican public at the same time, compared the Land Law to the U.S. Homestead Act, passed by radical Republicans during the Civil War and signed into law by Abraham Lincoln in 1862. See Luis Muñoz Marín, Recordatorio de Luis Muñoz Marín para el dictado en ingles, April 14, 1944, Cartapacio 330, Tierras, series 10, Legislatura, 1948–40, subsection 22, Leyes, section 4, Luis Muñoz Marín, Presidente del Senado, 1941–1948, Fundación Luis Muñoz Marín.

42 "Oppose Puerto Rican Land Law," *New York Times*, March 12, 1941, 15; "Fights Puerto Rico Land Law," *New York Times*, July 22, 1941, 19.

43 García-Colón, "Buscando ambiente," 10.

44 Luis Muñoz Marín to Franklin Roosevelt and Eleanor Roosevelt, Luis Muñoz Marín—Correspondence with Franklin Roosevelt, Cables, 1940–1944, Franklin D. Roosevelt Presidential Library; Michael Lapp, "The Rise and Fall of Puerto Rico as a Social Laboratory, 1945–1965," *Social Science History* 19, no. 2 (Summer 1995): 169–199; Tugwell, *Changing the Colonial Climate*, 67.

45 Tugwell, "Investigation into the Administrative Responsibilities under the Five Hundred Acre Limitation on Land Holdings in the Organic Act of Puerto Rico," in *Changing the Colonial Climate*, 40–44, 65. The Farm Security Administration had replaced the Resettlement Administration in 1937.

46 Tugwell to Roosevelt, January 29, 1942, folder 13, box 8, series 2, Confidential Files, Franklin D. Roosevelt Presidential Library.

47 Maldonado, *Boom and Bust*, 85–88.

48 Catherine Marsh Kennerley, "Cultural Negotiations: Puerto Rican Intellectuals in a State-Sponsored Community Education Project, 1948–1968," *Harvard Educational Review* 73, no. 3 (September 2003): 416–448; Mariam Colón Pizarro, "Poetic Pragmatism: The Puerto Rican Division of Community Education (DIVEDCO) and the Politics of Cultural Production, 1949–1968" (PhD diss., University of Michigan, 2011); Carmelo Esterrich, *Concrete and Countryside: The Urban and the Rural in 1950s Puerto Rican Culture* (Pittsburgh: University of Pittsburgh Press, 2018).

49 "Piñero, Jesús T., 1897–1952," U.S. House Historical Office, https://history.house .gov/People/Detail/19726. On how New Deal agencies such as the WPA performed similar political work in the continental United States, see Smith, *Building New Deal Liberalism*, 160–189.

50 Torruella, *Supreme Court and Puerto Rico*, 142–143; Maldonado, *Luis Muñoz Marín*, 258–261; El Archivo de las Elecciones en Puerto Rico. The law was sponsored by Senator Hugh Butler (R-NE) and Representative Fred Crawford (R-MI), the chair of the House Insular Affairs Subcommittee on Territories and Insular Possessions. See "Puerto Rican Migration and Political Participation," U.S. House History Office,

https://history.house.gov/Exhibitions-and-Publications/HAIC/Historical-Essays/Separate-Interests/Puerto-Rico/.

51 Ayala and Bernabe, *Puerto Rico in the American Century*, 167–171; James L. Dietz, *Economic History of Puerto Rico: Institutional Change and Capitalist Development* (Princeton, NJ: Princeton University Press, 1986), 236–237; Maldonado, *Luis Muñoz Marín*, 313–327.

BIBLIOGRAPHY

American National Red Cross. *The West Indies Hurricane Disaster, September 1928: Official Report of Relief Work in Porto Rico, the Virgin Islands and Florida.* Washington, D.C.: American National Red Cross, 1929.

Anderson, Robert W. *Party Politics in Puerto Rico.* Stanford, CA: Stanford University Press, 1965.

Argersinger, Jo Ann E. *Toward a New Deal in Baltimore: People and Government in the Great Depression.* Chapel Hill: University of North Carolina Press, 1988.

Ayala, César J. *American Sugar Kingdom: The Plantation Economy of the Spanish Caribbean, 1898–1934.* Chapel Hill: University of North Carolina Press, 1999.

Ayala, César J., and Laird W. Bergad. *Agrarian Puerto Rico: Reconsidering Rural Economy and Society, 1899–1940.* Cambridge: Cambridge University Press, 2020.

Ayala, César J., and Rafael Bernabe. *Puerto Rico in the American Century: A History since 1898.* Chapel Hill: University of North Carolina Press, 2007.

Ayala, César J., and José L. Bolívar. *Battleship Vieques: Puerto Rico from World War II to the Korean War.* Princeton, NJ: Markus Wiener, 2011.

Bachman, George W. *Report of the Director of the School of Tropical Medicine for the Fiscal Year Ending June 1941.* San Juan: University of Puerto Rico, 1941.

Badger, Anthony. *The New Deal: The Depression Years, 1933–1940.* 1989. Reprint, Chicago: Ivan R. Dee, 2002.

Baldrich, Juan José. "Class and the State: The Origins of Populism in Puerto Rico, 1934–1952." PhD diss., Yale University, 1981.

Baptiste, Fitzroy André. *War, Cooperation and Conflict: The European Possessions in the Caribbean, 1939–1945.* New York: Greenwood, 1988.

Bauer, John, and Nathaniel Gold. *The Electric Power Industry: Development, Organization, and Public Policies.* New York: Harper & Brothers, 1939.

Beasley, Maurine H. *Ruby A. Black: Eleanor Roosevelt, Puerto Rico, and Political Journalism in Washington.* Lanham, MD: Lexington Books, 2017.

Bergad, Laird W. "Coffee and Rural Proletarianization in Puerto Rico, 1840–1898." *Journal of Latin American Studies* 15, no. 1 (May 1983).

———. *Coffee and the Growth of Agrarian Capitalism in Nineteenth Century Puerto Rico.* Princeton, NJ: Princeton University Press, 1983.

214 · Bibliography

_____. "Toward Puerto Rico's Grito de Lares: Coffee, Social Stratification, and Class Conflicts, 1828–1868." *Hispanic American Historical Review* 60, no. 4 (November 1980).

Bernabe, Rafael Alberto. "Prehistory of the Partido Popular Democrático: Muñoz Marin, the Partido Liberal and the Crisis of Sugar in Puerto Rico, 1930–35." PhD diss., State University of New York at Binghamton, 1989.

Beverley, James R. *Thirty-Second Annual Report of the Governor of Puerto Rico*. San Juan: Bureau of Supplies, Printing, and Transportation, 1932.

_____. *Thirty-Third Annual Report of the Governor of Puerto Rico*. San Juan: Bureau of Supplies, Printing, and Transportation, 1933.

Billington, David, and Donald Jackson. *Big Dams of the New Deal Era: A Confluence of Engineering and Politics*. Norman: University of Oklahoma Press, 2006.

Blanch-Miranda, Hilda. *"Discover Puerto Rico, U.S.A.": Propaganda, cultura, y marca pais, 1929–1941*. San Juan: Fundación Luis Muñoz Marín, 2021.

Bolívar Fresneda, José L. *The Caribbean Front in World War II: The Untold Story of U-Boats, Spies, and Economic Warfare*. Princeton, NJ: Markus Weiner, 2021.

_____. "The Development Bank and the Initial Failure of the Industrial Program in Puerto Rico, 1942–1948." *Centro Journal* 20, no. 2 (Fall 2008).

_____. *Guerra, banca y desarrollo: El Banco de Fomento y la industrialización de Puerto Rico*. San Juan: Fundación Luis Muñoz Marín / Instituto de Cultura Puertorriqueña, 2011.

Bourne, Dorothy Dulles, and James Russell Bourne. *Thirty Years of Change in Puerto Rico: A Case Study of Ten Selected Rural Areas*. New York: Praeger, 1966.

Brinkley, Alan. *The End of Reform: New Deal Liberalism in Recession and War*. New York: Vintage, 1995.

Brown, D. Clayton. *Electricity for Rural America: The Fight for the REA*. Westport, CT: Greenwood, 1980.

Burrows, Geoff G. "Rural Hydro-Electrification and the Colonial New Deal: Modernization, Experts, and Rural Life in Puerto Rico, 1935–1942." *Agricultural History* 91, no. 3 (Summer 2017).

Cabán, Pedro A. *Constructing a Colonial People: Puerto Rico and the United States, 1898–1932*. Boulder, CO: Westview, 1999.

_____. "Puerto Rico: State Formation in a Colonial Context." *Caribbean Studies* 30, no. 2 (2002).

Caribbean Research Council. *Caribbean Land Tenure Symposium of the Caribbean Committee on Agriculture, Nutrition, Fisheries, and Forestry of the Caribbean Research Council*. Washington, D.C.: 1946.

Carr, Raymond. *Puerto Rico: A Colonial Experiment*. New York: Vintage, 1984.

Carrero, Telesforo. *Housing in Puerto Rico*. Santurce: Puerto Rico Planning Board, 1950.

Christie, Jean. "Morris L. Cooke and Energy for America." In *Technology in America: A History of Individuals and Ideas*, 2nd ed., edited by Carroll W. Pursell Jr. Cambridge, MA: MIT Press, 1990.

Clark, Truman R. *Puerto Rico and the United States, 1917–1933*. Pittsburgh: University of Pittsburgh Press, 1975.

Clark, Victor S. *Porto Rico and Its Problems*. 1930. Reprint, New York: Arno Press, 1975.

Cohen, Lizbeth. *Making a New Deal: Industrial Workers in Chicago, 1919–1939*. Cambridge: Cambridge University Press, 1990.

Collazo, Luis G. *Pedro Albizu Campos: La espiritualidad de un revolucionario*. Río Piedras: Publicaciones Gaviota, 2015.

Conkin, Paul K. *Tomorrow a New World: The New Deal Community Program*. 1959. Reprint, Ithaca, NY: Cornell University Press, 2019.

———. *TVA: Fifty Years of Grass Roots Bureaucracy*. Urbana: University of Illinois Press, 1983.

Córdova, Gonzalo F. *Resident Commissioner Santiago Iglesias and His Times*. Río Piedras: Editorial de la Universidad de Puerto Rico, 1993.

Córdova, Nathaniel I. "In His Image and Likeness: The Puerto Rican Jíbaro as Political Icon." *Centro Journal* 17, no. 2 (Fall 2005).

———. "Luis Muñoz Marín's Stump Speech in the Partido Popular Democrático Campaign of 1938–1940." *Advances in the History of Rhetoric* 10 (2007).

Cramer, Lawrence W. *Annual Report of the Governor of the Virgin Islands to the Secretary of the Interior for the Fiscal Year Ended June 30, 1940*. Washington, D.C.: Government Printing Office, 1940.

Curbelo, Silvia Alvarez. *Un país del porvenir: El afán de modernidad en Puerto Rico*. San Juan: Ediciones Callejón, 2001.

Davis, George W. *Report of Brig. Gen. Geo. W. Davis, U.S.V., on Civil Affairs of Puerto Rico, 1899*. Washington, D.C.: Government Printing Office, 1900.

Del Cueto, Beatriz. "The Development of Hydraulic Mortars, Cement, and Concrete in Puerto Rico." *Journal of Preservation Technology* 42, no. 1 (2011).

———. "Portland Cements in the Spanish Caribbean as Agents of Change: Hydraulic Mosaics and Concrete Blocks." Paper presented at the Fifth International Congress on Construction History, Chicago, June 3–7, 2015.

Department of Health of Porto Rico. "The Public Health Aspects of the Hurricane of San Ciprian." *Puerto Rico Journal of Public Health and Tropical Medicine* 8, no. 2 (1932).

Dietz, James L. *Economic History of Puerto Rico: Institutional Change and Capitalist Development*. Princeton, NJ: Princeton University Press, 1986.

Dinzey-Flores, Zaire Z. *Locked In, Locked Out: Gated Communities in a Puerto Rican City*. Philadelphia: University of Pennsylvania Press, 2013.

———. "Temporary Housing, Permanent Communities: Public Housing Policy and Design in Puerto Rico." *Journal of Urban History* 33, no. 3 (March 2007).

Duffy Burnett, Christina, and Burke Marshall, eds. *Foreign in a Domestic Sense: Puerto Rico, American Expansion, and the Constitution*. Durham, NC: Duke University Press, 2002.

Earle, Walter C., Luis D. Palacios, and Antonio Arbona. "Methods Used to Control Malaria in Puerto Rico." *Puerto Rico Journal of Public Health and Tropical Medicine* 11, no. 3 (1936).

Edel, Matthew O. "Land Reform in Puerto Rico, 1940–1959: Part One." *Caribbean Studies* 2, no. 3 (1962).

216 · Bibliography

Elliott, R. N. *Decisions of the Acting Comptroller General of the United States*, vol. 17, *July 1, 1937 to June 30, 1938*. Washington, D.C.: Government Printing Office, 1938.

Esterrich, Carmelo. *Concrete and Countryside: The Urban and the Rural in 1950s Puerto Rican Culture*. Pittsburgh: University of Pittsburgh Press, 2018.

Esteves, Guillermo. "El Comienzo de la P.R.R.A." February 11, 1935. Serie de Charlas por la Radio. In *La PRRA según la prensa puertorriqueña*, vol. 2. San Juan: Puerto Rico Reconstruction Administration, 1936.

Fairbank, Miles H. *The Chardon Plan and the Puerto Rico Reconstruction Administration, 1934–1954*. San Juan: Fairbank Corporation, 1978.

_____. *The Economic Outlook for Puerto Rico: An Address Delivered before the Faculty and Student Body of the University of Puerto Rico*. San Juan: Bureau of Supplies, Printing, and Transportation, 1935.

_____. "Puerto Rico Reconstruction Administration." In *Annual Report of the Secretary of the Interior for the Fiscal Year Ending June 30, 1939*. Washington, D.C.: General Printing Office, 1939.

_____. "Statement of Miles H. Fairbank, Assistant Administrator, PRRA." In *Hearings before the Committee on Appropriations, United States Senate, May 16, 1938, on the Work Relief and Public Works Appropriation Act of 1938*, H. J. Res. 679, 75th Cong., 3rd sess. Washington, D.C.: Government Printing Office, 1938.

_____. "Testimony." In *Hearings before the Subcommittee of the Committee on Appropriations, Making Appropriations for Work Relief and Relief, Fiscal Year 1941*, United States Congress, House of Representatives, 76th Cong., 3rd sess. Washington, D.C.: Government Printing Office, 1940.

Fassig, Oliver L. "On the Average Monthly and Annual Rainfall of Porto Rico." *Porto Rico Journal of Public Health and Tropical Medicine* 5, no. 3 (1930).

_____. "San Felipe—The Hurricane of September 13, 1928, at San Juan, P.R." *Monthly Weather Review* 56, no. 9 (September 1928).

Federal Emergency Relief Administration. *Report of the Federal Emergency Relief Administration from October 1, 1935 to June 30, 1936*. Washington, D.C.: Government Printing Office, 1939.

Federal Works Agency. *Final Statistical Report of the Federal Emergency Relief Administration*. Washington, D.C.: Government Printing Office, 1942.

Fernández Garcia, E., Francis W. Hoadley, and Eugenio Astol, eds. *El Libro de Puerto Rico*. San Juan: El Libro Azul, 1923.

Ferraiolo, Nicole. "Charitable Imperialism and the Hurricane of San Ciriaco: Ideology, Humanitarian Partnerships and the Formation of American Relief Policy (Puerto Rico, 1899–1901)." MA/MSc thesis, Columbia University / London School of Economics, 2011.

Ferrao, Luis Angel. *Pedro Albizu Campos y el Nacionalismo Puertorriqueno*. San Juan: Editorial Cultural, 1990.

Findlay, Eileen J. Suárez. *Imposing Decency: The Politics of Sexuality and Race in Puerto Rico, 1870–1920*. Durham, NC: Duke University Press, 2000.

Franqui-Rivera, Harry. *Soldiers of the Nation: Military Service and Modern Puerto Rico, 1868–1952*. Lincoln: University of Nebraska Press, 2018.

Galvin, Miles. *The Organized Labor Movement in Puerto Rico*. London: Associated University Presses, 1979.

García Betancourt, Max E. "La influencia de la Escuela Institucionalista en la Administración de Reconstrucción de Puerto Rico (PRRA) Proyecto de Transformación económica y social (1935–1944)." PhD diss., University of Puerto Rico, Río Piedras, 2015.

García-Colón, Ismael. "Buscando ambiente: Hegemony and Subaltern Tactics of Survival in Puerto Rico's Land Distribution Program." *Latin American Perspectives* 33, no. 1 (January 2006).

———. "Developing a Comprehensive Health Service in Puerto Rico: An Address at the Inaugural Meeting of the Puerto Rico Public Health Association, San Juan, September 23, 1941." *American Journal of Public Health and the Nation's Health* 32, no. 1 (January 1942).

———. "Discurso pronunciado por el Honorable Comisionado de Sanidad en la Primera Asamblea de la Asociación de Salud Pública de Puerto Rico." *Puerto Rico Journal of Public Health and Tropical Medicine* 17, no. 3 (1942).

———. *Land Reform in Puerto Rico: Modernizing the Colonial State, 1941–1969*. Gainesville: University Press of Florida, 2009.

———. *Migrants at the Heart of Empire: Puerto Rican Workers on U.S. Farms*. Berkeley: University of California Press, February 2020.

———. "Playing and Eating Democracy: The Case of Puerto Rico's Land Distribution Program, 1940s–1960s." *Centro Journal* 18, no. 2 (Fall 2006).

———. "'We Like Mexican Laborers Better': Citizenship and Immigration Policies in the Formation of Puerto Rican Farm Labor in the United States." *Centro Journal* 29, no. 2 (Summer 2017).

Garrido Morales, Eduardo. *Report of the Commissioner of Health to the Hon. Governor of Porto Rico for the Fiscal Year 1937–1938*. San Juan: Bureau of Supplies, Printing, and Transportation, 1939.

Garwood, John D., and W. C. Tuthill. *The Rural Electrification Administration: An Evaluation*. Washington, D.C.: American Enterprise Institute, 1963.

Giusti Cordero, Juan A. "Labour, Ecology, and History in a Puerto Rican Plantation Region: 'Classic' Rural Proletarians Revisited." *International Review of Social History* 41 (1996).

González, Elisa M. "Food for Every Mouth: Nutrition, Agriculture, and Public Health in Puerto Rico, 1920s–1960s." PhD diss., Columbia University, 2016.

Grey, Michael. *New Deal Medicine: The Rural Health Programs of the Farm Security Administration*. Baltimore: Johns Hopkins University Press, 1999.

Hawley, Ellis W. *The Great War and the Search for a Modern World Order: A History of the American People and Their Institutions, 1917–1933*. 2nd ed. New York: St. Martin's, 1992.

Healey, Mark. *The Ruins of the New Argentina: Peronism and the Remaking of San Juan after the 1944 Earthquake*. Durham, NC: Duke University Press, 2011.

Heutchy, Alvin E. "The Rural Electrification Administration and Its Work in Pennsylvania." MA thesis, Pennsylvania State College, 1938.

218 · Bibliography

Ickes, Harold L. *Annual Report of the Secretary of the Interior for the Fiscal Year Ending June 30, 1937*. Washington, D.C.: Government Printing Office, 1937.

_____. *Annual Report of the Secretary of the Interior for the Fiscal Year Ended June 30, 1938*. Washington, D.C.: Government Printing Office, 1938.

_____. *Annual Report of the Secretary of the Interior for the Fiscal Year Ending June 30, 1939*. Washington, D.C.: General Printing Office, 1939.

_____. *The Secret Diary of Harold L. Ickes*. Vol. 1, *The First Thousand Days*. New York: Simon & Schuster, 1953.

_____. *The Secret Diary of Harold L. Ickes*. Vol. 2, *The Inside Struggle*. New York: Simon & Schuster, 1954.

Johnson, Robert David. *Ernest Gruening and the American Dissenting Tradition*. Cambridge, MA: Harvard University Press, 1998.

Jones, Marian Moser. *The American Red Cross from Clara Barton to the New Deal*. Baltimore: Johns Hopkins University Press, 2013.

Katznelson, Ira. *Fear Itself: The New Deal and the Origins of Our Time*. New York: W. W. Norton, 2013.

_____. *When Affirmative Action Was White: An Untold History of Racial Inequality in Twentieth-Century America*. New York: W. W. Norton, 2005.

Keller, Morton, ed. *The New Deal: What Was It?* New York: Holt, Rinehart & Winston, 1964.

Kelshall, Gaylord T. M. *The U-Boat War in the Caribbean*. 1988. Reprint, Annapolis, MD: Naval Institute Press, 1994.

Kennerley, Catherine Marsh. "Cultural Negotiations: Puerto Rican Intellectuals in a State-Sponsored Community Education Project, 1948–1968." *Harvard Educational Review* 73, no. 3 (September 2003).

Lapp, Michael. "The Rise and Fall of Puerto Rico as a Social Laboratory, 1945–1965." *Social Science History* 19, no. 2 (Summer 1995).

Leighninger, Robert D., Jr. *Long-Range Public Investment: The Forgotten Legacy of the New Deal*. Charleston: University of South Carolina Press, 2007.

Leuchtenburg, William E. *Flood Control Politics: The Connecticut River Valley Problem, 1927–1950*. Cambridge, MA: Harvard University Press, 1953.

_____. *Franklin D. Roosevelt and the New Deal: 1932–1940*. 1963. Reprint, New York: Harper Collins, 2009.

_____. *Herbert Hoover*. New York: Henry Holt, 2009.

Levy, Teresita A. *Puerto Ricans in the Empire: Tobacco Growers and U.S. Colonialism*. New Brunswick, NJ: Rutgers University Press, 2014.

Lucchetti, Antonio S. "Concerning the Construction and Operation of the Hydro-Electric and Irrigation Systems of the South Coast and of the Hydro-Electric System of Utilization of the Water Resources of the Government of Puerto Rico." In *Bulletin of the Department of the Interior*. San Juan: Government of Puerto Rico, 1936.

_____. "Creating the Puerto Rico Water Resources Authority: Hearings before the Committee of Insular Affairs on HR 8239," House of Representatives, 76th Congress, 3rd sess., March 19–22, 25–29, and April 15–16, 18–19, 1940. Washington, D.C.: Government Printing Office, 1940.

_____. "Rural Electricity in Puerto Rico, An Insular Government Undertaking." In *Third World Power Conference, 1936*. Washington, D.C.: Government Printing Office, 1936.

_____. *Second General Report on the Utilization of the Water Resources of Puerto Rico, 1935–45 / Segunda memoria general sobre la utilización de las fuentes fluviales de Puerto Rico, 1935–45*. San Juan: Government of Puerto Rico Printing Office, 1945.

MacPherson, Anne S. "Birth of the U.S. Colonial Minimum Wage: The Struggle over the Fair Labor Standards Act in Puerto Rico, 1938–1941." *Journal of American History* 104, no. 3 (December 2017).

Maldonado, A. W. *Boom and Bust in Puerto Rico: How Politics Destroyed an Economic Miracle*. Notre Dame, IN: University of Notre Dame Press, 2021.

_____. *Luis Muñoz Marín: Puerto Rico's Democratic Revolution*. San Juan: La Editorial, Universidad de Puerto Rico, 2006.

_____. *Teodoro Moscoso and Puerto Rico's Operation Bootstrap*. Gainesville: University Press of Florida, 1997.

Mathews, Thomas G. *Puerto Rican Politics and the New Deal*. Jacksonville: University of Florida Press, 1960.

Meléndez, Edgardo. *Puerto Rico's Statehood Movement*. New York: Greenwood, 1988.

_____. *Sponsored Migration: The State and Puerto Rican Postwar Migration to the United States*. Columbus: Ohio State University Press, 2017.

Meléndez-Badillo, Jorell. *The Lettered Barriada: Workers, Archival Power, and the Politics of Knowledge in Puerto Rico*. Durham, NC: Duke University Press, 2021.

Monteagudo, Antonio M., and Antonio Escámez, eds. *Album de Oro de Puerto Rico: Obra divulgación cultural en pro de la fraternidad americana*. Havana: Artes Graficas, 1939.

Morales Carrión, Arturo. *Puerto Rico: A Political and Cultural History*. New York: W. W. Norton, 1983.

Morales Otero, Pablo, and Oscar Costa Mandry. "Report of Studies of the 1932 Epidemic of Influenza in Puerto Rico." *Puerto Rico Journal of Public Health and Tropical Medicine* 8, no. 2 (1932).

Morales Otero, Pablo, José Rodríguez Pastor, George C. Payne, R. Ramírez Santos, and Euripides Silva. "Tuberculosis Surveys in Puerto Rico: II. A Study of Two Urban Communities. Preliminary Report." *Puerto Rico Journal of Public Health and Tropical Medicine* 10, no. 4 (1935).

Morales Otero, Pablo, and Manuel A. Pérez. "Health Work in the Rural Areas or Puerto Rico." *Puerto Rico Journal of Public Health and Tropical Medicine* 15, no. 1 (1939).

Morales Otero, Pablo, Manuel A. Pérez, R. Ramírez Santos, Rafaela Espino, Adriana Ramu, J. L. Fuster, Dolores González, and Mario Marrero. "Health and Socio Economic Conditions on a Sugar Cane Plantation (Part 1–6)." *Puerto Rico Journal of Public Health and Tropical Medicine* 12, no. 4 (1937).

Morales Otero, Pablo, Mario Marrero, Rafaela Espino, R. Ramírez Santos, and Manuel A. Pérez. "Health and Socio-Economic Conditions in the Tobacco, Coffee and Fruits Regions." *Puerto Rico Journal of Public Health and Tropical Medicine* 14, no. 3 (1939).

Morgan, Arthur. *The Making of the TVA*. Buffalo: Prometheus Books, 1974.

220 · Bibliography

Mújica-Baker, Frank, Manuel A. Valverde Jr., and Awilda Lozano. *Huracanes y tormentas tropicales que han afectado a Puerto Rico*. San Juan: Estado Libre Asociado de Puerto Rico Agencia Estatal para el Manejo de Emergencias y Administracion de Desastres, n.d.

New York Power Authority. *Bold Dream . . . Shining Legacy: A History of the New York Power Authority*. New York: New York Power Authority, 2006.

Ortiz, Santiago. *American Press Opinion with Reference to Politics and Government in Puerto Rico, 1932–1939*. Washington, D.C.: Office of the Commonwealth of Puerto Rico, 1946.

Pantojas-García, Emilio. *Development Strategies as Ideology: Puerto Rico's Export-led Industrialization Experience*. Boulder, CO: Lynne Rienner, 1990.

———. "End-of-the-Century Studies of Puerto Rico's Economy, Politics, and Culture: What Lies Ahead?" *Latin American Research Review* 35, no. 3 (2000).

———. "Puerto Rican Populism Revisited: The PPD during the 1940s." *Latin American Studies* 21, no. 3 (1989).

Park, Marlene, and Gerald E. Markowitz. *Democratic Vistas: Post Offices and Public Art in the New Deal*. Philadelphia: Temple University Press, 1984.

Patterson, James T. *Congressional Conservatism and the New Deal: The Growth of the Conservative Coalition in Congress, 1933–1939*. Lexington: University Press of Kentucky, 1967.

Pearcy, Matthew T. "After the Flood: A History of the 1928 Flood Control Act." *Journal of the Illinois State Historical Society* 95, no. 2 (Summer 2002).

Pearson, Paul M. *Annual Report of the Governor of the Virgin Islands for the Fiscal Year 1934*. Washington, D.C.: Government Printing Office, 1934.

Phillips, Sarah T. *This Land, This Nation: Conservation, Rural America, and the New Deal*. New York: Cambridge University Press, 2007.

Puerto Rico Emergency Relief Administration. *Second Report of the Puerto Rican Emergency Relief Administration, from September 1, 1934, to September 30, 1935 and Report of the Federal Emergency Relief Administration for Puerto Rico, from October 1, 1935 to June 30, 1936, in Liquidation to October 1937*. Washington, D.C.: Government Printing Office, 1939.

Puerto Rico Reconstruction Administration. *Facts about the Puerto Rico Reconstruction Administration*. San Juan: Puerto Rico Reconstruction Administration, 1938.

———. *Problems in Connection with Slum Clearance in Puerto Rico: With Special Reference to the San Juan Area*. Unpublished, 1939.

———. *Puerto Rico: A Guide to the Island and Boriquén: Compiled and Written by the Puerto Rico Reconstruction Administration in Co-Operation with the Writers' Program of the Works Progress Administration*. 1940. Reprint, New York: Gordon Press, 1979.

Puerto Rico Water Resources Authority. *Power and Irrigation in Puerto Rico, 1945–1955, Third General Report, Sol Luis Descartes, Executive Director*. San Juan: Commonwealth of Puerto Rico, 1958.

Radford, Gail. *The Rise of the Public Authority: Statebuilding and Economic Development in Twentieth-Century America*. Chicago: University of Chicago Press, 2013.

Resettlement Administration. *Greenbelt Towns: A Demonstration in Urban Planning.* Washington, D.C.: Resettlement Administration, 1936.

Ribes Tovar, Federico. *Albizu Campos: Puerto Rican Revolutionary.* New York: Plus Ultra, 1971.

Rippy, J. Fred. "Electrical Utilities in Puerto Rico." *Journal of Business of the University of Chicago* 19, no. 4 (1946).

Rodríguez, Luz Marie. "New Deal Communities for Puerto Rico: The Urban Housing Projects of the Puerto Rico Reconstruction Administration." MS thesis, Mississippi State University, 1994.

_____. "[Re]visions on Social Housing in San Juan: Notes on Workers' Housing (1930s–1950s)." In *Ambivalent Spaces: Memory and Oblivion in Modern Social Architecture,* edited by Jorge Lizardi and Matin Schwegmann. San Juan: Ediciones Callejón, 2012.

Rodríguez, Manuel R. *A New Deal for the Tropics: Puerto Rico during the Depression Era, 1932–1935.* Princeton, NJ: Markus Wiener, 2010.

_____. "Representing Development: New Perspectives about the New Deal in Puerto Rico, 1933–1936." *Centro Journal* 14, no. 2 (2002).

Rodríguez Beruff, Jorge. *Strategy as Politics: Puerto Rico on the Eve of the Second World War.* San Juan: La Editorial Universidad de Puerto Rico, 2007.

Rodríguez Beruff, Jorge, and José L. Bolívar Fresneda, eds. *Puerto Rico en la Segunda Guerra Mundial: Baluarte del Caribe.* San Juan: Ediciones Callejón, 2012.

Schwartz, Stuart B. "Differential Disasters: The 1928 Hurricane and the Shaping of the Circum-Caribbean Region." *ReVista: The Harvard Review of Latin America* (Winter 2007).

_____. "The Hurricane of San Ciriaco: Disaster, Politics, and Society in Puerto Rico, 1899–1901." *Hispanic American Historical Review* 72, no. 3 (August 1992).

_____. "Hurricanes and the Shaping of Circum-Caribbean Societies." *Florida Historical Quarterly* 83, no. 4 (Spring 2005).

_____. *Sea of Storms: A History of Hurricanes in the Greater Caribbean from Columbus to Katrina.* Princeton, NJ: Princeton University Press, 2015.

Silvestrini, Blanca G. *Los trabajadores puertorriqueqos y el Partido Socialista 1932–1940.* Río Piedras: University of Puerto Rico Press, 1979.

Smith, Jason Scott. *Building New Deal Liberalism: The Political Economy of Public Works, 1933–1956.* Cambridge: Cambridge University Press, 2006.

Solá, José O. "Colonialism, Planters, Sugarcane, and the Agrarian Economy of Caguas, Puerto Rico, between the 1890s and 1930." *Agricultural History* 85, no. 3 (Summer 2011).

Tapia Ríos, Gloria. *La Central Lafayette: Riqueza, desarrollo, y politica en el sureste de Puerto Rico.* San Juan: Magna Cultura Ediciones, 2014.

_____. "Central Lafayette de Arroyo: Eje económico y de cambio social en el sureste puertorriqueño." In *Los Pueblos de la Región Centro Oriental y su historia (Siglos XIX y XX),* edited by Félix R. Huertas González and Juan E. Roque Rivera. Gurabo, PR: Universidad del Turabo, Sistema Universitario Ana G. Méndez, 2013.

Torruella, Juan R. *The Supreme Court and Puerto Rico: The Doctrine of Separate and Unequal.* Rio Piedras: Editorial de la Universidad de Puerto Rico, 1985.

222 · Bibliography

Towner, Horace. *Twenty-Ninth Annual Report of the Governor of Puerto Rico.* Washington, D.C.: Government Printing Office, 1930.

Trias Monge, José. *Puerto Rico: The Trials of the Oldest Colony in the World.* New Haven, CT: Yale University Press, 1997.

Tugwell, Rexford G. *Changing the Colonial Climate.* 1942. Reprint, New York: Arno, 1970.

———. *The Diary of Rexford G. Tugwell: The New Deal, 1932–1935.* Edited by Michael Namorato. New York: Greenwood, 1992.

———. *The Puerto Rican Public Papers of R. G. Tugwell, Governor.* 1945. Reprint, New York: Arno, 1975.

Turner, Julie D. *Best-Laid Plans: The Promises and Pitfalls of the New Deal's Greenbelt Towns.* Cincinnati: University of Cincinnati Press, 2022.

Tyrrell, Marygrace. "Colonizing Citizens: Housing Puerto Ricans, 1917–1952." PhD diss., Northwestern University, 2009.

U.S. Bureau of the Census. *Electrical Industries of Porto Rico: 1907.* Washington, D.C.: Government Printing Office, 1909.

U.S. Congress, House Committee on Insular Affairs. *Creating the Puerto Rico Water Resources Authority: Hearings before the Committee of Insular Affairs on HR 8239.* 76th Cong., 3rd sess., Mar. 19–22, 25–29, Apr. 15, 16, 18, 19, 1940. Washington, D.C.: Government Printing Office, 1940.

———. Division of Territories and Island Possessions, Department of the Interior. *Investigation of Political, Economic, and Social Conditions in Puerto Rico: Hearings before the Subcommittee of the House Committee of Insular Affairs, Pursuant to HR 159.* 78th Cong., 2nd sess., 1944. Washington, D.C.: Government Printing Office, 1944.

U.S. Congress, House of Representatives. *Hearings before the Subcommittee of the Committee on Appropriations: Making Appropriations for Work Relief and Relief, 1941.* 76th Cong., 3rd sess., 1940. Washington, D.C.: Government Printing Office, 1940.

———. *Investigation of Political, Economic, and Social Conditions in Puerto Rico: Hearings before the Subcommittee of the House Committee of Insular Affairs, Part 19, Pursuant to HR 159.* 78th Cong., 2nd sess., 1944. Washington, D.C.: Government Printing Office, 1944.

U.S. Congress, Senate Committee on Appropriations. *Hearings on the Work Relief and Public Works Appropriation Act of 1938, H. J. Res. 679.* 75th Cong., 3rd sess., May 16, 1938. Washington, D.C.: Government Printing Office, 1938.

U.S. Department of Agriculture. *Caribbean National Forest of Puerto Rico.* Washington, D.C.: Government Printing Office, 1936.

Valdés Pizzini, Manuel, Michael González Cruz, and José Eduardo Martínez. *La transformación del paisaje puertorriqueño y la disciplina del Cuerpo Civil de Conservación, 1933–1942.* Rio Piedras: Centro de Investigaciones Sociales, Universidad de Puerto Rico, 2011.

Van Fleet, Alanson A. *The Tennessee Valley Authority.* New York: Chelsea House, 1987.

Villaronga, Gabriel. "Constructing Muñocismo: Colonial Politics and the Rise of the PPD, 1934–1940." *Centro Journal* 22, no. 2 (2010).

_____. *Toward a Discourse of Consent: Mass Mobilization and Colonial Politics in Puerto Rico, 1932–1948*. Westport, CT: Praeger, 2004.

Wells, Henry. *The Modernization of Puerto Rico: A Political Study of Changing Values and Institutions*. Cambridge, MA: Harvard University Press, 1969.

Wilson, Joan Hoff. *Herbert Hoover: Forgotten Progressive*. Boston: Little, Brown, 1975.

Winship, Blanton. *Thirty-Fourth Annual Report of the Governor of Puerto Rico*. San Juan: Bureau of Supplies, Printing, and Transportation, 1934.

_____. *Thirty-Ninth Annual Report of the Governor of Puerto Rico*. San Juan: Bureau of Supplies, Printing, and Transportation, 1939.

Zulawski, Ann. "Urban Development, Public Health, and the Environment: A Historical Case Study in San Juan, Puerto Rico and Possibilities for the Future." *Brown Journal of World Affairs* 27, no. 2 (Spring/Summer 2016).

INDEX

Page numbers in *italics* refer to illustrations.

Adjuntas, 103, 113, 123, 128–29
Agregados, 22, 25, 28, 46, 49
Agricultor puertorriqueño, 29
Agricultural Adjustment Act, 9, 45
Agricultural Experiment Station, 35, 44, 61, 137
Aguada, 95, 108, 110
Aguadilla, 22, 28, 33, 61, 67, 93, 136
Aguas Buenas, 54, 108
Aibonito, 108
Albizu Campos, Pedro, 8, 31–32, 34, 52–56, 58, 119. *See also* Nationalist Party
Alliance for Progress, 73–74
American Red Cross, 25–30, 74, 79
American Society of Civil Engineers, 66–67
Andino, Augustín M., 69, 77, 104
Antonetti, Salvador, 106
Aqueduct Act, 14, 136–37
Arecibo, 21, 33, 65, 77, 93, 95, 97, 103, 108, 123, 128, 136, 144
Arrabales. *See* Barriadas obreras
Arroyo, *83, 86,* 104–5, 107
Asociación de Agricultores Puertorriqueños, 29, 112, 133
Asociación de Choferes, 33, 119
Atlanta Federal Penitentiary, 55

Baerga, Pablo, 28
Baker, Jacob, 45
Bananas, 21, 91, 103–4, 127. *See also* Plantains
Barceló, Antonio, 58
Barceloneta, 95, 108
Barriadas obreras, 15, 30, 46, 63, 74–76, 77–82, 91–92, 95, 97
Bayamón, 33, 93, 103
Benítez, José R., 58, 69

Benítez Gautier, José, 98, 123
Benítez Rexach, Félix, 75
Bernardini Palés, Tomás, 130
Bird Arias, Jorge, 28
Black, Ruby, 59
Blanco, Heliodoro, 98, 123
Boiling Nuclear Superheater, 141
Bourne, Dorothy, 41, 43
Bourne, James R., 41, 43, 77, 126
Bovine tuberculosis, 46. *See also* Cattle tick eradication
Bridges, 12, 65, 90, 101–2, 111, 144
Bureau of Insular Affairs, 10, 27. *See also* War Department

Cabo Rojo, 65
Caguas, 30, 33, 54, *87,* 100–101, 136
Cardón, Francisco, 110
Carite hydoelectric plant #3, 122–23, 126
Carmoega, Rafael, 68, 110
Castañer, *86,* 103–4, 107–8
Castro, Fidel, 6. *See also* Cuba
Cataño cement plant, 15–16, 51, 63–64, 66–70, 71–73, 75, 82, *83,* 90, 114, 122, 124, 134, 136, 139, 141, 143–44
Cattle tick eradication, 46, 51, 100–101, 147
Cayey, 33, *89,* 93, 101, 109, 136, 142, 144
Chapman, Oscar L., 45
Chardón, Carlos, 10, 28, 35, 44–50, 52–54, 57, 59–60, 64, 70, 96, 104, 121, 126, 139, 149–53
Chardón Plan, 35, 44–50, 64, 104, 149, 153
Cidra, 109, 113
Cigars, 21, 33
Citizenship, 6–7, 9, 39, 59, 69, 79, 142
Citrus fruit, 20–22, 35, 45–46, 80, 99, 103–4
Civil Works Administration, 42
Civilian Conservation Corps, 9, 12, 60, 101–2

226 · Index

Claiborne, Robert W., 106

Coalition, 7–9, 18, 31–32, 34–36, 40, 43, 45, 47–48, 53, 57, 60–61, 64, 66, 75, 94, 104–5, 126, 132–34, 147, 149, 151

Coconuts, 20–22, 46, 51, 103; Coconut beetle, 100–101

Coffee, 4, 20–25, 33, 35, 45–46, 48, 80, *88*, 90, 98–99, 102–4, 106–8, 112, 127–29, 145, 148

Cold War, 4, 6, 73–74, 143

Coll y Cuchí, Cayetano, 61

Coll y Cuchí, José, 31

Comites de Defensa Social, 34

Commonwealth of Puerto Rico. *See* Estado Libre Asociado

Community and recreation centers, 16, 82, 90, 101–2, 113, 152

Confederación General de Trabajadores, 71–72

Congreso Obrero de Mujeres, 33

Congress of Industrial Organizations, 71

Coolidge, Calvin, 4, 8, 26, 79

Cooper, Robert A., 55

Cooperatives, 11, 32, 91, 102–4

Cordillera Central, 11, 16, 20–21, 90, 109, 113–14, 124–25, 132

Cornell University, 44, 110, 121, 137

COVID-19, 138

Crawford, Fred L., 131–32

Cruz y Nieves, Antonio, 66, 147

Cuba, 5–6, 24–25, 40, 71–73, 117–18, 120, 147

Cuban-Spanish-American War, 5, 25, 40

Culebra, 21, 144

Culture of Poverty thesis, 78

Davis, George W., 25

Debt, 20, 46, 48, 74, 104, 125–26, 128–29, 132, 135, 138, 140, 142–43

Delano, Jack and Irene, 152

Del Toro, Emilio, 28

Democratic Party, 39–40

Dental exams, 69, 95

Department of Education, 41, 61

Department of Health, 30, 91–92, 107, 136

Department of the Interior (Puerto Rico), 65, 75

Department of the Interior (U.S.), 10, 47–48, 61

Díaz, Rafael B., 107

Dickey, James A., 45

Division of Community Education, 151–52

Division of Territories and Island Possessions, 10, 48

Dominican Republic, 5, 71, 75, 118, 147, 183

Dorado, 21, 144

Dos Bocas hydroelectric dam, 123–24, 127–29, 134–35

Dust Bowl, 2

Dysentery, 30, 116

Earthquakes, 65, 68, 96, 138, 142; Earthquake-proof construction 98, 110

Eckel, Edwin, 67–68

Egozcue, Manuel, 58, 75, 77, 96

Eleanor Roosevelt housing development, 97

Election of 1928, 27

Election of 1932 (in Puerto Rico), 7–8, 15, 31–33

Election of 1932 (in U.S.), 8, 37

Emergency Relief Appropriation Act, 49, 70

Estado Libre Asociado, 14, 152

Esteves, Guillermo, 10, 12, 15, 28, 58–59, 61–62, 64, 66, 68, 71, 75, *86*, 98, 102, 121, 124, 148

Esteves, Luis Raul, 58

Fairbank, Miles H., 10, 15, 48, 59–62, 66, 71, 74–75, *86*, 100–101, 105, 108, 112, 121–22, 124, 130, 147–49

Fair Labor Standards Act, 10, 33, 106

Fajardo, 21, 24, 79, 93, 105, 144

Falansterio, *84,* 96–97

Farley, James A., 39

Farm Credit Administration, 45, 60

Farm Security Administration, 12, 151

Federación Libre de Trabajadores, 7, 33–34, 71

Federal Emergency Relief Administration, 9, 38–39

Federal Land Bank of Baltimore, 48

Federal Surplus Relief Corporation, 41

Federal Works Agency, 10

Fernández García, Benigno, 31, 35, 49–50, 52, 54, 57, 149

Fernández García, Rafael, 35, 46, 49, 52, 98

Ferré, José, 73, 143

Ferré, Luis A., 143, 152

Fertilizer, *87,* 91, 98

Index · 227

500-Acre Law, 35, 45–48, 52, 57, 133, 149, 151.
   See also Land reform
Florida, 19, 24, 39
Font Jiménez, Manuel, 64, 66, 69, 75, 96, 124
Foraker Act, 6–7, 24
Forestry, 11, 46, 49, 91, 101–2
Fort Buchanan, 64
Freshwater fish industry, 46, 103

Gallardo, José M., 108
García Méndez, Miguel Angel, 32, 105
Garrido Morales, Eduardo, 93–94
Garzas hydroelectric dam, 123–24, 127–30,
   134–35
Goats, 101, 106
González, Rafael A., 58, 67, 95, 106
Good Neighbor Policy, 4, 10
Gore, Robert H., 39–41, 43, 47
Gore, Thomas P., 13
Greenbelt towns, 96
Gruening, Ernest, 10, 14, 48–50, 52–53, 55,
   57–60, 70, 121
Guánica, 5
Guayama, 19, 34, 107, 123, 142, 144
Guayanilla, 130, 141
Guaynabo, 64, 66–67, 73, *83*, 107, 110
Gurabo, 30, 33, 99

Harding, Warren G., 8
Hawaii, 39
Hernández, Rafael J., 110
Hirshberg, Henry, 110
Hitchman, J. C., 95
Hoff, John Van Rensselaer, 25
Hookworm, 23, 74, 92–93, 95, 116
Hoover, Herbert, 3, 8, 26–27, 29, 39, 79, 128
Hopkins, Harry, 59
Horizontal integration, 117–18
Hospitals and health clinics, 16, 22, 51, 69, 90,
   94, 104, 107–8, 110–11, 152
Houses and housing construction, 12, 15–16,
   19–23, 26, 30, 41, 48–49, 52, 62, 73–82, *86,
   87*, 90–99, 100–101, 105, 107–8, 111–16, 118,
   120, 142, 150, 153
Humacao, 25, 33, 99, 144
Hurricanes, 1–2, 5, 13, 19, 23–24, 37–39, 65, 69,
   79, 81, 92–93, 95–96, 113, 128–29, 138, 148;

Fiona, 16, 138; Irma, 16, 138, 142; María,
   16, 138, 142; Okeechobee, 19; San Ciprián,
   2, 4, 7, 14–15, 19–23, 25–35, 42, 76–79, 93,
   115, 122, 138, 145, 153; San Ciriaco, 4, 24–26;
   San Felipe, 2, 4, 13–15, 19–23, 25–35, 63, 76,
   93–94, 111, 115, 122, 128, 138, 144–45, 153;
   San Liborio, 20

Ickes, Harold, 10, 14, 40, 45, 47–49, 53, 56–61,
   72, 108
Iglesias, Santiago, 8, 31, 33, 53, 55
Influenza, 23, 74
Insular Cases, 6
Isabela, 51, 95, 101, 113, 124

Jíbaros, 17, 25, 52, 116, 148, 151
Jones-Shafroth Act, 6–7, 119
Juan Morel Campos housing development, 97
Juncos, 33, 99

Kennedy, John F. 73–74

Lafayette, *86*, 94, 103–8
Lafayette Cooperative Sugar Association, 103,
   106
Laissez faire political economy, 8, 26–27, 29
Lámela, Félix, 94, 107
Land reform, 12, 14, 35, 45, 48, 146, 148–50, 152.
   See also 500-Acre Law
Lares, 33, 103; Grito de Lares, 24
Latin America, 2, 4, 10, 14, 52–54, 71, 73–75, 94,
   120, 127, 141, 145–47
Leper asylum, 20, 34, 94
Liberal Party, 7–8, 14, 18, 31, 33–35, 40, 43, 45–
   46, 53, 57–58, 60, 66, 93–94, 105, 147–48
López Domínguez, Francisco A., 98, 104
Lucchetti Otero, Antonio S., 12, 69, 104, 114,
   120–24, 126, 130–33, 135–37, 140, 148
Luquillo National Forest. *See* Yunque National
   Forest

Malaria, 23, 51, 74–75, 92, 95, 116
Malnutrition, 23, 74, 81, 92, 115–16
Mangroves, 51, 63, 76, 81, 92
Marcantonio, Vito, 132
Marí, Mariano, 99
Maricao Fish Hatchery, 102

228 · Index

Maricao State Forest, 51, 101–2
Martínez Nadal, Rafael, 31, 40, 43, 46–47, 57, 60, 75, 132, 148
Martín Peña Canal, 77
Maryland Farm Bureau, 59
Massachusetts Institute of Technology, 66
Maunabo, 104–5, 107, 144
Mayagüez, 12, 25, 33–34, 45, 52, 66–67, 77, 81, 93, 97, 100–101, 110–13, 117, 133–34, 144, 149; Liga de Defensa de Mayagüez, 34
Mayagüez Light, Ice, and Power Company, 32, 34, 117, 134, 136
McKinley, William, 24
Medina González, Julio, 31
Menéndez Ramos, Rafael, 35, 44, 46, 86, 151
Meyers, William I., 45
Mississippi River, 26–27
Monopolies, 12, 16, 32, 34, 51, 114, 117–20, 133, 135, 140, 142–43
Morales Otero, Pablo, 58, 93, 95, 107
Moscoso, Teodoro, 73, 143
Muñoz, Conchita R., 107
Muñoz Marín, Luis, 14, 16, 31, 40, 43, 46–48, 53, 57–58, 66, 73, 132–33, 137, 143, 146–49, 151–52
Muñoz Rivera, Luis, 31, 58; Parque Luis Muñoz Rivera, 149

Naguabo, 109
National Guard, 27–28, 30, 34, 54, 144
National Industrial Recovery Act, 9
Nationalist Party, 7–8, 31–34, 38, 40, 46, 52–53, 55–58, 119–20. See also Albizu Campos, Pedro
National Labor Relations Act, 9, 56, 71
National Recovery Administration, 56
Nazi Germany, 4, 144–46
Needlework industry, 10, 33
New Deal: First New Deal, 9–10, 38, 70, 79; New Deal political coalition, 8–9, 11, 13–14, 18, 36, 151; Second New Deal, 1–2, 9–10, 38, 48, 74, 114, 139
New Progressive Party, 142–43, 152. See also Statehood movement
New York Power Authority, 131

Obama, Barack, 138
Occupation of Puerto Rico, 24–25, 90, 114, 117–18
Operation Bootstrap, 73, 137
Orbeta, Enrique de, 57

Padín, José, 41
Panama Canal, 6, 25, 68
Partido Autonomista Puertorriqueño, 31
Partido Comunista Puertorriqueño, 33–34, 71, 119
Partido Popular Democrático, 14, 66, 93–94, 133, 136, 143, 146–52
Patillas, 99–100, 104–5, 107–8, 111, 113, 118, 144
Pearl Harbor, 4, 144–45
Pérez Mercado, Rafael B., 109, 129
Philippines, 55
Picó, Rafael, 151
Pilard, Augusto R., 110
Piñero, Jesus T., 66, 152
Plantains, 21, 91, 103. See also Bananas
Ponce, 12, 20, 32–34, 45, 51–52, 57–58, 65–67, 72–73, 77–81, 93, 97, 109–10, 117–19, 121, 123, 130, 134, 136–37, 141, 143–44
Ponce Cement Corporation, 73, 143–44
Ponce Electric Company, 34, 117–19, 130, 134, 136–37
Ponce massacre, 15, 57–58, 66
Populism, 5, 13–14, 16, 146–47, 151–53
Porto Rico Hurricane Relief Commission, 28–29
Porto Rico Railway, Light, and Power Company, 34, 117, 134, 136
Poverty, 3, 39, 48, 77–78, 80–82
Progressive era, 24, 26–28, 63, 67, 77, 118, 120
Public Works Administration, 10, 12, 42, 59, 61, 69, 101
Puerta de Tierra, 53, 78–79, 96, 110, 149
Puerto Rico British West Indies Sugar Association, 133
Puerto Rico Cement Corporation, 13–14, 68–69, 71–74, 81, 114, 139, 143–44, 153
Puerto Rico Electric Power Authority, 140–43
Puerto Rico Emergency Relief Administration, 1, 9–10, 14–15, 36–44, 48, 51, 56, 59, 74, 77, 79, 93, 99, 111, 126, 145

Puerto Rico Housing Authority, 73, 97, 109
Puerto Rico Hurricane Relief Loan Section, 125, 128–29
Puerto Rico Industrial Development Company, 73, 137, 143
Puerto Rico Iron Works, 73
Puerto Rico Irrigation Service, 118–19, 130, 133
Puerto Rico Oversight, Management, and Economic Stability Act, 138
Puerto Rico Reconstruction Administration: Engineering Division, 11–12, 15–18, 23, 42, 50–52, 59, 61–63, 66, 70–71, 79–82, 87, 90–91, 94–95, 98–99, 102–3, 111, 144–45, 152–53; Information and Research Section, 66, 147, 151; Payroll and personnel, 1, 50, 149; Rural Electrification Division, 11, 51, 114, 121–26, 129, 135; Rural Rehabilitation Division, 11, 16, 50, 58–60, 77, 87, 98–103, 147, 149
Puerto Rico Water Resources Authority, 13–14, 16, 120, 122, 131, 137, 139–41, 143–44

Quebradillas, 113

Racism, 3, 6, 52
Ramírez de Arellano, Germán, 98, 110, 149
Ramírez de Arellano, Jorge, 97–98, 107
Reconstruction Finance Corporation, 29, 39
Republican Party (Puerto Rico), 7–8, 31–35, 38, 40, 45–47, 75, 94, 105–6, 149–50
Republican Party (U.S.), 8, 70, 118, 132, 135
Reservoirs, 78, 90, 102, 114, 118, 123, 128
Resettlement Administration, 12, 96
Resident commissioner, 7, 31, 66, 142, 152
Riggs, E. Francis, 15, 54–55, 66
Rincón, 109, 141
Río Piedras, 33–34, 45, 53–54, 68, 88, 94, 97, 109–12, 133
Río Piedras massacre, 15, 53–54
Río Piedras State Penitentiary, 68
Rockefeller, John D., 118
Rockefeller Foundation, 92–93
Rodríguez Pastor, José, 93
Roldán, Francisco, 68
Romero Barceló, Carlos, 142
Roosevelt, Eleanor, 47, 151

Roosevelt, Franklin D., 1–4, 10, 13, 33, 39–41, 45, 47–50, 53, 56–57, 59–60, 100, 136, 150–51; Roosevelt administration, 3, 8, 13, 17, 32–37, 45–47, 56, 59, 120
Roosevelt, Theodore, 25, 118
Rosselló, Pedro, 142
Rosskam, Edwin and Louise, 152
Ruiz, Eloy, 110

Sabana Grande, 95, 101
Saldana, Eduardo J., 58
Salinas, 104, 141, 144
Sánchez Vilella, Roberto, 152
San Germán, 33, 95
San Juan, 10, 12, 19–22, 25, 27, 29–30, 33–34, 40, 45, 51–53, 58–60, 64–65, 67, 72, 77–81, 93, 97–98, 100, 110, 112, 117, 128, 131, 134, 136, 141, 144, 146, 148
San Juan (Viejo), 40, 67, 79
San Lorenzo, 30, 33, 99, 113
Santurce, 33, 53, 67, 77–81, 94, 97, 100, 113, 117, 134
School of Tropical Medicine, 22, 51, 91–93, 107, 110; Department of Bacteriology, 22
Schools, 22, 42, 51, 80, 99, 108–11, 120
Schoolteachers, 17, 28, 30, 42, 61, 72, 75, 96, 108–10
Section 936 of U.S. tax code, 16, 142–43
Serra Colón, Emilio, 98, 123
Serrallés, Pedro Juan, 133
Sewer Authority Act, 14, 137
Sewers, 12, 14, 20, 48, 51, 82, 90, 96–99, 111–14, 116, 137
Sixty-Fifth Infantry, 28, 30, 78
"Slum clearance," 11, 15, 41, 46, 58, 63, 74–77, 80–82, 112, 119
"Slums." See Barriadas obreras
Socialist Party, 7–8, 32–35, 46, 65, 148
Social Security Administration, 9–10, 44, 56
Social work, 2, 11, 41, 72, 139
Soil erosion, 4, 25, 46, 100–101, 132
South Porto Rico Sugar Company, 150
Statehood movement, 7–8, 31–35, 38, 40, 60, 142–43
Status question, 7, 9, 35, 40, 115, 139, 152
Storm drains, 12, 82, 90, 97, 113

230 · Index

Strikes, 33–34, 37, 40, 53, 71, 105, 134
Subsistence farming, 4, 21–23, 46, 61, *83*, 99, 103–4, 127, 150
Sugar, 4, 7–10, 19–23, 26, 32–35, 44–47, 53, 79–80, 92, 100, 103–7, 114, 118–19, 132, 137, 145, 148–52
Sugar question. *See* 500-Acre Law
Supreme Court (Puerto Rico), 6, 28, 136, 149
Supreme Court (U.S.), 9, 70, 135
Swope, Guy J., 132

Taft, William Howard, 118
Tallaboa, 66–67, 130
Taylor, Frederick, 67–68
Tennessee Valley Authority, 12, 56, 67, 121, 131–33, 140
Thomson, John W., 147
Tobacco, 4, 10, 20–23, 29, 33, 35, 45–46, 61, 80, 98–103, 118, 127, 129, 145
Toro Negro electric plant, 122–23, 126
Towner, Horace, 27
Trujillo Alto, 33, 94, 144
Trujillo Molina, Rafael, 71, 75
Truman, Harry S., 152
Tuberculosis, 92–93, 116
Tufts University, 28, 61
Tugwell, Rexford G., 14, 45–48, 56, 77, 96, 124, 137, 150–52
Tydings, Millard, 13, 55–56; Tydings Bill, 13, 55–57, 66
Typhoid, 30, 74, 95, 116

U-boats, 4, 144–46
Union Party, 31, 58
University of California, 44
University of Puerto Rico, 11, 35, 40–41, 44–45, 51, 53, 67, 75, *88*, 91, 94, 107, 110–11, 137, 151
Usufruct rights, 22–23, 79, 99, 150
U.S. Virgin Islands, 10, 39, 71, 106, 148

U.S. Weather Bureau, 21
Utilización de las Fuentes Fluviales, 121, 134–36
Utuado, 54, 95, 113, 127–28, 140

Valdés Cobián, Alfonso, 32
Vega Baja, 33, 136, 144
Vertical integration, 117–18
Vieques, 21, 141, 144
Villalba, 95, 108, 122
Vivoni, Armando, 68

Wagner-Steagall Housing Act, 97
War Department, 10, 27, 41, 48, 144, 146
War Powers Act, 136
Washington, D.C., 4, 6, 10–11, 29, 44–49, 52–55, 58–59, 73, 98, 112, 119, 131, 134, 148
Water Resources Authority. *See* Puerto Rico Water Resources Authority
Water supply, 12–13, 16, 20, 32–34, 48, 51, 69–70, 78, 81–82, 90, 96–97, 99–100, 102, 105, 111–13, 114–20, 124, 128, 130–37, 140–42, 153
Will, Ralph, 151
Wilson, Woodrow, 6, 118
Winship, Blanton, 40–43, 47, 53–55, 57–60, 126, 132
Works Progress Administration, 9–10, 12, 59, 69, 144–45, 147
World War I, 27, 40, 66, 98, 132
World War II, 3–4, 6, 10–11, 44, 64, 69, 98, 106–7, 136, 143, 146

X-rays, 93, 107

Yabucoa, 95, 99, 107–8
Yauco, 65, 103, 108, 112–13
Yunque National Forest, 30, 51, 102, 116–17

Zayas, Don Taso, 19
Zeno Gandia, Manuel, 90

Geoff G. Burrows is a senior program officer at the National Endowment for the Humanities. A historian of Latin America, the Caribbean, and the United States, he received a PhD from the CUNY Graduate Center and has taught at Seton Hall University, Hunter College, Queens College, and the College of Staten Island. Burrows is the author of an article, a book chapter, and several book reviews.